The Rise of
Big Government
in the
United States

The Rise *of* Big Government *in the* United States

John F. Walker

Harold G. Vatter

M.E. Sharpe
Armonk, New York
London, England

Library of Congress Cataloging-in-Publication Data

Walker, John F.
The rise of big government in the United States / John F. Walker
and Harold G. Vatter.
p. cm.
Includes bibliographical references and index.
ISBN 0-7656-0066-8 (alk. paper). —
ISBN 0-7656-0067-6 (pbk. : alk. paper)
1. United States—Economic policy.   2. United States—Politics and
government—20th century.   3. Fiscal policy—United States—
History—20th century.   4. Free enterprise—United States—
History—20th century.   5. Mixed economy—United States—
History—20th century.   6. Industrial policy—United States—
History—20th century.   7. United States—Foreign relations—
20th century.   I. Vatter, Harold G.   II. Title.
HC106.W15   1997
330.973—dc21   96-40286
CIP

Printed in the United States of America

The paper used in this publication meets the minimum requirements of
American National Standard for Information Sciences—
Permanence of Paper for Printed Library Materials,
ANSI Z 39.48-1984.

BM (c)   10   9   8   7   6   5   4   3   2   1
BM (p)   10   9   8   7   6   5   4   3   2   1

For
Susan and Timothy Walker,
Asa Redmond, Simeon Redmond, and Andrew Culpepper

CONTENTS

LIST OF TABLES

PREFACE

While there is a vast literature on the growth of government in the United States, the contemporary attack on the public sector warrants an updated historical, comprehensive analysis of its roots and prospects. The present work undertakes this task.

The unfolding of this analysis brings out certain specific features of public-sector development that fill important gaps in existing treatments purporting to be comprehensive. In the first place, an analytical format is explicitly employed. This format connects evolving public programs and policies with their sources. Those sources are to be found in three basic historical currents: the private market system's evolution, changing social and ideological streams in the larger culture, and the history of international relations. The impulses emanating from these sources prompt people and their related organizations to press for government participation in human affairs.

To establish the connection between those impulses and the resulting governmental interventions requires an ongoing examination of relevant changes in these three sources of public action. This is one major contribution of the present work. An integration of source and response, therefore, is the focus of this analysis. The integration typically reveals the deep roots of a growing public establishment.

The market's technological advances, economic cycles, and wars, as well as the ratchet effects of leaps in public-sector size are integrated into what is viewed as more basic, long-run influences at work. Shorter-period developments simply bring to the surface precisely those long-simmering pressures impatient for expression.

No clearer example of this approach and its analytical cogency is available than an examination of the Great Depression of the 1930s—the founding decade of our mixed economy. Depressions in general reveal most starkly the human costs and the deficiencies of business enterprise in the private market system. There were depressions recurrently before the 1930s, some of them—such as those of the 1870s and 1890s—were quite severe in their impact on people and business. Why did the mixed economy of big government not result then? Was the social reaction to the 1890s stillborn? The answer is that societal and ideological hostility to such shocks, with its attendant public interventionist demands, had not yet ripened.

The severity and long duration of the 1930s Depression were the final stimulus needed to bring the interventionist process to fruition. Many elements of welfare interventionism and government responsibility for market system management set seed in the laissez-faire decades that then sprouted quantitatively and qualitatively during that grim period. There was no turning back; the economic shock revealed enormous long-run forces at work. No 1929 government "bureaucracy," no "great man" president, could have executed such a devastating blow to laissez-faire, and the enormity of the turnaround ensured that more intervention was to come.

Until the 1930s and 1940s, a technologically advanced, high-income market system had been engendering a welfare state outcome, with a continuing need for more infrastructure and rectification of the ever more severe damage to the environment. This was happening in other industrial market economies as well, but in the United States international developments contributed a peculiar component to government's role. Historic anti-Sovietism eventuating in the Cold War gave a unique, chronic, superpower character to the American form of a mixed economy, supported by a public consensus. In contrast to other advanced market systems, the military establishment acquired the bureaucratic clout to constrain the welfare component of big government's expansion, particularly the public health element in the welfare state.

As a result, the American community did not confront the historical necessity for big government in such overwhelmingly civilian terms as did other countries —at least not until the Cold War subsided. The next welfare crisis is thus being generated in this last decade of the twentieth century.

All of these observations dictate this comprehensive survey of the major components of the burgeoning public sector. They also require careful treatment in this work of the relative growth contributions of the federal versus the state and local roles in the American federal system. A considerable effort is made to present in detail the widely neglected, administrative management component of government's growth. This is viewed as the chief contemporary expression of Wagner's Law.

Finally, the book provides empirical and analytical support for the hypothesis that the sources responsible for government's continuing growth ensure its irreversibility. Reliance on irreversibility is viewed as primarily in the administrative management component, rather than in revenue-expenditure flows.

Some works on public-sector growth consider selected ideas presented in this book, but this analysis is an integrated look at all such elements. In so doing, it differs from all works that rely primarily on either the median voter theory or the bureaucratic Leviathan presumption.

ACKNOWLEDGMENTS

Our special thanks needs to be extended here to Portland State's Provost Michael F. Reardon and College of Liberal Arts and Sciences Dean Marvin Kaiser for their continuing support of the research and manuscript preparation necessary for this work. Ongoing encouragement was also forthcoming from the Economics Department chair, Professor Helen Youngelson-Neal, for which we take this occasion to express our appreciation.

Particular thanks are due to Economics Department Office Coordinator Rita Spears for her unremitting assistance with the production tasks emanating from this project—on top of her daily flood of office work.

This work could not have been completed without the consummate proficiency of and untiring effort by Bahar Jaberi of Portland State University. Our gratitude to her much exceeds what can be expressed here.

A very special acknowledgment is due Warren Samuels, who made the original recommendation that a book, authored such as this and employing an institutionalist approach, was urgently needed. It is our earnest hope that he will find the work a reasonable approximation of his expectations.

We also owe a large debt of thanks to Richard Bartel, Stephen Dalphin, Aud Thiessen, Christine Florie, and Steven Martin of M.E. Sharpe, Inc. for their lucid instructions, encouragement, sharp editing, cooperation in manuscript processing, and patience regarding deadlines not quite met.

The Rise *of* Big Government *in the* United States

CHAPTER ONE

The Erosion of Laissez-Faire

The enlargement of government's role in the industrialized market economies during the twentieth century is one of the most striking historical transformations of modern times. The widespread nineteenth-century laissez-faire era of moderate, pro-business intervention experienced a significant shock in the 1880s, when the conservative German government under Otto von Bismarck introduced a package of social measures. The purpose of Bismarck's welfare measures was to forestall the presumed threat of a socialist attack on the private market system. That configuration of capitalist industrial development, social action, and government reformist intervention was prophetic of much future history.

In Japan, on the other hand, the giant industrial market system that developed after the Meiji Restoration in 1867 never experienced laissez-faire. Japan was a state-guided capitalist system from the start of modernization, and it remains such to a very large degree. But the other industrially advancing market systems of the world that had accepted the laissez-faire arrangement in the nineteenth century gradually discarded it in the twentieth century.

In the United States, the prevailing domestic laissez-faire relationship between government and the market was, in fact, slowly undermined—although not ideologically—in the decades between the end of the Civil War and the Great Depression of the 1930s. Prior to 1933, restraints were indeed placed on the customary assistance given to the private market. Regulatory restraints were instituted at both federal and state and local levels. The period from the turn of the twentieth century to about 1915 in particular was marked by a wave of reform legislation. But like reform programs generally, the objective was to maintain a "social balance" to obviate possible turmoil brought on by contentious groups. These programs were instigated largely by middle-class people who were both appalled by the market system's harsh treatment of the economically disadvantaged and fearful of the emerging labor discontent. The middle class was also seriously hurt by the increasing predation by great industrial, transportation, utility, and commercial monopolies, which took over more and more markets in the late nineteenth and early twentieth centuries.

However, the U.S. experience is rather unusual among the industrially advanced nations for the distinct historical break evinced by the New Deal's sudden public activism at the federal level in the span of less than a decade. The activism first appeared in 1933 as a set of emergency measures, but it soon produced a package of abiding interventionist reforms, such as the Social Security Act, the National Labor Relations Act, and the Fair Labor Standards Act. The reform package was a far-reaching expression of two forces: the most severe market system breakdown in U.S. history and a powerful surge of specific societal responses in the context of a deep-rooted humanistic and progressive cultural current. The combination introduced the "mixed economy" to the American experience.

The purpose of this survey is neither to view with alarm nor to condone the rise of big government—federal and/or state and local—but to determine its sources. We find those sources to be neither episodic nor transient. The competitive interest groups, generated by the evolving market system, are driven by their maximization goals to invoke lasting governmental intervention on their behalf. Expanding political reflection of the growing market system's rewards and punishments is ensured by the persistence, increasing sophistication, and greater organizational power of those rival interest groups.

An essential and encompassing fact about the twentieth-century interventionist developments is that, in the first place, they have not been confined to one or two countries, but have occurred in quite a few major market economies. In the second place, despite unrelenting attacks on the allegedly Leviathan character of those developments, they have apparently gained sufficient social acceptability to forestall any serious efforts toward reversibility.

The endurance over time shown by large-scale public interventionism suggests the hypothesis that a profound social insistence or approval must underlie it. The hypothesis acquires persuasiveness from the fact that the substitution of "big government" and welfare states for laissez-faire has taken place in countries enjoying what are customarily considered to be democratic political institutions.

In the United States, as elsewhere, laissez-faire governments at all three levels played for the most part a selective, pro-business development role. They also pursued a sort of balancing act designed to make adjustments for particular weaknesses, vulnerabilities, and inequities in the market system's impact on people. Examples of such diverse activities are the minimization of business regulation; various direct subsidies and grants to business; protective tariffs; general incorporation laws; direct infrastructure investment such as sewage and potable water systems in cities; indirect infrastructure encouragement such as the 1916 Federal Highway Act and state and local highway construction; encouragement of easy natural resource exploitation such as the provision of grazing lands to cattle ranchers, particularly free mining privileges; official subversion of Na-tive American land claims; acquisition of continental land areas; free homesteading; the 1862 Land Grant College Act; agricultural experiment stations; rural free postal delivery; an open immigration policy to increase the labor supply; and the establishment in 1913 of an economy-wide central banking system (the Federal Reserve).

Examples of social-balance policies under laissez-faire are the *Commonwealth v. Hunt* court decision in Massachusetts in 1842 ruling that labor unions were not per se illegal conspiracies; the extension of voting rights to the propertyless and later to women; state legislation overruling the "fellow servant" rule that had judged employees responsible for injury or death on the job; and the Sherman Anti-Trust Act designed to restrain exploitive business monopolies. Government spending on education was both an aid to social balance through its contribution to enriching the quality of life and a contributor to the market's need for better-quality human capital. On the other hand, so far as the rights of labor were concerned, laissez-faire government was as anti-labor as possible because such a stance was deemed good for business, that is, it kept wages down and profits, the source of savings, up.

The fiscal policies of laissez-faire government were classical political economy to the core: minimize the public budget, balance it every year to obviate debt growth, tax consumption (tariffs, excises, property, no income levies), and tax only in order to finance the work of the spare government personnel. Transfer payments to persons were undreamed of. Regressive taxation was designed to reinforce householders' frugality and augment private savings, all of which would presumably be invested for economic progress. The imperviousness of this philosophy to inimical institutional change throughout the nineteenth and twentieth centuries, however violated in practice, is one of the more incredible continuities in modern history. Indeed, the staying power of the general philosophy of domestic laissez-faire defies almost all explanations of intellectual history.

It needs to be recognized, of course, that during the entire evolution of the capitalist market system, laissez-faire and thereafter, government has provided the indispensable, basic, legal framework protecting the essentials of private property and the security of the person, guaranteeing the "sanctity of contracts" and assuring national defense. The vital contribution of this protective institutional framework to the very existence of a national market system has been dramatically demonstrated in the Eastern European transformations during the present decade. Furthermore, U.S. history along with the history of other similar economies has shown that, with a growing population and rising per capita incomes, the legal framework itself has changed as to its role, its personnel, and its complement of physical facilities. The size of the judicial and law enforcement apparatus has therefore of necessity had to grow.

The size of the government establishment under laissez-faire was historically small—one fact that provides a critical indicator of the meaning of laissez-faire itself. Charles William Eliot, president of Harvard University for forty years, dramatically pinpointed this fact of smallness as early as 1888, with a shocking contrast between the large size of a "certain railroad" corporation and the government of the important state of Massachusetts.[1] Eliot's figures for annual totals may be tabulated as follows:

	"A certain railroad"	State of Massachusetts
Gross receipts	$40,000,000	$7,000,000
Employees	18,000	6,000
Top salary paid	$35,000	$6,500

Eliot's essay, "The Working of the American Democracy," was dated early in the career of the big business era.

For the United States, small laissez-faire government may also be appraised quantitatively by a comparison of its size before and after about 1930, the census year that will be used here as a rough benchmark for the final demise of an era already in a state of decline.

Two readily available measures showing the small size of government during laissez-faire are public employment and purchases of goods and services. For example, in the United States, the ratio of all-government (federal, state, and local) *civilian* employment to the total civilian labor force averaged at census dates over the period from 1890 to 1929 about 4.7 percent. But the average over the initial mixed economy period 1939 to 1959 had already become twice that size at about 9.5 percent.

To be sure, before 1929 the public employment ratio slowly crept upward, even as laissez-faire was being undermined. While the ratio was less than 4 percent in 1900, it was more than 6 percent by 1929 (Table 1.1). Over 80 percent of this 1929 proportion was accounted for by state and local employees. This gradual rise in the total proportion through 1929 was empirically quite supportive of the famous "law" of the nineteenth-century German social theorist Adolf Wagner, who forecasted absolute and relative growth in society's demand for government services as economic development in capitalist economies brought about increasing industrialization and urbanization.

A second customary measure of all-government size in the United States is purchases of goods and services by federal, state, and local governments (G) in comparison with GNP, also shown in Table 1.1. The G/GNP ratio in current dollars from the mid-1870s to about 1900 rose about a percentage point from a little over 5 percent to a little over 6 percent. In the next twenty years, as the table shows, the ratio drifted upward, but it remained historically small compared to what the future had in store. A similar comparison holds for the employment ratio, which also jumped dramatically by 2 percent a year between 1929 and 1959 with the great transformation to the mixed economy. A slowdown to six-tenths of 1 percent annually for the ratio's succeeding thirty-five years, 1959–

Table 1.1

Growth in Government Size, Twentieth-Century Purchases, and Employment, 1900, 1929, 1959, 1989, 1994

	Percent purchases/GNP (current $) (1)	Percent civilian employees/ civilian labor force (2)	Ratio (1)/(2)
1900	6.02	3.86	1.56
1929	8.12	6.42	1.27
1959	20.27	11.65	1.72
1989	18.70	14.35	1.30
1994	17.43	14.53	1.20

Sources: Historical Statistics and *Economic Reports of the President* for 1967, 1992, and 1996.

1994, indicates that the selection of 1959 reveals nicely the break in the historical trend.

The New Deal year 1939 would also show a trend break insofar as the G/GNP percentage at 14.7 for that year is concerned. Apparently the New Deal was busy increasing aggregate demand. But the all-government employment ratio by that year had risen to only 7.23, a modest 13 percent above 1929. It is true, however, that the ratio of federal civilian employees to state and local workers rose from 21 percent in 1929 to 29 percent in 1939.

The last column in Table 1.1 satisfies one's curiosity but otherwise tells us very little. It does not measure efficiency in a strict output/input sense. The drop shown between 1959 and 1994 might superficially appear to be some indicator of a growing bureaucracy that raises government jobs without raising work done (purchases). However, "purchases" contains a very large component of government wages and salaries. Furthermore, transfer-payment work by public employees is not contained in purchases, whereas total government transfers to persons (such as Social Security payments) exploded from $28 billion in 1959 to $956 billion in 1994 (real transfers from $109 billion to $758 billion in 1987 dollars).

In making these long-run historical comparisons it is important to remember that the national defense purchases of the federal component of all-government purchases became for the first time chronically very large after 1948. Hence, *civilian* G in ratio to total GNP averaged 11.2 percent for the three dates 1939, 1949, and 1959. Nevertheless, this was still about 58 percent higher than the average of the two percentages for 1900 and 1929, as shown in Table 1.1. It would be still higher if civilian GNP were the denominator of the fraction.

The record shows that the demise of the domestic laissez-faire relationship occurred in two phases in the United States: a more or less gradual, long-drawn-out decline in the half-century before 1929, followed by a relatively sudden jump in government's role as the mixed economy was inaugurated during the decade of the Great Depression. It also shows that the long rise in big government has always entailed in quantitative terms, as distinguished from discretionary public policies, a strong rise in the state and local component. The state and local sector was by far the largest part of the public sector throughout the laissez-faire era and also in the mixed economy era. To be sure, some of its growth was financially supported by the federal government. Such a pattern is to be expected in a culture that worships grass roots. The financial support pattern will be looked at in Chapters 3 and 5. In any case, in 1994 there were 16,171,000 state and local employees and 2,870,000 civilian federal employees. However, about 1 million of those "civilian" federal employees worked for the Department of Defense. On a truly civilian comparison, state and local employees outnumbered federal by about 8 to 1.

Changes Driven by the Market's Evolution

Up to this point the concern has been primarily with description. We now turn to Wagner's Law, which treats some major aspects of the decline of laissez-faire. To appreciate the operation of the law in the United States, we can take as examples a number of chiefly long-run changes in the enterprise: household nexus comprising the market system and changes that induced responses in both society and government. Such examples reveal the mutual interactions between all three of the major institutional players in the evolutionary drama with which we are chiefly concerned: the business-consumer and employer-employee complex at the heart of the market system; the societal groups that have an intimate set of specific connections with that complex; and the governmental establishment. These three institutional sets continually interact as they evolve, but Wagner's great empirical insight, which is embraced herein, made market system changes the prime movers in the totality of change.

As an example, take per capita income. The market's operation during the laissez-faire era achieved total output growth rates that, given the falling growth rate of population, impressively raised income per head. Two among the several pertinent long-run effects of that rise were the creation of an ever larger (urban) middle class and an enormous increase in both enterprise and household fossil fuel energy use.

It was primarily this new and growing middle class that as early as the first two decades of the twentieth century mounted the Progressive movement. That organizational groundswell affected a remarkable variety of modest governmental intrusions into society at large, as well as the behavior of the market system itself. The government interventions were designed to ameliorate a number of perceived inequities that the Progressives and their supporters attributed to market system defects. The Progressive years from the end of the 1890s to about 1915 showed that "defects" or "failures" (1) are generated by the market's own functioning, (2) become at some point big enough to reach a threshold of social perception that they are defects or failures of the market system, and (3) can induce organized group counteraction.

As for the vast expansion of energy use with the rise in per capita income, the gestation period for the social perception threshold to be reached took many decades that spanned the entire laissez-faire period. With the consumption of energy materials rising annually at twice the population rate, by the end of World War II per capita energy consumption had more than doubled since 1900. By that time, a full two decades after the end of laissez-faire, the social recognition of the damage being wrought on the environment and on human health by the production and consumption of energy was soon to crystallize in the form of the environmental movement, with its demands for public and private restraints.

Another far-reaching change wrought primarily by the market system's economic growth during the declining laissez-faire era was the relative growth in the nonfarm economy and the attendant proportionate fall in the agricultural sector. While both supply and demand influences within the market nexus were at work, domestic demand was predominant by virtue of the community's high income elasticity of demand for nonfarm products contrasted with the low elasticity for farm food products. The sectoral effect of the differing elasticities was, of course, facilitated by nonfarm business supplier decisions.

The enormous, gradual shift toward nonfarm consumption and production had a powerful impact on all three of the great institutional configurations. The effects on the economy and on people included, for example:

1. Some decline in the numerical and relative economic importance of small proprietorship enterprise in the economy.
2. A loss in a part of the community's insulation from the market cyclical contractions that had been enjoyed by most farm families, since they had usually kept possession of their housing and grew some of their own foods. Urban households lacked these cushions when their incomes fell or were cut off in depressions.
3. The creation of an ever greater need for the social provision of community sanitation and potable water systems, waste disposal facilities, and commutation transit.
4. An expanded need for job training and higher levels of education.
5. A greater institutionalization of health care and care for the elderly as the farm home and family disappeared.

The burgeoning nonfarm sector produced by demand-supply interaction in the womb of the market created a dramatic transformation in its structure. While the sector's industrialization, transport modernization, and urbanization generated a great number of small enterprises, the spread of the large corporation with its accompanying concentration of business wealth increasingly supplanted the earlier, more atomistic competitive market structures and policies. The dominant group industry, with its powerful oligopoly core and a small-firm fringe, became ever more typical. Small competitors with erratic competitive behavior provided the numbers, but the big corporations, with a devotion to profit-assuring price stability, administered each industry's important internal and external relationships.

At the same time, wage-earning employees without claims to production property came to dominate the labor force. That creation of a market system with a labor force made up overwhelmingly of employees, instead of the former large contingent of petty farm and urban proprietors, brought on a quite new set of socioeconomic conditions with interpersonal group relationships that were profoundly inimical to continuation of a laissez-faire, overwhelmingly pro-business minimum government.

In the first place, the always unequal distribution of income and wealth became more unequal and was viewed as such particularly by an urban population lacking the possession of production wealth that, for example, farmers had. This intensified the old, deep-rooted, resentful egalitarianism in American society on the part of property-short groups.

In the second place, the impact of recurrent cyclical depressions was much more severe on the nonfarm wage earner than on the family farmer. This cyclical incidence of chronic job uncertainty, depression unemployment, sudden eviction from housing, and outright hunger generated the preconditions for wage-worker group action that was both hostile to the unalloyed market system and likely to elicit an appeal to government for redress.

In the third place, mustering large masses of employees in job markets with large corporate buyers of labor services created fertile grounds for labor organization designed to exercise countervailing bargaining power. The violent opposition of business to a collective bargaining solution was usually supported by government intervention under laissez-faire. But in the long run that coalition of business and government became a great public issue and proved socially intolerable.

In a further development, nonfarm rural and urban employees faced aging and ill health without the former agrarian family support system. In particular, the numbers and the proportion of elderly of all classes in the population rose because of the declining population rate and the increase in life span. Consequently, at some point laissez-faire insensitivity to retirement and its human problems would generate a threshold of intolerableness, giving rise to organized demands for private and public pensions.

Parallel with these effects in the growing nonfarm economy, the small farm firms in the relatively declining agricultural sector found themselves confronting implacable discrimination in their markets. Here were many small enterprises facing a few large buyers in the transportation and commodity markets in which they sold (monopsony or oligopsony). Likewise, they confronted one or a few large sellers in the markets in which they bought commodities and services for production or household use (monopoly or oligopoly). Those product markets were not competitive and did not afford a "fair" (competitive) price. The farmers' terms of trade were below "par" (again, competitive). Hence the call for "parity."

In the market for credit, the problem was not price exploitation by big business. Rather, private bankers recognized the greater risks represented by farm borrowers and on strict "business" grounds had to charge higher interest rates on farm loans. This looked like discrimination to farmers, but it was largely discounting the risk factor. It would be better to say that private financial market institutions were not equipped to provide agriculture with inexpensive credit and capital.

In brief, the market's operation prepared the groundwork for the farmers to become a *disadvantaged group*. But for that label to emerge the farmers had to develop their own *perception* of disadvantage and fashion an appropriate *organization*. Only then could the label receive long-run public credibility. And only then could an appeal to government succeed.

Despite their famed rugged individualism, after their private market producer cooperatives failed to correct the perceived inequities, the farmers organized an "agrarian revolt" against railroad and middleman monopolies and against the "money trusts." The revolt inaugurated a century of appeals to government for subsidies to correct for the farmers' chronic disadvantaged status in the market. That persistent political campaign spanned both the last decades of laissez-faire and more than a half-century of the subsequent mixed economy.

Almost all of these ominous changes in the market system, and the sociopolitical turmoil associated therewith, began in earnest around the last quarter of the nineteenth century. It was in that quarter-century that the "organizational revolution," with its highly political potential, sprang from the industrially maturing market system. Its most dramatic manifestation was the agrarian revolt and labor's craft-focused trade unionism. Those organizations represented *countervailing power centers* responding primarily to the initial rise of the big-business power center, to use John Kenneth Galbraith's insightful phrases.[2]

While laissez-faire thrived in a largely rural world of small business proprietors, the new world of big group organizations and giant corporations proved subversive of it. The farm organizations made no bones about turning to the states, and later the federal government, but the American Federation of Labor (AFL) was laggard about it. For decades prior to the 1930s the AFL touted its devotion to laissez-faire and an apolitical stance, even as it gave support to legislation to improve conditions on the job.

Meanwhile, as the laissez-faire relationship waned, additional disruptive changes took place *within the market system's business component itself.* That process in economic history was insightfully recognized and analyzed by the brilliant theoretical and empirical economist, Joseph Schumpeter:

> The opening up of new markets, foreign or domestic, and the organizational development . . . illustrate the same process of industrial mutation—if I may

use that biological term—that incessantly revolutionizes the economic structure **from within,** incessantly destroying the old one, incessantly creating a new one.[3]

These changes were fated to undermine domestic laissez-faire in the long run. By 1900 the giant corporations had become the major economic and political power center in the private sphere of society. But paradoxically as such they had made themselves "affected with a public interest."

For example, in the case of the public utility industry, so vital to an urban society, the monopoly power position of its component firms led very early to public regulation. The "public interest" phrase just quoted was applied to such firms by virtue of two community judgments: (1) the firms had huge investments in fixed plant and equipment with consequent high fixed costs and long-run falling average costs that made them "natural monopolies"; and (2) they supplied essential community services like water, sewage disposal, electricity, communication and transportation. In most cases regulation allowed private ownership, but the government influenced the firm's prices at levels designed to underwrite their profitability. This was a far cry from a laissez-faire "free market." The public utility sector came to occupy in the twentieth century a very notable portion of the total "private" economy—about 10 percent of total production by the 1920s, for example. There it remained into the 1990s.

In other industries in which the leading corporations had large fixed assets and costs but were considered not to be producing socially essential products, such firms nonetheless were likely to be "affected with a public interest" in a nonlegal sense. One reason for this was that as oligopolists their recognition of mutual interdependence and their drive for price stability often led to cooperative uniform behavior that bordered on monopoly. In a society that worshipped the god of competition, monopolistic market structures, behavior, or results were anathema. While the antitrust "conspiracy" laws were ill-adapted to restraint of monopolistic behavior, they nevertheless attested to society's willingness to intrude at any time into an enterprise system that had moved far away from pure competition.

Furthermore, in many markets having a large-firm oligopoly core and a small-firm fringe the unequal competitive struggle between the two groups led to bitter policy collisions. It was thus no accident that a high percentage of cases under the antitrust laws were initiated by small competitors. In general, an industry's "leaders" wanted much more stability in the market than did the small firms. The latter were likely to try to buttress their tenuous share of sales by price cuts or some form of product differentiation. They were consequently looked upon as "destructive" and "cutthroat" threats to the power of the leaders to assure uniform, stable prices high enough to cover the high fixed costs on the big firms' differentially large fixed investments in plant and equipment.

Industry leaders used widely the business trade associations to implement their stability goals. For example, the so-called open-price trade associations were designed to further common pricing among all the enterprises in the market. The same purpose was served by publication of standard cost-accounting formulae in the house organs of the industry. The hope was that if all concerns adhered to the formula, uniform prices would be more readily developed. Thus tacit collusion could be substituted for illegal Sherman Act "conspiracy." It is small wonder that the ancient, outmoded conspiracy doctrine contributed to a very weakened and checkered career for antitrust enforcement.

In retaliation to small-firm disruptions, the giants might initiate their own price war to drive out the small-firm disrupters. The inequality between the market system contestants gradually became a public issue: there was a "small business problem." Small enterprise was another "disadvantaged group." As a result, government protection was belatedly extended during the Great Depression, for example, in such regulatory legislation as the 1936 Robinson-Patman Act prohibiting firms from giving special discounts or rebates to large buyers (the "anti-chainstore act"); and the 1937 Miller-Tydings amendment to the Sherman Anti-Trust Law, legalizing agreements by small retailers under state "fair trade" resale price maintenance laws they had gotten adopted, laws preventing price cuts below a manufacturer's list price. It was ironic that Miller-Tydings prevented price competition even between small-firm "disrupters," thus assuring the price stability and uniformity so desired by large firms. Social control of business was not without its paradoxes. Of course, in that event it was the inarticulate consumers who paid for their lack of participation in the organizational revolution.

Both Miller-Tydings and Robinson-Patman violated the great American commitment to competition by the public sponsorship of business-prompted cartelization. A similar monopolistic measure had been made official government policy in the 1933 Agricultural Adjustment Act. But such violations were acceptable because they purported to benefit more or less "disadvantaged groups" of small enterprises.

The burgeoning giant corporations, bolstered by often ruthless methods against labor and smaller competitors, by acquisitions, through use of the holding company device, and with the help of the first merger movement during 1897–1904, also magnified the concentration of wealth and income. The muckraker literature of protest and exposure and a nineteen-volume report by the Federal Industrial Commission struck at business concentration and the cavalier exercise of economic power with accusations such as "robber baron" and "octopus." A growing public recognition also surfaced regarding the alleged adverse effects of big business's exercise of political clout over every level of government. All of the popular rumblings pyramided into the development of a new public insistence on the "social responsibility" of big business—a close substitute for "affected with a public interest."

Nevertheless, the pro–laissez-faire stance of the large corporations and their small-firm "fellow travelers" had substantial support among the populace. The big firms were big in the local economy, and the community's economic dependency on them was thought to be paramount. President Calvin Coolidge was merely echoing public opinion when he declared in the Roaring Twenties that "the business of America is business." Any governmental restrictions on business—as sharply distinguished from subsidies—always had to be very specific, ad hoc, or "crisis" related. Indeed, while Americans had a strong traditional propensity to make an accommodation with big business, they never ideologically came to approve big government, especially a big civilian *federal* government. They were much more prone to pin the Leviathan and bureaucracy labels on government than on business organizations. Ironically, however, over the very long run many piecemeal, "temporary," or ad hoc interventions proved to be abiding, and they added up to bigger government.

Technological Advance and Market Evolution

The remarkable economic growth record of the market system through most of the laissez-faire era involved significant advances in production technology and business management. The rising class of corporate managers, increasingly separated as to decision making from the owners of their firms, founded great new technologically innovative industries such as the modernized railroads, motor vehicles, electric power generation from coal, and petrochemicals. Those giant advances flowed of necessity from the cost-minimization and profit-maximization drives of the growing firms as they channeled retained income and borrowings from the new financial markets into plant and equipment investment.

Government worshipped and encouraged that untrammeled investment as much as business itself and everybody else in the tradition-bound establishment as well as the general public. Private investment was almost universally viewed as the prime source of all economic progress and the only escape from cyclical economic instability. The fact that wide investment fluctuations were overwhelmingly responsible for cyclical instability was either ignored or viewed as an unfortunate feature of the market's "natural" *modus operandi*. The veneration of private investment was the great ideological foundation of laissez-faire policy. The enduring power of that ideology to guide private and public policy can be appreciated by scanning the orthodox policy stance in the 1990s.

Investment in human capital such as education, on the other hand, long played second fiddle, relegated largely to the practical sphere of on-the-job training. As late as 1900, only slightly over half of the population five to twenty years old was enrolled in the already overwhelmingly public schools (less than one-third for blacks). The average number of days in school per enrolled pupil was only ninety-nine a year. A bare 6 percent of youths seventeen years old had graduated from high school in that year; and only about 2.3 percent of the eighteen- to twenty-four-year-old population was enrolled in institutions of higher education.

However, the popular demand for public education spread rapidly after 1900, contributing to and expressing a greater role for government in that crucial sphere. Indeed, the advance of public education during the three laissez-faire decades—1900 to 1930—proceeded at a faster pace than it did thereafter.

The progress of publicly provided education resulted from many factors. But it stemmed in particular from three major determinants, two of which were connected directly with the market system. The first was business's chronic failure to invest sufficiently in human capital. The second was the progress of production technology to ever higher levels of complexity. The third, largely external to the market system's operation, was social group pressures for intellectual competence and enrichment.

Public education's generally gradual growth pattern after 1930 embraced three leaps. The first was the immediate post–World War II surge in higher education enrollments owing to the federal GI Bill, designed to support the transition to civilian life for demobilized service personnel. This was a far cry from the irresponsible federal role in demobilization in laissez-faire's post–World War I years. Of course, the numbers involved were vastly different. The second leap was in response to the baby boom, also coming out of World War II. In this case, society's demand for intellectual competence soared again. The American social consensus left no doubt that the enormous public resources necessary to provide educationally for the baby boomer generation had to be mobilized. The third educational leap was the rapid, belated rise in women's college enrollments. That leap reflected the post–World War II jump in women's labor force participation and the feminist movement that began to flower in the 1960s.

The end result of all these developments, spanning both the laissez-faire decades after 1900 and the later mixed economy era, was a very large public educational sector in the economy and society. For example, by 1990, directly involved public education employment accounted for almost 4 percent of all civilian employment. In the state and local government sector, education-connected employees amounted to 42 percent of all employees working in that big sector.

The progress of technology from steam engines to electric generators and then internal combustion engines created a market system requirement for broadbased and high-level education. That same "gale of creative destruction" (Schumpeter) generated great new investment-embodied innovations that initiated major new production techniques and capital-using growth industries. The new giant steel, chemical, petroleum, petrochemical, electric power, motor vehicle, and the later government-aided nuclear energy industries, with their continuous production technology ("mass production"), also became veritable social icons worshipped by the public at large.

However, as time passed and these giant industries continued to grow, certain side effects developed that were destined to undermine the public's free market euphoria characterizing the early decades of their expansion. In the first place, there were the adverse side effects of the previously mentioned explosion of energy use in the spheres of both production and consumption. In addition, there were spillover effects from the application of the great new industries' technological base. Two famous British economists, Alfred Marshall (writing in the 1890s) and A.C. Pigou (*The Economics of Welfare,* 1920), noted that both businesses and households make maximizing decisions that affect beneficially or adversely persons who are not parties to their individual decisions. Such effects are thus "external" to the economic activity of those decision makers. Hence the effects, following Marshall and Pigou, came to be called *externalities.* The type that is relevant here is the technological externality.

Pigou observed the coal-burning, smokestack industries of industrial Britain. He noted, for example, that a railroad's (private or governmental) decision to let fly into the surrounding atmosphere the sparks and soot from its locomotives might impose costly damages on nearby farmers' crops. Running the trains generated *private* costs (and benefits) for the railroad business, but the railroad incurred none of the *external costs* perpetrated upon the farmers located near the railroad's right-of-way. The sum of the two costs comprised the *social costs* of the railroad's business.

A hallmark of the laissez-faire era, even in its declining phase, was the customary "freedom" permitted a business firm or household not to incorporate into its own private costs the external costs it might impose on others in the larger environment. And it goes without saying that the same liberties prevailed for government organs.

The growth of large external costs emanating from the technological externalities of the great, expanding modern industries only gradually became a matter of governmental concern. It was a long road from smokestack energy use and soot to the threat of global warming. A threshold of public perception always had to be generated. Besides, there were many varieties of technological externalities, and they developed at uneven rates—most from business, some from households, some even from government. important thresholds in the emergence of major public concerns, leading to significant government intervention, were in general reached in the United States only in the post–World War II era. The prime example of the crossing of a threshold was the formation of the many-faceted environmental movement. The resulting variety of ecological agencies that were set up by all levels of domestic government and by international bodies became dramatic testimony to the historic linkages between the market system's technological progress, the social responses thereto, and the consequent establishment of public interventionist agencies and policies.

The advancing mechanized production technology was embodied particularly in producers' durable equipment (PDE) investment as distinguished from fixed investment in industrial and commercial structures. Indeed, while the former enjoyed a quite buoyant career in the twentieth century, the career of structures was slow-growing. The incidence of PDE on skill requirements was split. While some equipment required greater technical education ("human capital"), as pointed out earlier, much of it was skill diluting. This was especially so with electrified, assembly-line, continuous-production equipment. One result of this schism in technology was to make the older craft distinctions irrelevant in those so-called mass production activities. The technological basis for the craft-based organizations at the heart of the trade union movement was drastically undermined. The consequent spreading obsolescence of craft union structure was partly responsible for the failure of the AFL to expand its membership after World War I. When the Committee for Industrial Organization (CIO) emerged in 1935 to organize the huge establishments and firms in the mass production industries, the issue of craft vs. industrial organizational form was central to the schism in labor's ranks. It was not merely a formal, structural matter, either. Rather, the conflict at that time over organizational form concealed a conflict over whether the unorganized, unskilled were to be organized at all.

Those conflicts came to a head during the C ʒaᵗ Depression of the 1930s, at a time when the split in the character of technology had matured. This also meant that the unions, like almost everybody else in that grim decade, quite suddenly acquired a stronger political stance. Such politicalization had been very much, although not entirely, lacking in the decidedly pro–laissez-faire, voluntarist philosophy of the AFL.

Consequently, in subsequent years the raised level of political activity of the CIO unions pushed even the AFL in the direction of demands for government help. No branch of the much bigger, more politically conscious, labor union movement after the mid-thirties could ignore, for example, the strengthening of labor's status under the New Deal's Section 7(a) of the 1933 National Industrial Recovery Act and the 1935 National Labor Relations Act. The CIO response in particular to a changing industrial technology and to New Deal reforms had insinuated an important new labor potential for post–laissez-faire government intervention.

The Unfettered Market Often Undermined Its Own Autonomy

The historical examples presented above have shown that the slowly growing demand for government intervention constituted an institutionalized set of social responses that were inherent in some of the private market system's own developmental patterns. A number of the adaptive responses reach far back in time. Such is the case with demands for redistribution of income and wealth. But the history of those demands was episodic, not steady. For example, passage of the Federal Income Tax Amendment in 1913 was an episodic milestone in a long and spotty record of agitation for greater progressivity in the tax structure. Subsequently, as per capita real income continued to rise, the redistributive demand became both weakened because more people became well-off and indifferent, and strengthened because the continued existence of an impoverished underclass appeared patently absurd to the large humanistic elements in society.

Other popular demands arose over the long run to become significant influences on the size of government only when the evolving market system faults reached a similar threshold of intensity and public perception. A major case in point was the emergence of a belated widespread demand for high, steady employment, whose episodic milestone was the Employment Act of 1946. That most important piece of bipartisan congressional commitment in the twentieth century made the federal government responsible for "maximum" employment and purchasing power—that is, the ultimate guarantor of aggregate business sales. Another case in point was the overdue demand for environmental damage avoidance, which reached a political pinnacle with the first Earth Day and the establishment of the Environmental Protection Agency, both in the year 1970.

The higher the level of per capita income achieved over the long run, the more demands society has made on the market's potential capacity to provide for "deserving" groups and to function in a socially acceptable way. Since business enterprise operates the production side of the market, particular failures to meet the needs of some groups have been considered ground enough for blaming business and prompting government to step in to correct the inadequacies through either regulation, supervision, or direct programs. As Robert Kuttner has aptly expressed it, "market relations carried to an extreme drove out other necessary forms of relation and led to deeply antiliberal spasms of response. Laissez-faire, in short, wrecked the civil society on which capitalism depended."[4]

The private market system was never well equipped to cope on its own, not only with some of its internal needs but also with some of the social concomitants that developed out of its endogenous evolutionary changes. This fact has been explored to some degree in the preceding discussion. The main point in that discussion was that, along with the market's material achievements, society has increasingly insisted that the economy have a human face—a "fair" division of the rising income and wealth; full employment; educational opportunity for personal development, not just human capital for the market; access to health care; decent housing; security in old age; equal opportunity for women and minorities; environmental well-being, and so on.

In those cases in which the evolving market's social impact has been perceived by the community as unsatisfactory, the government has again and again been selected by the affected strata in society to provide an appropriate compensating response. That such public intervention itself might be defective was not a big issue for reformers in the laissez-faire era of small government, although it did become an issue in more recent times.

It required a long time for the interactions between market change and societal response in each case to develop the respective thresholds of community demand for intervention. The laissez-faire era may be viewed as a gestation period for those thresholds—that is, a period during which the groundwork for a larger government role was laid.

Evolution of Public Demands for Intervention and the Government Responses, 1870–1929

The career of public pressures for the subversion of domestic laissez-faire policy in response to the market's changes prior to 1929 went through three phases. The first spanned the decades from about 1870 to 1900. It is both ironic and prophetic that the agrarian crusade dominated that phase. The most "rugged individualists" of all—the family farmers—relinquished a big part of their previous individualism, acted collectively, and invoked government help. Other millions of individualistic Americans, but only in later times, did much the same thing.

The agrarian revolt organized countervailing power against the new corporate titans in railroad transport and shipping services, manufacturing, and finance. In the process, agriculture's political populism created an enduring public image to the effect that farming was a disadvantaged occupation within a discriminatory system of big industry and finance. The image of a competitively disadvantaged group would prove useful to numerous other groups in the future.

The agricultural organizations and the agrarian-based Populist Party in the 1890s initiated a custom of correcting perceived market defects by means of an organized appeal to government for compensatory action. They thus endowed this early historical phase of interventionism with the character of a model and a gestation period for the wider public demands that rose in the future in response to other structural and functional transformations in the market.

In the midst of this phase was the 1894 march on Washington of Jacob Coxey's nonagrarian "army" of the unemployed with its New Deal–type program demanding relief and public works. But the demonstration, while exhibiting the worker's counteraction to the market's cyclical contraction, could at that early date be only historically anticipatory. It lacked the urban, industrial, mass, ethnically homogeneous wage-earner base that was necessary for more advanced and organized interventionist demands of that character.

The second phase in the evolution of public pressures for government intrusion into the market's functioning may be dated by such well-known phrases as "the age of reform" or "the quest for social justice" or as in the classic economic history by Harold U. Faulkner, "the decline of laissez-faire."[5] It spans the years from the late 1890s to about World War I. As those expressions suggest, the period was outstanding for its famous upsurge of organized social and political response to the market system's developments reviewed above. The Progressive movement of elements in the new, predominantly urban, middle class, in loose coalition with the liberal turn taken by the Democratic Party under Woodrow Wilson, mounted a running attack on the market's perceived economic inequities. The attack sought *social balance* through state action. The Progressives thus propounded the normative doctrine of an "adjudicative state" responsive to a general will presumably favoring a harmonious balance among conflicting interests. Organized extremism like radical socialism, labor violence, and brutally exploitive business was abhorred by the Progressives. This middle-of-the-road stance of the urban middle class was destined to become an abiding influence on the subsequent history of government-economy relations. Powerful as that general influence later became, it was, strangely enough, never institutionalized into an integrated, coherent, firmly established form at that time.

The Progressive's reform activities in those two decades were a lagged reaction to the imbalances previously generated by market changes but addressed only parochially and narrowly by the agrarian crusade. The adjustments in market-government relations that were accomplished in the two decades of this phase were extremely modest. But they were nevertheless the most significant penetrations into the armor of laissez-faire in the whole era from the nineteenth century's last quarter to the end of the 1920s.

Reform meant mainly nonsocialistic restrictions and regulations imposed on swashbuckling private corporate predaciousness. The list of modest public policy corrections achieved by Progressive pressures is well known:[6] unseating of corrupt municipal governments, the Oregon ten-hour laws, the 1906 Pure Food and Drug Act, the Massachusetts 1912 minimum wage law, New York's 1910 compulsory workmen's compensation act, child-labor protection laws, railroad rate controls in the 1906 Hepburn Act and 1910 Man-Elkins Act, the federal income tax amendment (ratified in 1913), natural resources conservation and reclamation regulation, the 1914 Clayton Anti-Trust and Federal Trade Commission acts, the direct election of senators (Seventeenth Amendment, 1913), women's suffrage (Nineteenth Amendment, 1920), and various state regulatory commissions for the control of corporate behavior. The attempts to strengthen antitrust were modestly bolstered by the U.S. Senate's famous 1913 Pujo Committee Report on business concentration and the "money monopoly."

The third phase of laissez-faire's declining career was one of arrested deterioration or, as the "cycle" theorist of affirmative government growth Arthur Schlesinger Jr. would call it, "recession from social liberalism," spanning the "prosperity decade" of the 1920s. But between the second and this third phase lay the World War I interlude. That interlude brought about an end to the "age of reform."

In the course of that short and economically rather small war there was only one development of long-run significance for laissez-faire's decline. That was the explosion of business organization into a multitude of trade associations. The war was administered at home by corporate executives, stockholders, and editors, with a bare sprinkling of professional people. In the guise of administrative desirability, the proliferation of trade associations completed the institutionalization of business's organizational revolution. Thus was laid additional solid groundwork for business interest-group roles in the future history of government-market system relationships that bypassed householder participation. That experience is emphasized as an important empirical component of Robert Higgs's "crisis" theory of the episodic growth of big government.

A second wartime development has been viewed by some historians as also of long-run import. That was the official recognition by the federal government of labor-management collective bargaining. However, in the ensuing decade unions were subjected to an unrelenting attack by business with government support. Unions lost hundreds of thousands of members as a result. Except for the Norris-LaGuardia anti-injunction act of 1928, labor organization had to wait until the 1933 National Industrial Recovery Act of the New Deal to again receive official approval of collective bargaining—and that for reasons very different from those prompting the World War I recognition.

In World War I, the government centrally planned and controlled agricultural output and distribution; overland transportation through a temporarily national-ized railway system; and manufacturing in all industries producing war-related goods or manufacturing using materials the war industries needed. The system of controls developed largely by teams led by the great capitalists Bernard Baruch and Herbert Hoover were deemed successful. They provided the models for controls used in the much bigger and economically significant World War II. However, it remained a firm belief of most Americans that economic planning could not succeed. The exception of war was a special case of planning for a generally accepted goal: unconditional surrender of the enemy. Even recovery from depression was not sufficiently generally accepted as a goal for the govern-ment to adopt the kinds of controls it used in the two wars. Hoover, who had personally controlled the production and distribution of food for most of the Northern Hemisphere in 1919, was unwilling to apply that remarkable central management skill to the amelioration of the Great Depression.

Some writers have also suggested that another lasting effect of World War I on the expansion of the federal government was the large increase in the number of veteran claimants on the treasury's resources.[7] It is true that there were 773,000 veterans in civil life in 1915; and that the average during the 1920s was close to 5 million; and that the American Legion was founded as a pressure group in 1919. It is also true that federal expenditures for veterans' benefits and services exploded from $174 million in 1915 to $665 million in 1929. That latter sum accounted for over a fifth of all outlays of the federal government in 1929.

However, a review of the federal government's expenditures for veterans since the Civil War shows that as a percentage of total federal outlays the period of greatest support in all U.S. history since that time was about twenty years after the Civil War. A focus on the 1920s is deceptive. There has been no long-run persistent relative rise in veterans' claims since World War I that could explain the rise in big government thereafter. Historically, there have been only episodic, exogenously determined fluctuations in veterans' payments as a share of the federal budget. These fluctuations have stemmed mainly from the timing of wars and to a lesser extent the ebb and flow of pressures from veterans' organizations.

When the war ended, the crisis administrative machinery was dismantled in favor of a return to a smaller federal establishment and a shift by business leaders back to their traditional tasks of running economic affairs in the private sector with the aid of the state and local governments. That shift was paralleled by a haphazard, irresponsible demobilization of the armed forces. "Wartime planning" was therefore not institutionalized—that is, it did not generate a lasting, purposeful, ideologically substantiated pattern of group behavior with its requisite internal administrative guidance and physical facilities. There was no Higgs-type ratchet effect.

A number of writers aver that the successful planning experience significantly affected government's role later, as some of the World War I business executives and other advisers reappeared in the New Deal administration.[8] The implied power of such a presumed continuity seems exaggerated in view of the many intervening years of undirected economic activity. "Government-business cooperation" is very different from World War I planning. Such cooperation was always prevalent on specific matters and in specific industries or activities throughout the era of laissez-faire and afterwards.

The eminent economist Joseph Schumpeter once referred to the prosperity decade as one of "intact capitalism." Indeed, it was pro-business, laissez-faire with a vengeance. Fiscal policy was distinctly classical in its thrust: small federal budgets, annual budget surpluses with debt retirement, increased tariff rates, reduction of the meager progressivity of the new income tax—all designed to bolster savings on the traditional assumption that private real fixed investment was a function of savings. Labor organization was both attacked and hypocritically wooed by "welfare capitalism" into a state of drastic membership decline. State and local welfare legislation all but came to a stop.

What had happened to the progressive upsurge? We cannot turn to the maturation of the agrarian political crusade with the formation of the Farm Bloc lobby in the twenties, because Progressivism, as distinguished from Populism, expressed the moral aspirations of the urban middle class, as Hofstadter maintains. It is true that Robert LaFollette's 1924 presidential campaign found considerable support in eleven states that were strongly farm production economies, entities that were suffering not only from historic relative decline but now even from absolute decreases in persons engaged. It is also true that there were many socially minded crusaders, particularly in the social work profession, crying out for aid to the underclass.

But the former progressives among the city middle classes failed to mount the *organizational* vehicles necessary to sustain a level of reform activity such as had been achieved in the pre–World War I years. Historians have not come up with an interpretive consensus on this matter. But some partial explanations are plausible. For one thing, pervasive Republican claims, asserting the impeccable virtues of the private market, derived much across-the-board, continuous community support from the sustained economic expansion following the sharp slump of 1921, from the high levels of employment, from the stable prices that forestalled any group attempt (except for the farmers) to overcome differential inflation, and from the upward drift in real income per head that bolstered the folklore of "trickle down" benefits for all. Per capita income increased for the middle classes in particular, while private labor incomes lagged spottily behind the relative rise in property incomes. Government wages, however, were outstanding for reflecting the general expansion quite accurately.

Business corporations and spokespeople concocted an additional opiate to channel the attention of the middle classes, and even elements within the blue-collar strata: a tidal wave of consumerism. The emphasis was on bright new electrical household durables and automobiles, the markets for which were flooded by vast sales promotion outlays and provision of liberal installment credits.

Furthermore, establishment spokespeople and the mass media busied themselves with quite successfully touting the doctrines of "permanent prosperity," of a business class that allegedly embraced a heightened sense of social responsibility, of the untold dangers in any government policies designed to aid the underlying masses as distinguished from the propertied classes. Thus the middle classes and most other Americans were brainwashed into a state of apathy or disinterestedness. The Social Darwinist belief prevailed that everybody except incompetents could be an economic success if they were patient and frugal. The reform impulse was suffocated.

Hofstadter advances among other hypotheses the notion that the middle class became unduly focused on working out of Prohibition, which had been one of the Progressives' goals. Additionally, he suggests that by the end of World War I the Progressives had begun to become apathetic "tired radicals."[9] Leuchtenburg, in a chapter by that title, agrees, adding cogent points regarding the war-induced split in Progressive ranks, the conservative content of the Progressive platform in the 1916 election campaign, and the disillusionment pervading most of American society about the paltry results of the "war for democracy."[10] These speculations may all be correct as partial explanations. But the important point is that the reform movement languished, leaving laissez-faire to be merely nibbled at over the prosperity decade.

The absence of significant organized pressure for government social reform slowed the decline of domestic laissez-faire in the twenties but did not completely arrest it. However, what action there was occurred primarily on the state and local level. Federal total outlays, for example, after 1922 when World War I military expenditures had finally wound down, failed to increase at all (in current dollars). Federal government civilian employment did increase some: about 13 percent between 1922 and 1930, but barely kept up with the 14 percent rise in the civilian labor force.[11]

On the other hand, the growth of state and local government, always much larger than the federal, attested to the slow, continued attrition of laissez-faire. For example, the total full-time equivalent (FTE) employment in that sector increased 34 percent between 1922 and 1930. School FTE employment rose 25 percent, and nonschool 42 percent. By 1930, total state and local FTE employment, at 2,436,000, amounted to 5 percent of the economy's civilian labor force.

In general the expenditures of the state and local governments, other than the big-ticket item of education, more or less directly contributed to the functioning of the private market system rather than directly contributing to the population's well-being. Estimates available for 1927 show that of all state and local nonroutine expenditures of $6,188 million, public education for, among other things, the education of the market system's labor force at $2,235 million, and public infrastructure, also supporting the private market, at $2,121 million, summed to 70 percent of the total. Highway outlays alone, providing "road bed" for the great new "private" motor vehicle industry aggregated $1,809 million in that year.[12] Welfare expenditures, by contrast, totaled only $506 million, about 8 percent of nonroutine expenditures.

Government before 1929 had been growing absolutely and relatively to total economic activity, but remained small relative to that total. Such intervention as had been successfully demanded by interest groups was largely of a regulatory or supervisory character that left the basic performance of the economy to the vagaries of the market. A "social market economy," to use German Ludwig Erhard's term, did not exist. Neither did a welfare state. The United States was far behind other western democracies in these respects. Nor did "state capitalism" of the German and Italian fascist variety or the Japanese type exist. In the tradition of laissez-faire, the federal government was still largely the executive committee of the dominant corporate business interests, and the state and local governments kept the market system's house in order. Nobody who was anybody was seriously concerned at that "moment of truth" on the edge of the Great Depression about the distribution of income and wealth, the level of employment, inflation or deflation, the business mortality rate, rate of economic growth, the rights of labor, the security of the elderly, protection against ill health, environmental damage, or the increasing global interconnections facing the American economy in the years ahead.

Harold U. Faulkner's brilliant economic history dates the decline of laissez-faire in the progressive years 1897–1917. He insightfully calls attention to the fact that much of the interventionist reform legislation in that period was designed to restore a Paradise Lost of free competition and laissez-faire.[13] Until this utopianism was overcome laissez-faire could not be overcome. The paradox was resolved beginning in the Great Depression. It is for that reason that the Depression and the New Deal represented a discontinuity in economic history and in the relationships between government and the market system. The decline of laissez-faire was transformed into its demise with the rise of the early mixed economy. To that institutional transformation in the relationships between government and the market system we now turn.

Notes

1. Referred to in Richard Hofstadter, *The Age of Reform* (New York: Random House, 1955), p. 231.

2. John Kenneth Galbraith, *American Capitalism: The Concept of Countervailing Power* (Boston: Houghton Mifflin, Sentry ed., 1962).

3. Cited in Janet A. Napoli, "Derivative Markets and Competitiveness," Federal Reserve Bank of Chicago, *Economic Perspectives,* July/August 1992, p. 13.

4. Robert Kuttner, *The End of Laissez Faire* (New York: Alfred A. Knopf, 1991), pp. 4–5.

5. Harold U. Faulkner, *The Decline of Laissez Faire* (New York: Rinehart, 1951).

6. See also the more comprehensive summary in Harold G. Vatter, *The Drive to Industrial Maturity* (Westport, Conn.: Greenwood, 1975), pp. 208–209.

7. See, for example, Robert Higgs, *Crisis and Leviathan* (New York: Oxford University Press, 1987), p. 150.

8. See, for example, William E. Leuchtenburg, *The Perils of Prosperity* (Chicago: University of Chicago Press, 1958), p. 41.

9. See Hofstadter, *Age of Reform,* pp. 292, 288–289; 286–287.

10. Leuchtenburg, *Perils of Prosperity,* pp. 120–139 *passim.*

11. The significant employment figures used for this calculation are what might be called the "discretionary" totals: civilian defense and postal employment have been removed. This leaves a total of only 200,000 discretionary federal employees in 1930—less than 1/2 of 1 percent of the civilian labor force.

12. In this calculation, based on data in *Historical Statistics,* p. 1128, the "routine" expenditures deducted to get "nonroutine" are police and fire protection, general administration, parks and recreation, and interest on debt. Welfare expenditures include the listed "public welfare," hospitals and health.

13. Faulkner, *Decline of Laissez Faire,* p. 367.

CHAPTER TWO

The Beginnings of the Mixed Economy, 1930–46

No radical change is easy. Radical change is only necessary when
we fail to learn from our past in anticipating the future.
—attributed to Attila, The Hun

A social and political upheaval during the Great Depression of the thirties destroyed the old laissez-faire relationships among the institutional triad: market system, society, and government. The years immediately following World War II solidified public acceptance of the new, augmented government role in the triad. Acceptance was powerfully represented in the 1946 Employment Act. In the context of public fear that severe depression might recur, the act's new radical thrust asserted, with the customary caution, federal responsibility for socially satisfactory macroeconomic performance.

While the Employment Act was a major new direction in short-run public policy, an explicit commitment to underwrite long-run growth in total output was lacking. Yet such a commitment had to be implicit because to *sustain* "maximum employment and purchasing power" output (and therefore aggregate business sales) would have to rise in pace with labor force and any participation growth. As things worked out in the postwar era, however, the growth implication was generally shunted into the policy background, always denigrated by the lingering reliance on the old faith in private investment as prime mover of the growth process.

The critical years for the great public policy transformation were not during World War II, but from 1930 to 1940. Those years produced an explosive conjuncture of several powerful long- and short-run forces making for a massive change in government's role and size. Indeed, those forces irreparably dismantled the very foundations of the traditional relationships among government, the market system, and society.

In the case of the market system itself, the growth of GNP and the private investment rate had been beset by slowdown forces ever since the end of the first decade of the twentieth century. The average long-run GNP rate had dropped from well over 4 percent a year for the period 1870–1910 to about 3 percent for the period 1910–29. The average long-run ratio of gross business fixed nonresidential investment to GNP had drastically fallen, from well over 13 percent to 10 percent, largely because of a serious drop in the growth rate of business structures.[1] Residential construction investment had also experienced a continuing long-run slowdown, primarily owing to the fall in the population and urbanization rates. While hardly anybody was aware of these arresting changes, they were operating during the long, grim years of the Depression to accentuate the market system's more apparent short-run inadequacies.

In the case of pertinent societal changes, the shock of economic collapse brought to the surface the potential for social activism contained in certain long-run structural, organizational, and ideological developments. For one thing, the farmers, even with their declining numbers, still made up about 10 percent of the civilian labor force, and had established themselves as a permanent disadvantaged group. They now had a Farm Bloc in Congress and a long tradition of demand for government support. Furthermore, the middle class, so decisive in the earlier progressive reform era, had continued to grow. While pushed into quiescence in the twenties, it was in a stronger position to come forward in the next outbreak of market operational deficiencies and inequities.

The dominant social class of wage workers, always a particularly fertile source of income and related demands, and a social category where numbers count politically, had become enormous. The wage-earning labor force in the commodity producing and transport activities, which was at the center of labor's organizational potential, numbered in 1930 over 12 million out of a total nonfarm employment of about 29 million. Much of the divisions in labor's ranks stemming from heterogeneous national origins had been dissipated by the termination of the open immigration policy and by public school educational homogenization.

The decline in job-conscious craft union organization under the employer offensive and the AFL's sickly organizing efforts during the twenties should not deceive one into overlooking the enormous potential for labor activism that had accumulated by 1930. Wage workers had continued to fare unequally in both the long run and in the preceding prosperity period with its typical cyclical shift in favor of property incomes. The business propaganda in the twenties about labor's potential for becoming a "stockholding proletariat" had not materialized. The same went for the promise of "two chickens in every pot, two cars in every garage." The existence of strong, politically active, labor movements in the comparable market systems of Western Europe well before 1930 suggests that the forces within the employee strata making for greater activism in the United States were overripe by the 1930s.

A closer look at long-run societal changes suggests that the influence of institutional evolution in society might have been (and may still be) rising, relative to the career of noninterventionist business influence rooted in the private market system. This interpretation may be illustrated by the acceleration in the advance of education, always overwhelmingly public, even during the laissez-faire era. Thus in the later years of laissez-faire, total elementary and secondary school enrollment embraced about 73 percent of all persons five to seventeen years old in 1913, but jumped to almost 81 percent in 1930. It had been 69 percent in 1890. It is difficult to believe that the jump in the seventeen years after 1913, contrasted with the very slow increase in the previous twenty-three years, was primarily a response to an accelerated rise in the market's production technology requirements rather than primarily to social demands for mental enrichment and its attendant enhancement of the quality of life.

There can be no question about the educational acceleration between 1913 and 1930. High school graduates as a percent of seventeen-year-olds, for example, increased 4 percent a year from 1870 to 1913, but rose 6 percent annually between 1913 and 1929. The relative advance in higher education degree-credit enrollment was even more striking: 6 percent a year over 1913–29 compared to about 2 percent annually between 1870 and 1913.

The education case supports the interpretation that some of the pressures for greater government provision and/or controls, augmented by the accumulation and institutionalization of experience with the appeal to government, can emanate primarily from societal wellsprings. This is not to say that the evolving market's own total or partial requirements are unimportant in the generation of pressures for government intervention. Those requirements have continued to generate pressures for more government intervention, addressed in some cases directly to government and in others indirectly or inadvertently through the market's impacts on some part of society.

The experience of public education enrollment growth up to 1930 also illustrates the fact that institutional histories, including the growth of government, exhibit continuities as well as discontinuities over the long run. The laissez-faire era and the subsequent mixed economy era are so different that we observe a discontinuous break between the two in the historical process. But many developments in the former era, like the erratic expansion of public education, unfolded in precursor patterns or at episodic rates closely resembling their subsequent patterns and rates as new societal demand thresholds were reached in the mixed economy era. (It is such resemblances that feed grist to the mill of gradualist historians who, unlike good physicists, can find no discontinuities in the universe.)

Continuity spanning both eras may also be found in the case of government's special attention to agriculture, in antimonopoly policy, and in the tariff. More generally, there is historical continuity in government's persistent policy of underwriting the operation and development of the business component of the market system. But that policy underwent a transformation after 1930 that is suggestive of discontinuity: from underwriting with an overwhelming emphasis on supply-side considerations to heightened, however reluctant, consideration for civilian demand-side factors in the upcoming mixed economy.

Collapse and Shock

Beginning in 1930 the market system collapsed into a state of devastating disarray. The resultant shock to society and the unprepared government establishment suddenly created thresholds for a number of social and ideological developments that had been brewing for a long time. As the thresholds were reached they surfaced in a surge of societal demands for large government responses. The responses were forthcoming.

The economic setting needs to be called to mind. Briefly, the contraction phase alone lasted forty-three dreary months, from August 1929 to March 1933. The drops in all the cyclically sensitive areas were catastrophic: business asset values, corporate profits, prices (especially farm prices), private investment, GNP, consumption, employment, wages and salaries, business proprietors' income. *Almost everything collapsed except farm production and all-government purchases of goods and services.*

One in every four persons in the civilian labor force was out of work in the trough year 1933. But all that was only in the contraction phase; there was plenty of depression still to come. While the recovery beginning in April 1933 was quite robust in terms of percentage, it had begun from such a calamitously low level that the subsequent peak-year real GNP in 1937 was barely higher than the preceding cycle peak eight long years earlier. Then came a recession in 1937–38, so that even the 1939 real GNP level was only 4 percent above ten years earlier. Business gross fixed nonresidential investment in 1939 was still only 60 percent of its 1929 level. With the labor force growing all the while, it is small wonder that the unemployment rate in 1939 was still a shocking 17 percent (it was only down to 15 percent in 1940). A monumental, decade-long fiasco in the operation of the business component of the market, complicated by disarray in the household component and social turmoil plus large-scale governmental experimentation, were among the more dramatic hallmarks of the period. In the process the market irrevocably destroyed many of its traditional warranties for self-governance.

The 1929–33 collapse was both severe and sudden. Its severity made the private market appear almost helpless to provide its touted mass material security. The suddenness of the collapse produced a devastating shock to the public's ideology about that institution. The shock waves on ideology began with widespread disillusionments, followed by rejection of some major long-established beliefs, followed in turn by a surge of reformist precepts about government's responsibilities.

Attitudinal disillusionment spread from the stark contrast between the preceding roseate promises of permanent prosperity and the immediately ensuing economic demolition. Closely connected therewith was attitudinal disillusionment toward the country's business and laissez-faire political leadership. The ruling "aristocracy of wealth" tended to become the culprit, just as it had in the Progressive era.

The culture of laissez-faire preached above all that there was a close link between its presumed competitive private markets and equality of opportunity. But how could it be claimed that the market provided equal opportunity when *total* opportunities, as evinced by the available hours of work, collapsed by 30 percent? The full employment assumption behind the equal opportunity ideology was exposed as fraudulent in the Depression world. How was it that if equal opportunity prevailed, many millions were ill-housed, ill-clad, ill-nourished, and ill-equipped to exploit "equal opportunity"? Clearly, equality of opportunity was an inoperative ideology if its alleged embodiment in the private market could not ensure a material minimum for millions in the world's richest country. Then there was the Social Darwinist assumption behind the equality of opportunity ideology: the individual was solely responsible for the opportunity niche he or she had carved out in the economy by 1929 when the unemployment rate was only 3.2 percent. But if so, millions wondered, why was it that they all suddenly became too incompetent to hold on to their opportunity niche? It didn't make sense. This social, collective character of the mass unemployment experience thus exposed the unfolding inapplicability of Social Darwinism's individualistic ideology.

The laissez-faire ideological package was also wrapped in a theory of natural law: this was just another cycle, and the cycle was the "natural" mode of the market economy. Economic laws, like all natural laws, are not made by humans, and humans cannot change them. This ideology too, while basically embraced by government during the Hoover presidency, could not withstand the hammer blows of the severe and prolonged crisis. The subsequent federal regime made it explicit that economic laws are not made by nature, they are made by people. In the 1980s and 1990s some economists began again to use a modified natural law. They referred to natural rates of economic growth and unemployment—somehow set but by unchangeable man, with or without government's help. We are not aware of direct citation of God in these uses of "natural." However, the argument that man cannot change a natural rate would be comfortable to a (Chicago) schoolman.

Government in the Great Contraction, 1929–33

The policy-strategic federal government, along with the state and local governments, struggled to adhere to the laissez-faire philosophy and its restrictive fiscal precepts during the contraction years. The leading policy makers at all levels of government, as well as in the private sector, were continually chanting that prosperity was "just around the corner." They viewed cyclical contractions as untouchable natural purges—the "castor oil theory," as Virgil Jordan expressed it. The purges corrected the private policy excesses (like speculation) of the preceding prosperity. The collapse of asset values offered entrepreneurs with "animal spirits" and intrepid optimism a chance to buy up properties cheaply and thus boost the imminent recovery. These notions of the eminent Harvard economist Joseph Schumpeter were congenial with the hoary views of the other supply-side theorists who insisted that "the answer to underproduction is more production."

The dominant views thus denigrated the demand side of the market. Production created its own demand in the private sphere. Public demand could only interfere with the natural recovery process. Public spending also had many other things wrong with it. The Republican Contract with America of the 1990s was a resounding echo of 1929–32. Budget deficits would be unfortunately required since tax revenues had collapsed. But deficits threatened the soundness of the government's credit standing and distorted the channeling of funds from private savings, the source of sacrosanct investment and therefore recovery. To cap it off, deficits meant bigger government, bigger government was self-expanding, all government, especially federal, was bureaucratic, and so on. Only the handy doctrine of emergency could "temporarily" shelve these everlasting precepts, and emergency was basically unacceptable. But even after 1929–32 the New Deal had to draw upon the emergency rationale when almost four years of depression had piled up.

In the face of the accumulating social discontent, governments did not dare to cut expenditures to match the revenue drops. At the federal level the alarming deficits mounted, so that Roosevelt in the 1932 campaign was able to unscrupulously attack Hoover for them. At the state and local level deficits were held down partly by spending cuts, but mainly by tax increases. This was a time when general sales taxes were "temporarily" instituted like wildfire. The repeal of Prohibition in 1933 also helped, with the resulting liquor excises adding to the spread of tax regressiveness at that governmental level. Local governments got some assistance from the states. So if traditional balanced-budget fiscal doctrines were good for recovery, the state and local governments surely did their part. Keynesians later wrote of the "perversity" of state and local fiscal patterns. For example, in the contraction period 1929–33, state and local real purchases were the same in 1932 as in 1929 and then fell in 1933. As late as 1940 they were only 15 percent above 1929. *Practically all of the Depression decade's two-thirds increase in all-government real purchases came from the federal government.* State and local employment rose only .67 percent annually between 1929 and 1933, although it did show a noteworthy rise thereafter. It would not appear that a state and local "bureaucracy" exploited the great contraction to accelerate its bureaucratization, although it could conceivably be so accused after 1933.

State and local government employment rose almost 4 percent yearly between

1933 and 1939, faster than the civilian labor force but at only one-third the federal employment rate rise. The states' public welfare expenditures did exhibit some sensitivity. But as the mixed economy was launched in the Great Depression, we must conclude that state and local governments as a whole were lagging participants at best.

The federal government, with regard to both size and interventionist policies during the years of the Hoover presidency spanning the great contraction, reflected the profound ambivalence of an institution with its ideologies caught in a historical cross-fire. The executive authority in general pushed for the laissez-faire program of minimum intervention coupled with minimal props for a market system that was wreaking havoc on its own business and household components and on society at large.

The Congress was somewhat differently oriented. Already in the elections of 1930 the Republican majority in the House was eliminated, and the Senate retained only a very small Republican majority. This meant that Congress became increasingly responsive to the change taking place in public attitudes. The divided federal government consequently came up with policies that in general hewed to a noninterventionist line but that also made some concessions to the emerging popular interventionist pressures.

The call for government action came overwhelmingly from society with its changing ideologies rather than from the alleged federal government bureaucracy itself. Various social groups were rapidly developing what they thought at first was a temporary "human rights" counterattack against the business element in the market system. The attack was channeled toward the governmental arena, particularly the federal arena. Indeed, at several junctures during the later phase of the contraction the exhausted state and local governments joined societal vehicles in putting pressure on the federal regime for relief and public works. The rising clamor for help was directed primarily toward the federal rather than the state and local arena during the Hoover interregnum. But the administration in those years was hardly a bureaucratic Leviathan. On the contrary, it exerted vigorous efforts to keep itself and its budget small by calling on others to institute remedial action. It directed the needy to get help from private charity, from their families in the cities or in the old farm homestead, from city garden plots, and if worse came to worst, from the state and local governments. But all these sources, themselves flattened by the contraction, failed to cope, as George Bush's "thousand points of light" did sixty years later. Thus the increasing popular focus on the federal government was the end product of the process whereby all those other channels urged by the federal government were exhausted long before the New Deal entered the fray in March 1933.

During the contraction years, federal budget expenditures in the context of a drastically falling price level were therefore pressured to be maintained and to increase, from $3.44 billion in fiscal 1930 to $4.85 billion in 1933. With dropping revenues, the annual deficits after fiscal 1930 ran up the gross debt from

$16.2 billion to $22.5 billion by 1933. The precious balanced-budget "principles" had to be agonizingly discarded, despite the largest peacetime tax increase in history in June 1932, including a 33 percent cut in the personal income tax exemptions, and a small expenditure cut in the same action.

One response late in the contraction was the passage with Hoover's approval of the Norris-LaGuardia Act, at long last limiting the use of federal court injunctions in industrial disputes, outlawing "yellow dog contracts," and more important, making labor's right to organize explicit public policy. The AFL and an organized group of progressives had been active for some time in pursuance of the anti-injunction provision in particular. Also, the AFL building trades unions had already in 1931 successfully won union-scale wages on public construction projects in the Davis-Bacon Act. Despite the fact that organized labor was a minuscule portion of the labor force and generally resisted government help, the social drift was toward government involvement in pro-labor policies, a trend hastened by the severe effects of contraction on the blue-collar class in particular and the barest beginnings of political activism on the part of the AFL. Indeed, in 1932 the AFL surprisingly came out for federal funding of unemployment compensation, "a drastic break with a half century of pure voluntarism."[2]

Other responses to the contraction appeared on the expenditures side of the government's ledger. There was the rise in previously delayed outlays for federal building construction in early 1930 and again in early 1931 to help relieve unemployment. There was federal assistance to drought victims in 1930. There was the beginning of construction of the Boulder Dam in the same year. There was a Veterans Loan Bill passed in February 1931 over Hoover's gleeful veto.[3] It was reported that partiality by Hoover to budget balancing as a political issue led him to hope that Congress would pass the bonus bill so he could veto it.

The historic, chronic fear of inflation by the Federal Reserve Board (the Fed) was partially set aside in February 1932 by the Glass-Steagall Act permitting federal securities to be used as collateral for currency issue. Unfortunately, this did little to offset the Fed's inadequate open-market purchases of government securities, the shrinking money stock, the sharp drop in the velocity of money use, the Fed's increase in the discount rate in 1931 and again in the winter of 1932–33. Chronic fear of inflation, protection of the foreign exchange rate, anxiety over the growing budget deficits after fiscal 1930, and piecemeal cuts in the discount rates rather than bold open-market purchases marked the old-fashioned tight money policy of the Fed. All this has been highlighted over the years by the economist Milton Friedman.

Most of the spending moves were of little impact for the long-run growth of the federal government except insofar as they represented a responsiveness toward market failure and its adverse social effects. But by 1932 the continued severity of the contraction and the consequent dispersal of illusions about imminent recovery produced two major legislative moves that were definite precursors of the forthcoming enlargement in the federal government's role in the economy.

The first was the creation by Congress of the "temporary" Reconstruction Finance Corporation (RFC), destined to last until 1957. The RFC was proposed by Hoover "in support of credit" as part of his annual message to Congress in December 1931, inaugurated by Congress as a U.S. government corporation in January 1932, and put into operation within a month.

In the act of January 1932 the object was to shore up the financial sector by federal loans ("the shield of government credit") to banks, insurance companies, building and loan associations (i.e., aid to housing), farm-mortgage associations, livestock-loan associations, and railroads. Home mortgages were additionally to a small degree underwritten in July by the extension of more RFC funds to a newly set up Home Loan Bank system. Hoover proudly argued that, through the aid to financial firms, 5,000 institutions and "25,000,000 American families" would be "saved" from disaster.[4] Critics irreverently called the financially modest RFC policy approach a "theory of feeding the sparrows by feeding the horse."[5]

Nevertheless, the RFC act was historically significant for the rise of big government. This is so not because it illustrated again the power of temporary institutions to enjoy a long life, nor is it because a public policy to shore up a particular industry, or even a whole private sector, necessarily represented a significant departure from the laissez-faire tradition. Rather, it is because the recipients of much of the aid were in the large, highly sensitive, and uniquely strategic financial sector, which is the connecting tissue of potential disaster for the entire private market economy. The general performance of the economy was at stake. It was precisely such concern of the federal government for the economy's general performance, however inadequate pecuniarily, that represented a clear connection with the forthcoming mixed economy. While it was not suspected at the time, the RFC commitment to give crisis support to the vital financial sector—Hoover's "very basis of our economic life"—anticipated permanent government policy toward that sector. The vast scale that the commitment might involve was of course also undreamed of, and would only be grasped when the savings and loan and related government bailouts exploded in the late 1980s and early 1990s.

The second major legislative precursor of the forthcoming New Deal enlargement in government's role was the Emergency Relief and Construction Act of July 1932 (ERCA). The act was a pro-Hoover, "divided government" compromise following the president's veto of a much more generous bill that would have provided $2.3 billion to the clamoring states for relief and public works. Under ERCA the RFC could make loans funneling a paltry $300 million to absolutely financially distressed states for individual relief. (Congress converted the loans into gifts in 1934.)

The miserly amount, so typical of federal policy during even the last years of the great contraction, is not the important point here. It is rather the fact that ERCA "closed a chapter in American financial history by writing finis to the doctrine that welfare payments to individuals were outside the scope of the Federal government."[6] Mass agitation transmitted through the Congress gave the president "no choice but to retreat from his oft-expressed opposition to federal aid."[7] ERCA also foreshadowed welfare *grants-in-aid* (as distinguished from highway trust fund dispensations) that much later became major components for "revenue sharing," a central feature of intergovernmental fiscal relations in the mixed economy.

A growing, pre–New Deal federal responsibility for the human condition was in process, destroying the remaining foundations of laissez-faire. This development reflecting the "quickened social conscience,"[8] emerged also in legislative attempts that did not quite succeed. A case in point is the failed Costigan-LaFollette bill, which passed the more liberal House but was defeated in the Senate in early 1932. Here was a measure that would have brought to the forefront a welfare policy executed by federal grants-in-aid to the state and local governments: $375 million for relief by that channel.

The RFC and ERCA anticipated during the year of the contraction's worst drop in real GNP the later permanent assumption by the federal government of ultimate responsibility for the economy's socially acceptable performance and the relief of human insecurity and material want. But the commitment was only anticipatory because it was essentially stopgap rather than long-run reform, and it was too woefully inadequate to even approach those two socioeconomic goals.

The federal establishment in the great contraction tried to "stay the course" of minimizing its role and size. But forces overwhelming and external to it—business elements that deviated from tradition, various social groups, state and local governments—coerced it into taking some interventionist measures. The pressures primarily responsible for the upcoming New Deal were already near the boiling point. As a result, federal purchases of goods and services rose 15 percent in current dollars and 30 percent in constant dollars between 1929 and 1932. All federal expenditures in current dollars increased 12 percent a year from fiscal 1930 through fiscal 1933. The federal increases, alarming at the time, contrasted with a sluggish state and local performance as noted earlier. Thus, almost the whole burden of the 10 percent rise in real all-government purchases between 1929 and 1932 was assumed by the federal government.

The expansion in the number of federal workers in the contraction period should have been as "alarming" as the rise in federal spending and debt. To estimate that expansion, let us extract from the total workers an employee category that in a broad, loose sense may be considered relevant from the standpoint of potential domestic policy making. This is our "discretionary" employee group, calculated by subtracting Defense Department and postal employees from the total of federal civilian employment. The calculation yields an impressively modest 181,000 employees in 1929 and 209,000 in 1932, an increase of 28,000 for the three years. This is 16 percent, a rise almost identical with the percentage rise in federal current dollar purchases of goods and services.

These employee totals increased the ratio of federal discretionary employment to the civilian labor force from .38 percent in 1929 to .42 percent in 1932 (and the same in 1933). Frightening as this relative increase may have appeared to the traditionalists in those years, it was soon dwarfed by the New Deal's increase in the ratio to .80 percent in 1937–39 and .83 percent in 1940.

As a historical note of considerable significance for the present study, this federal discretionary ratio evolved as follows:

1929	0.38
1932	0.42
1940	0.83
1949	1.18
1960	1.13
1970	1.23
1975	1.22
1980	1.20
1989	.99
1992	1.03
1993	1.04

From this measure it may be inferred that the "big bang" in long-run federal employee growth rate occurred in the dramatic six or seven years after 1933. The inference is close to the facts. The rise from .42 to .83 over the seven years from 1933 to 1940 amounts to an annual increase of 10.22 percent. From .83 to 1.18 over the nine years from 1940 to 1949 amounts to an annual increase of 4 percent, which is still quite robust. Thereafter, over the long run, the above federal discretionary ratios column shows a slow rise to a peak in the early 1970s with a fall thereafter that has a 1992 level well below the immediate postwar's 1.18 ratio.

Let us pursue the federal employment pattern a bit further. For this purpose we take total federal instead of the discretionary employment just referred to. The totals over the very long run evolved as follows:

1933	603,587
1939	953,891
1949	2,102,109
1960	2,398,704
1970	2,981,574
1980	2,876,000
1989	3,124,000
1992	3,085,000
1993	3,043,000

The annual percentage rates for these increases were:

1933–39	7.93
1939–49	8.22
1949–70	1.68
1970–93	0.09

The increase of about 350,000 civilian employees in the New Deal years, 1933 to 1939, was overwhelmingly for civilian functions. The civilian employees of the Defense Department increased by about 95,000 however. This 95,000 meant a yearly rise of 12 percent, but active-duty military personnel rose at only 5.4 percent. About a third of the total federal employment growth was in old-line regular departments, Agriculture in particular, and a fourth was in new agencies, some of which were to endure, like the Tennessee Valley Authority (TVA).

A similarly large total federal employment annual percentage rise in the forties shows that we must modify the conclusion about the thirties that was drawn on the basis of the federal discretionary ratio data. There it appeared that the explosion of federal employment was overwhelmingly concentrated in the thirties. We can see here, using simply total federal employment growth, that the forties was at least as explosive. The great expansion of the forties, however, had a quite different complexion from the thirties. Of the numerical increase of 1,148,218 between 1939 and 1949, almost 90 percent was due to only three branches: civilians in the Defense Department, postal employees, and the Veterans Administration! The first of these three accounted for almost 60 percent of the total increase. The Cold War and America's new international orientation was gathering momentum by 1949. Defense outlays were rising after their 1947 nadir, and military personnel on active duty were bottoming out in 1948 at 1,446,000—some four-and-a-half times their size in the New Deal's 1939.

Employment in the old-line agencies as a group rose only about 8 percent between 1939 and 1949. This contrasted sharply with the aforementioned New Deal pattern. The Department of Agriculture staff failed to increase at all. Also, the new agencies of the thirties as a group rose by a tiny 2 percent or so over the decade. To be sure, it was a heterogeneous group, some of them being phased out, some of the enduring ones growing.

In any case, the 1949 disaggregated pattern by agency had pretty much set the stage for the next forty years, with most of the old-line agencies roughly following the growth rate path of total federal employment as outlined above. There were, however, four noteworthy exceptions to that generalization, all of which were big growers: Treasury, Post Office, Justice, and the Veterans Administration. The first three would be expected to grow with GNP and population. The Veterans Administration growth no doubt expressed a combination of two influences: hot and cold wars plus a very powerful lobby. So much for the career of one important measure of the growth of big government—civilian variety—at the federal level.

Inauguration of the Mixed Economy Era

Unbeknownst to the participants, the famous "hundred days" of federal legislative policy breakthroughs, beginning with the Emergency Banking Act of March 9, 1933, initiated a historical upheaval in government's role in the market economy and society. The state and local governments did not attend that three-month inauguration ceremony, although they gradually came to participate and solidify the new institutional order.

The continued "sickness" of the free market system overshadowed the fact that cyclical forces indigenous to that system launched a recovery in the very month after Franklin Roosevelt took office. The cyclical upturn was independent of the new policy package. Of course, the subsequent career of the incomplete expansion was influenced by New Deal policies. The pressures for federal intrusive actions came from many sources. While some surely expressed the New Deal executive-congressional coalition, most emanated from business elements representing that market system component and from various other depression-afflicted societal strata. The majority of the initial demands leveled at the federal regime were impelled by immediate crisis conditions. Others, however, expressed continuing critical imperatives rooted in the laissez-faire past and brought to the boiling point by the Depression.

Both sets of basic pressures proved capable of creating durable new policy orientations. The prominence of certain short-lived New Deal measures, such as the National Industrial Recovery Act (NIRA) with its Public Works Administration, the Civilian Conservation Corps, the Works Progress Administration (later called Works Projects Administration), and the Civil Works Administration, should not be allowed to deflect historical interpretation from appreciating the permanent *policy orientation* represented by those measures. That reorientation tossed onto the scrap heap of history Hoover's professed policy dictum that "though the people support the government, the government should not support the people."

Many of the demands for federal intervention in the market system came from business sources. The NIRA, for example, initially had wide support in the business community since its codes of "fair competition" (actually highly monopolistic cartels) embodied the Swope Plan of 1931–32 backed by the U.S. Chamber of Commerce. The general scope of the National Recovery Administration surpassed by far the industry-specific supports more typical of the laissez-faire era. Business exporters were largely responsible for establishment in 1934 of the Export-Import Bank designed to further the sale of U.S. products overseas, augmenting thereby a policy similar to that contained in the 1918 Webb-Pomerene Act. Similar business objectives in the form of mutually profitable trade were incorporated in the Trade Agreements Act in the same year.

Then there was the Merchant Marine Act of 1936, providing a system of direct subsidies for construction and vessel operation. The railroad business came in for its share of help with the 1933 Railroad Emergency Act, as well as grants from the Hoover-endowed RFC. Then there was the economically backward South. Within the South there was Appalachia, a vast, underdeveloped, poverty-stricken region. That problem area was addressed by the great Tennessee Valley Administration (TVA), which became an enduring addition to the governmental establishment.

The TVA is a prime example of government as entrepreneur, with an exceptionally distant time horizon. Its risky investment commitment was enormous and its impact on the private economy and society in a big region fantastically stimulative. Its construction contracts with private firms, and therefore those firms' employees, made the venture a joint public-private project, a pattern generally typical of government's entrepreneurial activities. Also with the TVA the government assumed a continuing regulatory responsibility with its attendant financial and personnel increases. By 1939, the TVA was one of the larger new agencies of the federal government, with 14,597 employees.

Farming is also a business. As might be expected, the Depression intensified the longstanding militant clamor of the farmers for sustained government assistance, just as it intensified their economic difficulties. That was enough to secure not only "temporary" aid but also a permanent program of planned output controls, price supports, and surplus disposal. Furthermore, a permanent program that dispensed food to the deserving was coupled with surplus disposal under the 1933 Federal Surplus Relief Corporation, the founding agency of the later Food Stamp Plan and School Lunch Plan serving over 40 million recipients in 1992. Farmers also benefited enormously from the establishment of the Rural Electrification Administration (REA) in 1935. Here was another example of a combination program, for the electric utility industry and business generally also gained from REA.

The New Deal responded further to the needs of financial business, greatly expanding the support network for that sector inaugurated under the Hoover administration. It not only extended the loan program of the RFC but also established lasting programs for underwriting farm business loans as well as farm and nonfarm home mortgages. Special credit institutions for farmers as producers began in the laissez-faire era with an act in 1916 setting up a system of Federal Land Banks for long-term production loans, and another in 1923 for intermediate credit. The New Deal continued and extended the policy with the Farm Credit Act of 1933 and the consolidation of federal credit agencies under a new Farm Credit Administration. Farm housing in general, and foreclosures in particular, received special attention under the Emergency Farm Mortgage Act of 1933 and three additional acts in 1934. Protecting farmers from bankers through special government lending goes back to preconstitutional Rhode Island.

A number of measures were designed to protect urban homeowners from losing their homes by protecting mortgage loan institutions. The policy was not to inaugurate a big program of public housing, although a bit was done on that score. Mainly, the policy was to underwrite lenders in the private mortgage market by creating a secondary market. That policy was represented in the Home Owners Loan Act (HOLA) of June 1933, the Federal Housing Administration (FHA) established a year later, and the 1938 Federal National Mortgage Association ("Fannie Mae"). The Hoover administration and its Congress had again modestly anticipated these programs with the previously mentioned Home Loan Bank Act of 1932. Credit assistance for farm homes and urban homeowners dovetailed policy-wise with support for firms in the mortgage market segment of the financial sector.

But there was a much bigger segment to be shored up by government action: the commercial banks. The wave of bank insolvencies and failures, together with the mass runs on banks by depositors withdrawing currency, unfortunately for hoarding, brought these financial institutions into the limelight and led to state government closures of commercial banks followed by FDR's bank "holiday" beginning on March 6, 1933. At that point the New Deal took two major, long-lived steps. In its Glass-Steagall Act of June 1933 investment banking and commercial banking were separated. That separation resulted primarily from the speculative financial fiascos connected with the combination of the two in the 1920s. De facto violation of the disengagement in the 1980s made enough trouble for the commercial banks to suggest that the lesson of the twenties had to be relearned. However the congressional initiative to repeal Glass-Steagall in the 1990s indicates that the lesson may have to be learned all over again.

Glass-Steagall also established a Federal Deposit Insurance Corporation (FDIC), guaranteeing individual deposits in all Federal Reserve member banks and qualifying state banks. Friedman and Schwartz describe the creation of that enduring new agency as "a nice example of how institutions are developed and shaped" because it "resulted from an amendment to the Banking Act of 1933 introduced by a Senator from the minority party and at least initially opposed by President Roosevelt."[9] Reference is to the amendment by Senator Arthur H. Vandenberg (Rep.) of Michigan. It should also be noted that some members of the New Deal inner circle favored the idea, notably Jesse Jones and Vice-President John Garner.[10]

Friedman and Schwartz go on to quote one Carter H. Golembe, writing in the *Political Science Quarterly,* to the effect that the FDIC was

> the only important piece of legislation during the New Deal's famous "one hundred days" which was neither requested nor supported by the new administration.
>
> Deposit insurance was purely a creature of Congress. For almost fifty years members had been attempting to secure legislation to this end, without success; while in individual states the record of experimentation with bank-obligation insurance systems dated back more than a century. The adoption of nationwide deposit insurance in 1933 was made possible by the times, by the perseverance of the Chairman of the House Committee on Banking and Currency [Henry B. Steagall], and by the fact that the legislation attracted support from

two groups which formerly had divergent aims and interests—those who were determined to end destruction of the circulating medium due to bank failures and those who sought to preserve the existing banking structure.[11]

The legislation was opposed by such powerful interests as the New York Federal Reserve Bank because it meant "by-passing the Reserve System"[12] and "to the last ditch" by the American Bankers' Association.[13] Friedman and Schwartz add that "protection of the circulating medium rather than protection of the small depositor against loss was one overriding concern of the legislator in establishing deposit insurance."[14]

Whichever of these two protections was paramount, it seems clear that the FDIC was a vital prop to the entire market system insofar as it greatly helped stabilize the monetary system ("circulating medium"), put a stop to mass runs on banks from then on, and contributed mightily to bringing down national commercial bank suspensions from 1,101 in 1933 to 45 for the years 1934–40.[15] It also protected the individual bank accounts of 90 percent of the millions of depositors.

The struggle for passage of the FDIC is in itself significant for our understanding of the process of government's enlargement. That struggle shows it should be no surprise that the addition of a new agency to the institution of government is typically the *net* result of opposing pressure groups, with one group or set of groups being the more effective. The FDIC case is also revealing in that elements *within* a divided government were at loggerheads, and the old laissez-faire record of defeats would likely have been repeated had not supporters been enormously helped by the times.

The subsequent institutionalized separation of commercial and investment banking and the FDIC illustrate the vital fact that new regulatory policies or bodies may be initiated by either *overt interest groups* or by *threatened social activism*. The record in these two cases suggests that where regulation endures, even in the presence of opposition, there is a supporting constituency that has created a coalition with the government regulatory policy or agency.

The FHA insured banks against default by householders. The FDIC insured homeowners against default by banks. Fannie Mae makes mortgage loan packages easily marketable so banks can get out from under the risk of holding long-term loans whose value can drop if interest rates rise. The Federal Reserve stands ready to bail out any reasonably managed major bank caught in unexpected economic events. The federal government has thus shouldered most of the risk of banking without accepting much of the profits.

If the FDIC was largely a creature of Congress and its supporters in the community rather than the federal executive branch, Section 7(a) of the NIRA emanated primarily from a coalition of the executive branch plus a handful of congressional New Dealers like Senators Robert F. Wagner, George Norris, and Burton Wheeler. Section 7(a) declared that all codes of fair competition include a guarantee to employees of the right to organize and bargain collectively through representatives of their own choosing. That provision greatly augmented a small inheritance of anticipatory federal, pro-labor, union-sponsored or supported legislation, such as the Railway Labor Act of 1926, the 1931 Davis-Bacon Act in the construction industry, and the 1932 Norris-LaGuardia Anti-injunction Act. But Section 7(a), while receiving the AFL's approval, was not a response to mass pressure from organized labor. The weakened AFL had rather been pushing for the Black-Connery Bill, unacceptable to the administration, favoring a five-day, thirty-hour week, designed to relieve unemployment by "spreading the work." The NIRA codes not only gave business minimum prices but under the President's Reemployment Agreement promulgated in July 1933 provided for minimum wages and maximum hours and banned child labor. All this was a powerful package for labor.

But organized labor was too weak to provide a plausible explanation of the labor provisions of the codes. Moreover, the AFL ostensibly opposed minimum wages for fear they would become a maximum. However, on the pro–minimum wage side was the recognition by the federal government, under both Hoover and FDR, that the nation's wage bill was the basic support of total consumer spending. Arthur Schlesinger has pointed out, for example that "even before his inauguration, Molly Dewson, once of the Consumer's League, more recently of the Women's Division of the Democratic Party, urged on Roosevelt the importance of wages and hours legislation to arrest the down-ward spiral. When New York passed a minimum-wage law in April 1933, Roosevelt called on governors of a dozen other states to take similar action."[16] An ideological transformation at the federal level was in the ascendancy, a shift from the supply-side belief that "the answer to underproduction is more production" to a demand-side recognition that escape from the Depression required not only "reflation" of prices but also rising consumption. Even President Hoover had sensed this in his appeal to business not to cut wages. And the link between organization rights and effective wage maintenance was irrefutable.

Thus we have a striking illustration of government-initiated legislation that had, as it turned out, far-reaching effects on government's role in the economy. The Roosevelt administration was quite autonomously pursuing (given the influence of the times) a traditional progressive policy aimed at securing not only recovery but "social balance" in the context of great inequality in industrial relations. That inequality had been made particularly glaring by business's many-pronged attack on organized labor in the preceding decade.

Section 7(a) was far-reaching because it was endowed with continuity three years later in the enduring National Labor Relations Act (NLRA), labor's Magna Carta. The NLRA strengthened and extended the independent collective bargaining provisions of Section 7(a). Furthermore, it was, much more than Section 7(a), the product of organized labor's demands. Total union membership, including the AFL and the new, more militant, industrial unions growing out of Section

7(a), increased by almost 800,000, or one-fourth, in 1934, a year of violent industrial conflicts. Organized labor, while still only 12 percent of nonagricultural employment, was not about to relinquish the advances won by the combination of New Deal policy and its own newfound power. When the New Deal's second greatest representative after FDR himself, Senator Robert Wagner, introduced the bill that was to became the NLRA, the AFL's eminent master of appeasement, President William Green, vented to the House of Representatives one of the most militant declarations of his lifetime:

> I do not mind telling you that the spirit of the workers in America has been aroused. They are going to find a way to bargain collectively. . . . Labor must have its place in the sun. We cannot and will not continue to urge workers to have patience, unless the Wagner bill is made law, and unless it is enforced, once it becomes law.[17]

It is historically significant that black political organization was too ineffective to persuade the equivocal Green and the AFL leadership to incorporate into the Wagner bill a provision that would have denied its benefits to any union that discriminated on the basis of race.[18] Clark Foreman, Interior Secretary Harold Ickes's adviser on black economic status, had laid bare the Jim Crow policy of American unionism during the NLRA's first year when he declared that both the industrialists and the AFL were "hostile to Negro labor, the former because they want to keep Negroes as a reserve of cheap labor, and the latter because they want to eliminate Negro competitive labor."[19] It is further testimony to the rapidity of the decade's social and political reversals that within two years the new CIO had inaugurated an end to union discrimination against immigrants, women, and blacks. Hence, by 1935 we can say that labor's Magna Carta was the product of an anti-business government-labor coalition that held sway until the burgeoning business attack on the New Deal was able to correct what it believed was a pro-labor "imbalance" by securing passage of the union-constraining Taft-Hartley Act in 1947. Taft-Hartley was a beautiful balancing act. While it did not meddle directly with the rights of labor provided in NLRA, it counteracted them by assuring comparable rights to employers. *As a result the federal government had become deeply and permanently involved in the market system's industrial disputes. Regulatory government was augmented as a result of the pressures of conflicting private interest groups.* It was an illustration of what might be called the "Law of Regulatory Augmentation."

There can be no doubt that the New Deal administration and its cohorts in the Congress were aware that their social programs were building constituency support. The 1936 landslide victory for FDR and the Democratic Party, for example, reflected the extensive popularity of those programs. It would seem to follow that in doubling its total of discretionary employees by that election year the New Deal was not merely passively responding to active or threatened popular pressures. On the other hand, the positive responses it got from powerful elements in the community unquestionably encouraged and reinforced its endeavors. The net result was continuation and expansion of the federal government's interventionist policies.

A major case in point was the recovery of labor organization beginning in 1934, and the formation of a new, more politically articulate, industrial union movement under the banner of the Congress of Industrial Organizations in 1937. The CIO was solidly Democratic. The New Deal's initiatives, expressed in "the president wants you to join the union," got its response in that labor upsurge. The AFL's historic resistance to governmental intrusion into labor-management relations was swamped by its bankruptcy in the twenties, New Deal encouragement, and rank-and-file militancy. The whole process, eventuating in more government, was self-reinforcing. Meanwhile, business antipathy was likewise accumulating, bitterly assailing that "laborist" process as "the road to serfdom."[20] By the late thirties business could blame government interventionism for the failure of the Depression to end. Sympathetic critics of the new interventionism, on the other hand, argued that it had been too weakly pursued.

The Mixed Economy and the Welfare State

The most prominent among the welfare components of the mixed economy is by far the institution of *social insurance* and the *transfer payments* connected with it. This fact enhances, for the present analysis, the acknowledged significance of the 1935 Social Security Act as the most outstanding piece of lasting social interventionism in the entire New Deal policy constellation.

Both the old-age benefit and the unemployment compensation provisions of the act were government-augmenting responses to popular demands for action to treat unmet, widespread, and growing human needs. The ameliorative powers of both the market system and episodic voluntarist group interventionism had proved over time unable to cope satisfactorily with those needs from society's standpoint. Most European market economies had already taken the social insurance route to attack the problems of support for the elderly and unemployed, as well as for health protection. The gap in the health insurance field was the New Deal's most conspicuous failure.

The pension movements, spearheaded by either prominent Progressives, or by business, or by nonprofit charity-type organizations, reached back at least into the early twentieth century. They were bolstered by increased superannuation resulting from advances in hygiene and preventive medicine, by urbanization, and by the spreading reliance of the labor force on money wage income. All of that is what one would expect from Wagner's Law of expanding government in market economies.

But the pension movement, insofar as it impacted the private sector of the economy rather than public employees, was split between business-supported, "voluntary," group pension advocates and other proponents of either voluntary or compulsory old-age insurance financed by contributions. Voluntarism, a hallmark of laissez-faire, had won the day in the private sector until the Great Depression and the New Deal.

There were only two major exceptions. The first was in the area of federal, state and municipal employment. The 300,000 federal employees in the classified civil service were blanketed with a contributory retirement system by the Lehlbach Act of 1920.[21] Police, firemen, teachers, and some others in the state and municipal services won noncontributory pensions beginning significantly around 1910. Voluntary contributory plans made major gains in the 1920s.

The other exception was, of course, pensions for the hundreds of thousands of veterans. They enjoyed the distinction of being both quasi-public and American patriots (215,000 of them in 1935). Besides, they had a powerful lobbying organization. However, one eminent progressive leader of the pension movement, Isaac Rubinow, took advantage of some possible momentum to be derived therefrom to comment critically that defending military pensions for sentimental or patriotic reasons was "childish," and that the basic issues involved with such measures had to do generally with "the problem of dependent old age and widowhood."[22] Rubinow might well have added that public systems in support of old age and widowhood partially freed adult offspring from the burden of supporting aged parents, a burden differentially greater in an urban as distinguished from a largely agrarian society.

The great issue of public unemployment aid in some form became politically and socially prominent as far back as the last quarter of the nineteenth century. The severity of the cyclical economic contractions, particularly in the 1890s, kept the issue very much alive. Organized proposals for government relief and public works in the contraction of the 1890s replaced earlier proposals for a western lands settlement solution, and have become acknowledged by historians as anticipations of the New Deal.

But as the economy moved through the early twentieth century, a mild contraction in 1907–1908 was followed by similar mild "lapses from full employment" over 1910–14 and in 1921. Additionally, there was a forty-four-month expansion over 1915–18, followed by the "prosperity decade." That stolid economic performance dampened the power of a primary market system failure to induce ameliorative public action on unemployment. Since mass cyclical unemployment had the greatest critical shock effect of all system failures, it is understandable that 1900–29 was a lengthy period of quiet before the storm.

That period of relative quietude, however, should not be allowed to conceal the concomitant evolution of an accumulating potential for corrective social action stemming from the growing recognition that recurrent unemployment was a built-in characteristic of the system's operation. Such recognition plus the heavy incidence of contractions on labor fostered the gradual growth of an attitudinal and programmatic revolt asserting unemployed labor's right to "a place in the sun."

Consequently, when the great cyclical shock hit the workforce after 1929 it quickly brought things to a focus. Thus, for example, in a November 1932 report of the Ohio Commission on Unemployment, the recommendations included a call for immediate implementation of "the classic European principles of social insurance."[23] This became the "Ohio Plan" and was an immediate forerunner of the Social Security Act's unemployment provisions. That it represented an advanced kind of reform is appreciated when one notes the response by the Ohio Chamber of Commerce to the effect that the plan was "indefensible and disloyal," an "attempt to foist on the United States foreign ideals and foreign practices," and the "most menacing and revolutionary piece of legislation ever proposed in the history of Ohio." That declaration well represented the tone of business opposition to the Social Security Act. It further shows why the New Deal had to carefully tailor the law in order to get it passed.

The great breakthrough in the act was that it featured *nationwide insurance* rather than localized public assistance, it inaugurated coverage of persons in the *private sector* of the economy, it was compulsory for persons covered, and its tax provisions were *contributory*. In the long run the design of the act was to phase out most public assistance and replace it with public insurance for the elderly and "employable" unemployed.[24] A special exception to that design was the act's "categorical assistance" for the needy aged, dependent children, and the blind through grants-in-aid to the states that would meet certain standards and provide matching funds.[25] Also, what later came to be called "entitlement" was to phase out welfare dependency. All these features of the act and its larger design were broadly typical of, albeit less comprehensive than, the social insurance systems characterizing welfare states everywhere else. In the main they were not the unique brainchild of a great president.

With such augmentation of the federal government's role, it was necessary, in order to get the legislation passed, to give states' rights its administrative due. While that bias was not reflected in the old-age provisions (until the later Great Society's Medicaid system was introduced in 1966), it was incorporated into the unemployment administration provisions. The federal role was confined to fiscal administration.

By calling the employment taxes "contributions," a politically facilitating concession was made to the almost universal antitax ideology; and at the same time an aura of free choice was created by the term since it could be linked with a belief that benefits received were "a matter of right and not a dole." "Contribution" also softened the regressivity of the tax's incidence from the standpoint of the covered employee. Regressivity helped sell the bill to conservatives. General revenues as a source would have been anathema. The act's trust fund reserve (held in the form of federal securities) inappropriately imitated private insurance and thus helped direct attention from alternative financing through more progressive general revenues. The reserve fund also contributed to fastening a tight, restrained benefits policy by falsely implying the system could become "insol-

vent." This also undermined the conservative threat to passage. The same political objective was served by the limited initial coverage (later greatly extended
during the Republican Eisenhower administration). Certainly the act failed to
provide FDR's cradle-to-grave security against the major material contingencies
of life.

The Social Security Act was not a bureaucratically perpetrated expense foisted
on a reluctant public by a dedicated president and a coterie of progressives.
Although "there was never, prior to the 1930s any serious consideration of compulsory, contributory old-age insurance in the United States,"[26] laissez-faire ante-
cedents of the act reached back at least three decades in the U.S. economy and
society, a period during which European exemplary models were multiplying.

The plight of the elderly and unemployed in the first half decade of the severe
depression crystallized a social consensus that was long in process of formation
as a result of agitation or example by prominent progressives, widespread organizational responses to severe unemployment in the contraction of the 1890s, the
National Committee of Organized Labor for promoting Old Age Pensions
(1898–99), the American Association for Old Age Security, the Massachusetts
Commission on Old Age Pensions (1907–10), the establishment of the U.S.
Employment Service (1918), the National Conference of Charities and Correc-
tions (1912), the United Mine Workers, the Fraternal Order of Elks, the Fraternal
Order of Eagles (1920s), the Progressive Party (1912), the AFL, the Catholic
National Welfare Conference, state retirement programs for state employees,
state legislators (compulsory pensions), members of the U.S. Congress, the
American Association for Labor Legislation, the President's Conference on Un-
employment in 1921, numerous ill-fated employment exchanges, the influential
Townsend pension movement in California, the Share Our Wealth movement led
by Senator Huey Long, the "National Union for Social Justice" (1933–34) led by
Father Charles Coughlin, the End Poverty in California movement spearheaded
by Upton Sinclair, the Ohio Commission on Unemployment (1932), and the
New Deal's own officialdom including the Committee on Economic Security
under the directorship of the great welfare advocate and future president of the
American Economic Association, Edwin E. Witte. Over all of those years of ebb
and flow, continuous and impetuous opposition to any form of social insurance
also contributed, ironically, to keeping the elderly and unemployment issues
politically alive.

The place of the Social Security Act in the historically evolving interplay
among the elements of our model's institutional triad—the market system, society at large, and government—has been well summarized by two members of the
University of Pennsylvania faculty.

> The enactment of Federal Old Age Insurance and of Grants to States for
> Unemployment Compensation recognized flaws in the country's private enter-
> prise market system and the need for institutional change to mitigate unavoid-

able economic and social distress. Insurance against the hazards of unemployment and of retirement in old age bolstered the security of beneficiaries and of the private enterprise system itself because these institutional reforms, aimed at meeting universal needs, guaranteed permanent economic stabilizers for both. Thus, social insurance benefits, based on a joint employee-employer contributory scheme, assured an income for individuals who had worked but could not necessarily be expected to maintain the burden of self-support in retirement or unemployment. The social insurance approach assumed the essential validity of the market system while acknowledging the need to support the public's purchasing power. This assumption by the federal government of responsibility for the worker's income security suggested that the flaws . . . were, after all, correctable.[27]

It is ironic that the business community generally, despite the existence of some reform elements within it, persistently opposed Social Security. Explanations may be found in ideological rigidity, an inability to recognize that such reform might be inevitable, the historic conservative proclivity to identify reform with revolution, and the fact that Social Security was a cornerstone of the whole threatening New Deal package in support of the "underlying masses." Again, we know that major social groups frequently act in ways that are against their own best interests—for example, the primarily business community's financial support for the recent Contract with America, directed largely to weakening income support for the poor and quality protections in private and public goods and services. Indeed, we shall have occasion to point out such behavior later in this work. It was the genius of Professor John Maynard Keynes—Lord Keynes, Baron of Tilton, Bursar of Kings College, advisor to the Treasury and all-around English old boy—to recognize that interventionist reforms by government bolstered the faulty capitalism he loved, and thereby dispelled the revolutionary forecasts of the Marxists.

The New Deal's Denouement

One final, major addition to the New Deal's pro-labor expansionism was enacted by Congress after Section 7(a), along with the entire NIRA, was declared unconstitutional. The Fair Labor Standards Act of June 1938 (FLSA) picked up the maximum hours–minimum wage stipulations in Section 7(a), just as the NLRA had picked up its collective bargaining provision. The FLSA also continued to set restraints on the employment of child labor in interstate commerce.

Passage of the FLSA cannot be ascribed to organized labor's pressures. Rather, it resulted largely from the New Deal's humanistic concerns for the lower income (and consumption) levels of the unorganized labor majority of urban society plus its acceptance of popular spread-the-work desires. This last social objective was embraced even by the AFL and also by the newborn CIO. One outstanding student of the Depression decade succinctly expressed the comparative roles of organized labor and the New Deal itself regarding the act's passage:

> Paradoxically enough, the president and his aides in Congress carried the Fair Labor Standards act through in face of apathy or downright skepticism from both CIO and A.F.of L. leaders, the latter tending to quote Gompers that the minimum wage often becomes the maximum. At least perhaps they had little interest in the welfare of the workers outside the pale of their own memberships, or else begrudged gains won in any other fashion than by collective bargaining.[28]

There were some federal precedents, in addition to Section 7(a), for action on the issues. One was the Davis-Bacon Act (1932) bolstering wages on federal construction projects, and another was the 1935 Walsh-Healy Public Contracts Act supporting both wages and maximum hours of private suppliers with federal government contracts. But these were minor influences on the FLSA passage. Besides, it was again the application of this new regulatory institution to the *private sector* that represented the significant breakthrough in government's role.

The New Deal was not acting alone. It had to deal with the times as well as the "quickened social conscience." Depression conditions were still pervasive despite remarkable economic expansion between 1933 and 1937.[29] Furthermore, a slowdown of the expansion set in during 1937, presaged the forthcoming excess inventory recession of 1938. Real GNP in 1937 barely topped its level of eight dreary years earlier. The falling civilian unemployment rate still exceeded 14 percent in 1937. And prices, those time-honored sources of optimism and pessimism, were still depressingly below their prosperity level. It was painfully obvious that prosperity was hardly "just around the corner." With that grim context, the New Deal was carrying the ball. It was still dedicated to helping the underdog regardless of whether to do so would augment the federal government's size.

A bureaucratic Leviathan explanation of the FLSA addition to the government's regulatory role is, of course, to be considered. However, one likely sophisticated defender of such an interpretation, Robert Higgs, merely mentions that the act was one of three legislative "jewels" of the New Deal's mid-Depression "stage" that produced "the full flowering of social justice progressivism."[30] Higgs then generalizes New Deal–societal relationships such as were expressed by the FLSA: "The great majority of Americans, regardless of party affiliations accepted and approved the new ideals of social welfare democracy."[31] This conclusion by a prominent critic of big government is congenial to the interpretation presented here. If a government institutes, expands, or maintains a particular activity, and that enlargement is interpreted as a step by an imperial bureaucracy bent on its own augmentation, it must have either a supporting constituency or a public lacking any significant element of resistance to the enlargement. This interpretive generalization embraces any combination of constituency strength and degree of apathy.

The material deprivation and insecurity of the millions of ordinary wage workers was fertile ground for planting an additional ameliorative, regulatory seed. Speaking of the FLSA, the president declared that "except perhaps for the Social Security Act, it is the most far-sighted program for the benefit of workers ever adopted in this or in any other country."[32] Allowing for the usual politicized exaggeration, the FLSA, while of distinctly less historical significance than the Social Security Act, was undoubtedly one of the three enduring "jewels" in the New Deal legacy. A more sober characterization of the act was offered by FDR's eminent social welfare aide Edwin E. Witte: "the most important protective labor law ever enacted by the national government."[33] It was indeed a fitting conclusion to the New Deal's very great lasting contribution to the welfare component of the mixed economy and to that economy's inaugural decade.

The great social welfare failure of the New Deal was in the health insurance area. The issue of national health care, like the other social issues to which the New Deal did address itself, was widely debated before 1929. (Veterans, of course, always had it.) For example, the Progressive Theodore Roosevelt called for universal health care in his presidential campaign in 1912. The American Medical Association (AMA) supported it! However, reversal of that stance subsequently by what became one of the most powerful political lobbies in American society destroyed any chance the New Dealers might have had to put through national compulsory health insurance. As Secretary of Labor Frances Perkins commented, "For the sake of passing the Social Security bill, we postponed the introduction of the bill on health insurance as the opposition was so great from the American Medical Association (principally) that it would have killed the whole Social Security Act if it had been pressed at that time."[34] The New Deal's decision to exclude compulsory health insurance from the Social Security bill is a clear case of governmental response to organized, articulate opposition.

That takes us through mid-1935. Then the intrepid Senator Wagner introduced a national health bill in February 1938, but it met "inflexible opposition" from the AMA, "even though a Gallup Poll found a majority of doctors favorable to schemes of voluntary health insurance."[35] If that poll expressed the opinion of physicians, a poll of the general public would surely have demonstrated overwhelming support for some kind of insurance, though not necessarily for mandatory insurance. Witte wrote the punch line in 1949 that in effect contrasts the compulsory systems in other advanced countries with the American situation: "Despite assumed but never expressed support from President Roosevelt and unequivocal endorsement on numerous occasions by President Truman, compulsory health insurance has never even gotten to a vote in either house of the Congress."[36] The main contribution to health care that did come out of the thirties was the inauguration and considerable proliferation of private voluntary group insurance schemes. Those were the wave of the future.

The Expanding New Deal Budgets

The federal government budget grew with the proliferation of New Deal short-run and long-run policy measures. The rise in tax receipts and other revenues, while substantial, failed to keep pace with outlays for farm supports, grants-in-aid to the states, public works, relief and work relief, the veterans' bonuses in 1936 and 1937, and beginning in fiscal 1936, the military. Hence budget deficits became the rule and added to a mounting debt that in nominal terms almost doubled between 1933 and 1940.

The deficits and debt were regarded with a mixture of repugnance and defensiveness by the New Dealers, but they were absolute outrages to the administration's vociferous opponents. The opposition attacked with the full armor of classical laissez-faire allegations that the deficits and debt would siphon saving away from funds that otherwise would be channeled into expansion-creating investment and bring full employment. Also, the debt would "bankrupt" the government. Not until many years later did a brilliant economist show that the New Deal's conventional budgets were so structured that as recovery proceeded toward high employment they typically dampened the expansion. The reason was, as his innovative concept of the "full-employment budget" showed that, given the existing revenue structure and its accompanying expenditure commitments, the deficits would typically turn toward surpluses as the GNP rose to higher levels.[37] The conclusion is that the New Deal's reluctant conventional budget deficits, relatively but little higher than Hoover's, were much too small to meet Keynesian robust recovery requirements. This was an appropriate beginning to the halting career of federal deficits throughout the subsequent history of the U.S. mixed economy.

There were other aspects of the federal budget in the thirties that were pregnant with similarity or contrast with the future contours of public demand that shaped the growing federal establishment. For example, real federal purchases of goods and services (FG) rose during the decade and generally rose also in ratio to real GNP. But this relative increase lasted only up to 1936. The FG/GNP ratio exhibited a plateau over 1933–35, averaging about 4.5 percent. There followed another plateau averaging about 5.9 percent. This considerable jump in the federal contribution to aggregate demand must certainly have helped sustain real GNP and employment. The ratio had been only 1.6 percent in laissez-faire 1929.

This 5.9 percent in the last years of the peacetime New Deal may revealingly be compared with the real FG/GDP ratio of 6.3 in 1994 over a half-century later. The ratio of 6.4 percent in 1940 was thus well on its way to the long-run mixed economy percentage. Alternatively, and perhaps more revealingly expressed, the ratio rose but little in the era following the New Deal.

But that is not all. In view of the long-run evolution in the composition of the absolutely growing real FG, it is instructive to break it down into military and civilian purchases. We know that the U.S. mixed economy of big government involved a very large rise in the military component of FG. During the inaugural decade of the mixed economy, however, the New Deal increased the absolute volume of military outlays but very little in relation to the total. Thus, for rough estimates, which have to be made in current dollars, we have the ratios of military and nonmilitary purchases to total purchases evolving as follows (in percent):[38]

	military	nonmilitary
1929	46	54
1933	30	70
1939	25	75

The striking change that came about subsequently in the mixed economy may be represented by the ratios for 1994. In that year the 1939 percentages were almost exactly reversed, with the military accounting for 67 percent and the nonmilitary for 33 percent. Even after the end of the Cold War, the military was 68 percent of the total. It is small wonder that Marxists and non-Marxists alike had a field day in the postwar years with labels such as "The Permanent War Economy" and "Pentagon Capitalism."[39] In such perspective, on the basis of FG alone, the New Deal's decade of substantial federal growth was primarily a civilian phenomenon. Another revealing change in the federal budget growth has to do with the proportion of total federal *expenditures* (FE) accounted for by FG alone. The FG/FE ratio unfolded for selected years as follows (in percent):[40]

1929	48
1933	48
1939	57
1947	39
1955	66
1965	58
1975	39
1985	38
1989	35
1994	29

The difference between FE and FG is composed overwhelmingly of transfer payments to persons, which are primarily Social Security benefits. The explosion of welfare transfers came after the 1950s; that is the main reason why the ratio drops from 66 to 29 in the long period after 1955. The rise in the military component of FG, despite its huge size, was swamped in total expenditures by the transfer payment explosion. That pattern describes well the career of two hallmarks of the U.S. mixed economy federal budget after World War II: military purchases come to dominate purchases, and welfare-type transfers dominate expenditures.

It is ironic and historically significant to observe the great extent of direct military and military-related outlays in the last laissez-faire federal budget in fiscal 1929. On the assumption that interest payments were essentially for war debt, plus the fact that veterans' payments of all sorts were also connected with past wars, then their sum when added to direct current outlays for the military establishment was $2.1 billion out of total expenditure of $3.1 billion, or 68 percent. That proportion fitted well Adam Smith's concept of government's appropriate concerns. Ten years later the proportion for the same components in total expenditures was only 30 percent. The inaugural federal budgets of the mixed economy reflected a predominantly *civilian* societal consensus.

The Introduction of Alternative Policy Precepts

The construction of the mixed economy after World War II owed much to the inauguration and widespread acceptance of certain dissident policy precepts arising in the thirties. They were dissenting because they were leveled at the market system and the established laissez-faire wisdom. Many of those dissident principles were projected by the New Deal as rationales for its programmatic responses to Depression-wrought pressures. They were, in other words, ideological accompaniments of short-run and long-run institutional innovations. They have been engaged ever since in a running battle with the persevering traditional policy ideologies.

The jump in the level of community dissatisfaction with the capacity of the market system to provide for basic human needs accelerated the rate of institutional and ideological innovation. In the first place, numerous collective social actions in fluctuating coalition with a growing government shifted the social balance of power toward the lower-income groups. In the process, the belief spread that economic laws are made by human action rather than by nature, as John Stuart Mill had insisted long ago regarding the laws of distribution. Since this implied human *group* action, individualism received a body blow in two senses: the individual was not only blameless for large, materially adverse economic events but also acting alone could accomplish but little.[41]

However, exclusively private group action to deal with certain kinds of economic adversity, as in the 1930–33 contraction, might well be inferior, it seemed, to a strong appeal to government for assistance. Indeed, as the Depression dragged on there emerged inklings of a belief that government should be the economy's underwriter of last resort. So far as employment and unemployment is concerned, such belief was soon to be embodied in the 1946 Employment Act. So far as other, more particular elements within the defective market economy are concerned, it has already been indicated that the principle of government underwriting was in varying degrees implicit with respect to the financial sector, the farm sector, the airlines, the labor market, the elderly, foreign traders, bank depositors, home mortgages, veterans, the unemployed, public utilities, and the poor. Indeed, as the newer public institutional arrangements evolved, the post–laissez-faire era could just as appropriately be called "the underwritten economy" as "the mixed economy." Many terms have been suggested, but they have a common denominator in the fact of a growing obliteration of the historic distinction between the private and the public spheres and the rejection of the traditional concept of "society as an adjunct of the market."[42]

There appeared also in the harrowing decade of the thirties some new normative propositions about economic policies and the theoretic rationales appropriate to them. For example, economic orthodoxy was challenged by the assertion that *full use* of resources is as important a policy goal as is the most *efficient allocation* of resources. Another challenge was contained in the New Deal, Keynesian-type precept that a domestic high employment policy should take precedence over an international policy consideration, such as stability of the foreign exchanges. Still another was connected with the fact that the New Deal introduced, among other major moves, a bit more progressivity into the federal income tax—that is, the implicit precept that some reduction in income inequality is compatible with economic progress in a market system. That assertion was especially in the "dangerous thoughts" category because orthodox wisdom was certain of its time-honored, enduring precept that the more inequality, the more savings, and the more savings, the more sacred investment. It was doubly dangerous because any inequality reduction through government was viewed as morally tantamount to officially sanctioned robbery—it encroached on the market's payments of "rewards for the services rendered by the owners of the factors for production." The new dissident precept, based squarely on the progressive rationale of the income tax movement, certainly faced a very powerful and enduring ideological opponent.

Major new dissident propositions were also necessarily advanced in the public finance arena. One of the more upsetting to traditionalists was the claim that government fiscal policy is more effective than monetary policy for the achievement of high employment and dampened cycles. This new belief was part of the endogenously created, Keynesian-type interventionism pursued by the New Deal.

The specific domestic Keynesian fiscal precepts presumed that an advanced capitalist economy chronically generates excess saving in the context of ever more limited investment opportunities. These ideas opened the door for government to tap those savings in the government securities market in order to deficit-finance its "net income-generating expenditures" for the relief of unemployment, and so on. The rest of the dissident fiscal rationale included the assertions that public debt is not analogous to private debt, that governments cannot go bankrupt, that debt growth no faster than GNP growth presents no serious problems, that the interest on it is paid overwhelmingly to "ourselves," and that the chief purpose of taxation is not revenue but control over the economy's performance ("functional finance," as Abba Lerner termed it).

The dissemination of these portentous propositions in the thirties should not obliterate the fact that almost everybody, then and subsequently, believed balanced budgets (preferably annually, but if impossible, then cyclically) are best, and deficits are to be avoided. That conviction was and is premised on the continued orthodox but questionable belief that the market's private investment mechanism still has the ability to assure tolerable cycles and long-run economic growth at high employment. Alternatively put, the likelihood that growth-assuring aggregate demand would henceforth require a big all-government–purchase (G) component, larger even than investment spending, was not even dreamed of by either the New Dealers or their opponents.[43] Had such a scenario been entertained by a significant group, it would have immediately been assailed by everybody who was anybody because it would violate almost totally the ruling beliefs that growth was a supply phenomenon, not demand; that long-run growth was driven exclusively by private investment; that nothing had happened historically to weaken investment's role as prime mover; that government demand diverted resources from the true, efficient, private use of growth-generating resources; and that it was only the long run that mattered policy-wise. Only a concession to the short run left the door ajar for public intercession—that is, to counteract temporary cyclical vicissitudes.

After World War II, when G became the second largest spending stream, it was reluctantly accepted, along with reluctant deficits to partially finance it, primarily because of its dominant national defense component. Large total state and local civilian purchases of goods and services (SLG), much larger than the federal civilian, were more acceptable though nevertheless chronically resisted. Acceptability was enhanced by virtue of the fact that much of the SLG paid for public schools. Also, a noteworthy proportion of the *expenditures* were financed by a big long-run rise in federal grants-in-aid. To understand the special governmental features of the postwar civilian mixed economy it is of the utmost importance to realize that "the chief clients of federal domestic expenditures are state and local government agencies."[44]

State and local government always has on its side the "traditional 'Jeffersonian' bias in favor of local as against Federal government administration."[45] If it is state and local, it is nonmonolithic, decentralized, grass roots, in accord with states' rights, and "more democratic." Finally, there is the legal state and local fiscal structure requiring an annually balanced budget.

Bypassed Issues and Responsibilities

A brief, selective review of some historically potential, government-augmenting responsibilities that were *not* assumed in the thirties will cast a heuristic light on the limits of augmentation reached in that decade. For such a review, we look at some of the important public issues that later on challenged government to either respond or abscond. The post–World War II developments of the government responses will be more fully examined in later chapters. Since these matters did not elicit any significant assumption of responsibility by government in the thirties, exploration of the likely reasons therefore should contribute to our understanding of the institutional and attitudinal forces that have prompted intervention.

Such a review was already begun earlier in this chapter with the discussion of the failure to adopt national health insurance. Programs were advocated, but with the notable, later emerging exceptions of Medicare and Medicaid, the organized pressures against it overwhelmed the proponents. The opposition has persisted, reinforced by the construction of private alternatives, successfully defeating all pro–social insurance pressure groups and their supportive influences emanating from, for example, a strong national health system just north of the border.

The failure of a national health insurance program in the thirties should not be interpreted to mean that government at all levels was fated to minimize expenditures and regulation regarding the health of the community. Quite the contrary. The Social Security Act itself authorized annual grants to the states for a variety of health purposes. The 1930s also saw passage of a National Cancer Act (1937), a Venereal Disease Control Act (1938), and a Federal Food, Drug and Cosmetic Act (1938). The Walsh-Healey Act of 1936 had stipulated that contractors on federal projects had to comply with the health and safety laws of the states in which they were operating.

More generally, the states and localities, as well as the federal government, had acted in the nineteenth century to treat the problems that had affected all classes from time immemorial: epidemics, sewage disposal, securing potable water, and preventing food contamination. All such problems were exacerbated by urbanization. Massachusetts finally set up the first state board of health in 1869; and all states had health departments of some sort by the end of World War I. Many states passed job safety laws to a great extent by virtue of the efforts of large employers and were committed to the provision of child health services, medical care under workers' compensation, and vocational rehabilitation.[46]

The U.S. Public Health Service had become a national agency in 1870. As government health programs grew in size, their functions became increasingly diversified, including even the maintenance of narcotic "farms" for the confinement and treatment of persons addicted to the use of habit-forming drugs.[47] Their much later progeny, the National Institutes of Health, was slated to become after World War II the largest supporter of medical research in the nation. The Public Health Service, along with the Food and Drug Administration, the Vocational Rehabilitation Administration, and the much older Children's Bureau, were all absorbed in 1953 into what was then a large civilian department of Health, Education and Welfare with 35,000 employees.

But state and local effort historically performed, and continued to perform the primary role, a role always unfolding with federal cooperation. Later on in this work we shall observe an enormous growth in the health and hospital expenditures and employment of the state and local governments after World War II. But the groundwork for that explosion was laid even under laissez-faire. It was extended substantially during the thirties. The pattern in the health sector of government growth has thus exhibited historical continuity with a trend acceleration rather than discontinuity. There are other similar cases. Higher education is one such, as we shall see.

The rapid expansion of governmental programs in the thirties generated at least three relevant public issues that were either not seriously considered at the time or not then explicitly concretized into programs. Indeed, the issues remained as abstract, general public problems or conflict matters throughout the subsequent history of the mixed economy.

The first of these issues was the question of the optimum proportion between the public and the private sectors of the economy. Failure to address the matter in any socioscientific sense is not surprising. The theoretically and historically minded people involved in the federal administration in the thirties were much too "pragmatically" embroiled in the specifics of reform to handle such a normative abstraction in any operational sense. The New Deal's opponents were quite confined to mouthing laissez-faire criticisms to the effect that government was getting so huge it was taking the very lifeblood out of the private market system.

This opposition to big government after World War II pretty much continued to monopolize the minimal discussion of the optimal proportion issue. While the opposition finally gave up hope of return to laissez-faire proportions, it insisted that growing government was a Leviathan bent on destroying the free market and should be reduced. Any nonpartisan discussion of the larger normative issue of public/private proportion was also pushed into the background by typical emphasis on disagreement over specific programs.

A second issue related to the expansion of government at the federal level arose out of allegations of bureaucracy, and in particular the increased role being played by the federal executive departments. The question of the political and economic power of overweening private bureaucracies was pushed off center stage, although the New Deal itself exhibited a touch of concern in connection with the investigation of the concentration of economic power by its Temporary National Economic Committee[48] and the Congress's Pecora Committee investigations of business financial frauds.

Of course, it was impossible to claim that the growing New Deal administration was the product of a preexisting federal bureaucracy intent on augmenting its political power. After all, the New Deal's predecessor regimes were Republican, small on any size measure, and dedicated to the unalloyed, "unfettered" free market. This left only the question of whether the decade's end had left the nation with a newly created political monster of overweening strength that would henceforth concentrate on its own imperial expansion. The ubiquitous critics of big government in the ensuing years answered the question with a resounding affirmative. They then proceeded to fuse bureaucracy allegations with their more general attack to the effect that the public/private sector ratio was being hope-lessly raised far beyond any reasonable optimum. The long-run growth of gov-ernment in the mixed economy at all levels after World War II added grist to the critic's mill. And there were few who would deny that the mixed economy did in fact produce bureaucratic tendencies.

A third issue was simmering under the surface of the new interventionism: did the government, the federal government in particular, have an enhanced role in determining the long-run growth of the economy? Neither the New Deal nor its opponents addressed themselves to the question at the time. Both concentrated on Depression problems and their possible solutions. Even if the New Dealers had uncovered Keynes's theories of unemployment equilibrium and deficit spending, they would have found there only a cyclically oriented—not a long-run growth—model. While the American Keynesian Alvin Hansen projected a "secular stagnation" thesis about the U.S. economy, his modest influence both inside and outside the profession was soon dissipated by the onset of war. After the war the thesis was illegitimately buried by the economics profession, whose leading lights claimed that the moderate postwar expansion rates "disproved" the thesis. That Hansen's argument called for Keynesian large-government spending to overcome stagnation—precisely what took place in the postwar years—was unconscionably ignored in the professors' "disproof."

In all generosity to the economics profession, it must be acknowledged that it was saddled with a doctrinal heritage that neglected a concern with any major growth determinants other than private business investment. Such investment would provide for growth if left alone. Economists embraced that classical, supply-side emphasis, but at the same time they forgot the classical concern with the long run and turned increasingly to the short-run questions. Thus one histo-rian of thought could say, "hardly a line is to be found in the writings of any professional economists between 1870 and 1940 in support of economic growth as a policy objective."[49] Hence it is not surprising that the bulk of the economics profession contributed to the general indifference toward the relation of public policy and long-term economic growth.

The New Deal not only was absorbed with the short run and the cycle, it also sided ideologically with the private investment emphasis in the orthodox heri-tage. It fostered policies that assumed that if the pump were primed to instigate recovery, private investment would respond and sooner or later (!) bring the economy up to the full employment level.[50]

After the war, a new field of Third World development inquiry absorbed much, though of course not all, of the energies of economists interested in long-run eco-nomic development. The profession thus bears a heavy responsibility for neglect of both growth policy in advanced economies and the Keynesian emphasis on demand as it might be applied to the long run. Of course, even had it not neglected the issue, it would still have had to deal with how to influence policy makers who remained, as in the thirties, locked in to short-run, largely supply-side, policy horizons.

There is a whole set of additional abiding public policy issues that for historical reasons could not be expected to have arisen as serious candidates for substantive government measures in the thirties. We know what to put into the set
because government did seriously concern itself with these matters subsequently,
but only when change in the market system and in society generated community
perceptions that major social actions should be taken, that government should
provide a substantive institutional response. This is why reference to the set of
issues performs an important heuristic role in a discussion of the long-run augmentation of government. The list of issues is long. It includes energy, urban
problems, crime, the extension of higher education, the quality of life, environmental damage, discrimination, inflation, a public welfare safety net (partially
attacked by the New Deal), international economic stabilization, Third World
development, and the Cold War. Of these, we treat at this time only two illustrative cases: environmental damage and the Cold War.

To simplify the point regarding the environmental issue, it may suffice to call
to mind the impact of major technological advances that were generated by the
development of the total capitalistic culture and the modified market system in
particular. Any society modeling itself after the capitalist industrial system will
have similar environmental problems.

We may selectively represent the technological advances by reference to the
traditional smokestack industries, motor vehicle, petrochemicals, and nuclear
power. Their spread and development created externalities that are exponentially
destructive of the natural and otherwise culturally produced environment, and
also are toxic to humans. The motor vehicles and petrochemicals existed in the
thirties. But the subsequent rise in per capita output and consumption embodying
their harmful technological fruits spread the damages at a rate far exceeding
population growth.

It took a long time for the magnitude of those spread effects to create and
register counteractions in community perceptions and organizations. When that
necessary gestation period had elapsed, the postwar environmental movement
appeared with its demands for institutionalized measures by government, business, and households. The 1930s was too soon. The market system was already
pregnant with the harmful externalities, but the accumulation was insufficient to
give birth to the requisite community recognition and organizational activity.

The nuclear power and weapons industry introduced an entirely new source of
environmental damage that developed many years after the 1930s. During the
long gestation period of the damage, its radioactive waste toxicity and disposal
costs were both ignored and concealed from the public by a combination of
nuclear power industrialists and Pentagon Cold Warriors.[51] Consequently the environmental movement, the nuclear power and weapons industry, and the government began to confront the monstrous cleanup costs most belatedly in the late
1980s. The disposal work in the nineties and after will unquestionably become the
biggest public-private works program in history. Government will have to grow

vastly to cope with it. In this case the growth will result from a technological innovation born of a gigantic public-private coalition.

Not only nuclear weaponry but also the Cold War itself became of overriding importance to federal government growth after World War II. It could not have been anticipated in the isolationist thirties. To be sure, there was a powerful current of anti-Sovietism in U.S. foreign policy from the time of the American invasion of Siberia during the Russian Revolution. But that anti-Sovietism in the interwar decades was ameliorated by isolationism. Vast military budgets, overwhelmingly dominating federal purchase, were not considered necessary. World War II transformed U.S. foreign policies and budgets. The federal establishment exploded as a result. Civilian employees of the Defense Department soared from 196,000 in 1939 to 1 million for most of the post–World War II years. They accounted for one-third of all federal "civilian" employment in the early 1990s.

Of course, the institutional roots of over four decades of a Cold War were not simply a powerful USSR. These roots, some of them substantially domestic in nature, need to be examined. But at this point it is necessary chiefly to emphasize that it insinuated a historically new growth stimulus after World War II to augment the federal government's size.

The Government as Administrator

The growth of government is by no means fully revealed by the usual criteria of size, such as number of employees and volume of revenues or expenditures. What we need for an adequate analysis of the rise of big government is a concept of its enlarging role in the economy and society. *Role* embraces governmental interaction with the components of the market system and society, not only through its budgetary but also through administrative management by its various agencies. Such managerial intervention is instituted, like all public policies, ostensibly to advance the interest of groups within the public.[52]

The degree of administrative management of the market system and society is but loosely correlated in many cases with agency staff or budget size. Also, the overall impact of such administration is extremely difficult to quantify, both on the specific and on the aggregate level.[53] Nevertheless, it is absolutely essential for the present subject to try to appraise the extent of government's long-run administrative policy growth. Our review of government in the 1930s has fortunately provided us with a body of empirical evidence that can contribute to such an appraisal by looking at the way things stood administratively on the eve of World War II. Using that evidence, together with our general knowledge of the relevant history, we can also project a taxonomic framework for subsequent appraisal.

The execution of government's growing managerial role with respect to institutions of long-run import in the thirties can be said to have taken three distinctive though overlapping forms:

1. Measures *providing for direct services,* such as finding employment for job applicants, administering the federal-state unemployment compensation system, and providing labor power training (Bureau of Employment Security, implementing the Wagner-Peyser Act of 1933 and the Social Security Act, 1935); extending loans to make electricity available to persons in rural areas lacking central station service (Rural Electrification Act, 1936); providing pensions for the elderly (Social Security Act); facilitating the multifaceted development of the Tennessee River watershed (Tennessee Valley Authority, 1933), along with other similar governmental entrepreneurial ventures—the Hoover, Grand Coulee, and Bonneville dams; delivering "surplus" foods to relief recipients (Food Stamp Plan, 1939–42, reactivated in 1961); delivering federal health, education, and welfare services (Federal Security Agency, 1939); and of course, expanding the postal service and the national defense establishment, and sustaining education at all levels of government.

2. Administrative measures *guiding the allocation of resources* among particular economic activities, such as Reconstruction Finance Corporation loans for lasting infrastructure projects like bridges, aqueducts, and power lines; various pro-agriculture programs (e.g., the Farm Credit Act, 1933; the Commodity Credit Corporation, 1933; the Soil Conservation and Domestic Allotment Act, 1936; the Agricultural Adjustment Act, 1938); support for exporters (Export-Import Bank, 1934; Gold Reserve Act, 1934; Reciprocal Trade Agreements Act, 1934); underwriting of residential construction (Homeowners' Loan Act, 1933; Federal Saving and Loan Insurance Corporation, FSLIC, 1934); stimulation of the flow of funds into the commercial banking system through "Regulation Q" (Banking Act of 1933, amended in 1935); state "fair trade" laws exempting from antitrust laws resale price fixing on particular brands of products (legalized by the federal Miller-Tydings Act, 1937); promotion and subsidization of the merchant marine industry (Maritime Administration, 1936); and promotion and subsidization, along with rate regulation, of transportation by air (Civil Aeronautics Board, 1938). Measures such as these are usually called simply "regulatory," but for analytical purposes it is desirable to segregate them from other regulation because they redirect the allocation of resources in the economy.

3. Administrative measures in the form of *manipulative regulation* of economic activities; regulation that has minimal allocative effects, such as the FSLIC and the Federal Deposit Insurance Corporation, FDIC, 1933, to greatly augment a depositors' "safety net" by insuring deposits of eligible commercial banks in the event of the latter bank failure (one provision of the Glass-Steagall Act, another being the separation of commercial from investment banking); the Securities and Exchange Commission, 1934, to protect investors on the stock exchanges by requiring public disclosure of basic information, and to regulate rates and practices of the exchanges as well as practices of investment advisers and public utility holding companies; the Federal Communications Commission, 1934, to regulate interstate and foreign communications media; the Public Utility

Holding Company Act, 1935, dismantling some of the concentration in that sector; the National Labor Relations Act, 1935, to dampen industrial conflict through support for labor's bargaining power, to supervise union representation elections, and to suppress "unfair" labor practices; the Federal Maritime Commission, 1936, to administer a number of shipping acts, including regulation of rates and practices of common carriers by water engaged in domestic, offshore, and foreign commerce; the Guffy-Vinson Bituminous Coal Act, 1937, to regulate prices, trade practices and marketing agreements in the bituminous coal industry; the Connally "Hot Oil" Act, 1935, to prohibit interstate shipments of oil produced in excess of the various state production quotas; the Motor Carriers' Act, 1935, which put interstate trucking firms under regulation by the Interstate Commerce Commission; the modest upsurge late in the decade in antitrust enforcement through Attorney General Thurman Arnold's "multiple litigation program" aimed at both business and labor monopolization; and the Robinson-Patman Act, 1936, forbidding manufacturers or wholesalers to give preferential discounts or rebates to large buyers.

This list of major New Deal legislative measures and agencies does not point up or distinguish income distribution effects. In one important sense there is no need to do so because all such programs have distributional effects to some not easily determined degree. More important, the list in the sometimes overlapping categories 2 and 3 provides qualitative evidence attesting to the fact that the mixed economy's first decade made a large contribution to the network of administrative management inherited from laissez-faire and the Hoover interregnum.

This list does not present an additional set of major administrative devices that will be treated later. These are known as *tax expenditures,* running into many billions of dollars. Tax expenditures are revenue losses attributable to provisions of the federal tax laws that allow special exclusions, exemptions, or deductions from gross income or that provide a special credit, preferential tax rate, or deferral of liability.

The so-called administrative state[54] had a great future in the long-run record of the mixed economy. The explanation therefore lies partly in the ongoing struggle for favored or protective treatment by government on the part of organizations representing some part of particular industries or sectors.[55] This *private interest* approach, emphasized by the late George Stigler, has been used extensively here in the review of the 1930s. It is also quite complementary with the *public interest* explanation of regulation that stresses governmental correction of market inefficiencies and failures.[56] That approach has also been used extensively in the present analysis.

But the public interest theory needs to be broadly applied if it is to contribute to an adequate explanation of some major long-run developments in the administrative management sphere. Such is particularly the case with regulatory institutions that cut across a wide spectrum of the economy—for example, the National

Labor Relations Act and the later Occupational Safety and Health Act (1970). These broad, public interest types have been labeled as "new style" social regulation to be distinguished from "old style," which was typically confined to specific industries or sectors.[57] The new style became increasingly characteristic of administrative management after World War II.

In any case, both the public and private interest approaches—sometimes useful in combination—are of value for explanation of the growth of direct services management (category 1, above). To round out the analysis, however, it is necessary also to examine the long-run changes in the disparate triad—market system, society, government—that generate the ever accumulating pressures for public intervention.

Ramifications of the World War II Years

The war ended the Great Depression and brought about an enormous, planned diversion of resources to the military establishment, with large attendant short-run socioeconomic effects. But the focus here is rather on the more lasting impact. Hence we need only note in passing the construction of the huge, successful emergency planning apparatus; the remarkably successful price control program belatedly beginning to take effect in late 1942; the temporary hump in the long-run rise of women's labor force participation rate; the surprising maintenance of civilian average per capita consumption; and the temporary alliance with the USSR. Rather, what needs to be extracted are the wartime developments and the war's immediate aftermath that contributed to the long-run augmentation of government's role.

We know that, as after World War I, the wartime planning apparatus was essentially dismantled—including, most unfortunately for the future, the greatest public child care network in American history. Nevertheless, the federal government's size and functions, both civilian and military, over the whole decade of the 1940s grew notably. All the old-line agencies, except for Labor and Agriculture, were affected. Employment growth in the Veterans Administration and in the civilian staff of the Defense Department was, of course, spectacular. After demobilization of most of the 12 million military personnel on active duty, the total by 1950 was still almost 1.5 million compared with about 0.5 million in 1940.

The state and local governments, on the other hand, expanded for the decade of the forties employment-wise at a much slower pace that approximated their long-run growth pattern. Nevertheless, state and local total employment in 1949 was still twice as large as federal civilian. Since the annual 7 percent rise in federal civilian employment in the forties ended the great surge that began in the early 1930s, it was destined to fall far behind the more vigorous state and local employment growth demanded by the American consensus thereafter.

Following 1949, the federal civilian personnel growth rate approximated a remarkably low 1 percent annually. We say "remarkably" because opinion makers chronically led the public to believe that the governmental Leviathan was primarily a federal creature. If so, it had to be revealed in phenomena other than personnel. Federal employment in the postwar era grew at only about one half the civilian labor force annual rate. It has been noted previously, and it bears repeating here, that in terms of government personnel, the civilian mixed economy of big government came to be administered primarily by state and local government workers.

Long-Run Effects of the War Years, 1941–45

The war brought overfull employment through a very large increase in deficit-financed federal purchases and consequent increase in the public debt. The public was not patriotic enough to tax-finance the war. That employment success story contrasted starkly in the public's economic images with the dreary preceding decade of government experiments clumsily designed with a hodgepodge of budgetary measures to counteract persistent mass unemployment and human suffering. The war showed how it could be done. Furthermore, as the war was coming to a successful close, the threat of a likely postwar depression created a spate of bills in the congressional legislative hopper calling for the federal government to try to again assume responsibility for some socially acceptable level of employment.[58] Herbert Stein has recorded the new component of the American political consensus: "There was never any real issue in the Congress about the idea that keeping unemployment low was an important national goal in the achievement of which the federal government had some responsibilities."[59] The groundwork had been laid for the historic 1946 Employment Act. Powerful intellectual support was at hand in the orb of the new Keynesian general theory of employment policy stressing the strategic role of aggregate demand, particularly government demand.

A second wartime change affecting government's future character was the rehabilitation of business's public image and influence. The Depression had been attributed in large part to business mismanagement in the twenties. Throughout that decade business had boastfully claimed full responsibility for the "permanent prosperity" that had turned frightfully sour. As a result of the debacle, business influence on public policy distinctly waned in the Depression years. Business was subjected to what it (mistakenly) considered punitive reforms by the New Deal. But the war brought large contingents of the corporate elite to Washington, and war production expanded, as it had to, under the direction of corporate managers who staffed the wartime agencies. Hence by the war's end the sullied image was a buried past. Big corporate management (not the much-touted and patronized small-enterprise segment) was again in the saddle, poised with all its internal conflicts, to shape public policies in its favor. In particular, "Roosevelt's wartime mobilization shaped the creation of a military-industrial complex whose influence was to persist and grow after World War II."[60]

The war also brought about a moderate shift in income distribution in the direction of greater equality. This "pre-fisc" (i.e., distribution before any reshaping owing to taxation and public expenditures) redistribution was apparently a structural change, for it was not, remarkably enough, reversed over the long run in the postwar era. So far as government is concerned, the shift slightly bolstered the revenue base available for long-run spending expansion and slightly dampened redistributive demands on public policy.

But by far the greatest contribution to the groundwork for an enlarged revenue role so necessary for conducting the future mixed economy was the wartime restructuring of the federal income tax. One of the changes was the institution in 1943 of withholding under the personal income tax on employees. Another was the reduction, despite the upward price drift, in personal exemptions; these were lowered, beginning even as early as 1940, from $2,800 in that year (married with two dependents) to $2,000 in 1944–46. The number of taxable individual income tax returns consequently soared—from 17.5 million in 1941 to 42.7 million in the last year of the war! With concomitant increases in tax rates, the ratio of total revenues from the individual income tax to the total from the corporate income tax jumped from 85 percent in 1940 to 134 percent in 1944. It was not the first time, of course, that war provided a handy patriotic rationale for lasting increases in direct tax revenues.[61] After the war, tax decreases were minimal. However, the wartime excess profits tax was promptly repealed.

There were also abiding developments in the labor field. In addition to large increases in union membership, the freeze on wages under the July 1942 "Little Steel Formula" prompted labor bargainers to demand, and business to concede, widespread compensatory "fringe benefits." Like workers' compensation for industrial accidents, some such benefits came to be required by law. As they became institutionalized in the postwar era, they shifted upward substantially the ratio of total labor compensation to money wages paid.[62] Since benefits included such things as employers' pension contributions and health insurance payments, these supplements to wages were fraught with large implications for governmental administrative involvement. Indeed, pensions became so important that the federal government, for example, found it necessary to underwrite the funding through the 1974 Pension Benefit Guaranty Corporation, an institution that within twenty years found itself precariously insuring some 40 million people. That long-term institutionalization of the fringe benefit, inaugurated firmly during the war, provides a prime example of private-public response to Michael Reagan's "community value changes,"[63] in this case the long march of humanism permeating the social fabric and reorienting the market system.

The effects of the war and the half-decade following on the black population were monumental and pregnant with implications for its long-run political power relationship to government. The implications flow from the changes shown in the census for 1940 and 1950 with respect to regional and rural-urban shifts, occupational advances, and educational progress. The strategically important outmigration from the oppressive South, together with national population rate increases, expanded the more politically vocal non-South black population by a very large 63 percent over the war decade—5 percent a year. The migratory drain and the exodus of blacks from southern farming to southern cities reduced the politically weakest black sharecroppers by a third. They were well on the way to extinction. Non-South urban blacks jumped by 71 percent, far outdistancing the strong 35 percent rise in the southern black urban population.

The war decade thus brought the urban black, largely ghetto population of the United States up from 49 percent to 62 percent of the total number of blacks in the country. In the same process, wartime and its aftermath also added to their economic and political potential through occupational betterment. Some 450,000 left agriculture and over half a million entered manufacturing to bring their total in that activity up to 1 million. Wholesale and retail trade acquired an additional 329,000, and 124,000 were added to the public service sector. As for education, the advances were less impressive, but they continued on a rising trend in terms of, for example, school enrollment and years of school completed.

In the context of an evolving, imminent conflict with superrace fascism even before Pearl Harbor, economic and political discrimination against blacks, which the New Deal had done but little to erase, was ripe for alleviation. But the amelioration process was sluggish because black awakening and organization were weak and establishment capitulation was a lengthy, tortuous process. A modest break came in June 1941. Under threat by A. Philip Randolph of the Brotherhood of Sleeping Car Porters that he would lead a mass march on Washington that summer, FDR issued a Presidential Order setting up an anti-discrimination Fair Employment Practices Commission (women excluded), or FEPC, to monitor federal contracts and employment. That FEPC lasted until a bill in 1946 to make the commission permanent was defeated in the Senate by southern white chauvinists presumably reflecting their major constituencies.

Nevertheless, despite that setback, the wartime FEPC, the large black representation in the armed forces, and the beginning of desegregation in the military initiated by President Truman in 1946 all anticipated the future civil rights movement, educational desegregation, the Equal Employment Opportunities Commission of 1964, the expansion of voting rights in 1965, and the landmark Civil Rights Act of 1964. World War II was indeed a seed time of recognition by government for blacks, although as much as half a century later there was still a very long way to go. This latter fact is a reminder of the ebb and flow pattern of group pressures, for affirmative action was brought under strong attack in the mid-1990s.

The ramifications of technological advance are a major determinant of governmental growth, as previously noted. The technological record of World War II was impressive in this respect. It included, by way of quiet preparedness, the establishment of the Office of Scientific Research and Development (OSRD) in 1940. In the sphere of national technology, it included advances in television; jet propulsion; plastics such as nylon; synthetic rubber; the development of electron tubes and their application to radar equipment; major improvements in electronic calculating apparatus, including the digital computer;[64] and the theoretical and experimental investigation of the properties of semiconductors at the Bell Telephone Laboratories that led to the invention of the transistor in December 1947. But atomic power from produced plutonium was the greatest innovation, a government-led breakthrough fraught with enormous import for public outlays and for the administration of big private activities. Aside from the impact on the electric utility industry and the federal military proper, the Energy Department's administration of contracts to private firms for weapons production was mainly responsible for its growth from 4,600 employees (Atomic Energy Commission) in 1949 to over 21,000 in 1992. Furthermore, the ultimate astronomical costs to government of radioactive waste management accumulating from nuclear power use were ignored and/or concealed for decades after the war; but as previously noted, by the 1990s those incredible costs, together with untold disposal problems, were becoming frightfully apparent.

The package of wartime technological innovations also contributed to the institutionalization of research. As symbolized by OSRD, the long-term trend toward a union of science with industrial technology was accelerated. The strategic financial and managerial role of government in that union was pinpointed. Connected therewith was the corollary demonstration that increased human capital investment through technical and higher education was an essential ingredient of a well-performing market system.

First Consequences: Setting the Stage for the Permanent Mixed Economy

By the last half of the war decade a permanent structural change in the composition of total demand had received social endorsement. In the new structure, gross business fixed nonresidential investment (I_f) was to remain in long-run stable ratio to GNP at approximately the 10 percent that had obtained over the last two decades of laissez-faire, 1910–30. As it turned out, without prior design, that demand ratio continued to accommodate, with its attendant technological advance, a post-1910 real long-run economic growth rate of approximately 3.25 percent annually up to 1970 (and 2.53 thereafter). But total household consumption (C) in ratio to GNP had permanently fallen from about 0.75 in the representative laissez-faire year 1929 to about 0.67 by 1948.

The accompanying rise after 1929 in all-government purchases of goods and services (G) had already by 1948 brought that spending stream up to about 12.5 percent of GNP, and soon thereafter it would reach its average postwar ratio of about 19 percent. It should be noted for possible international comparisons that the American societal consensus called a halt to its long-run G rise at a lower share of GNP than other developed mixed economies.

In relative terms, therefore, *the pickup in G demand filled the gap left by the fall in C demand, but only to an extent sufficient to accommodate the 3.25 and later 2.53 percent compound annual growth rate of real GNP* (given the I_f/GNP ratio). However, G became the economy's second largest demand stream through the entire postwar era.

Since the much enlarged G stream of demand was comparatively insensitive cyclically, it tended to reduce cyclical instability in the economy rather than aggravate it. The larger public employment did the same. To the extent that cyclical instability had in the past induced some of the social demands for governmental counteraction, this demand shift dampened such demands. The dampening effect was reinforced by the emergence of the so-called fiscal stabilizers embedded in the enlarged public budgets, particularly their federal component.

The demand requirements for sustained long-run economic growth now relied more heavily upon G and less on I_f than had historically been the case. Big government had become growth-decisive. To raise the long-run GNP growth rate above 3.25 percent, only small increases in I_f would be required, but large increases in G would be required. Capital goods productivity has significantly increased. Consequently small I_f increases could produce increasingly large output capacity increases that could only be utilized with increasingly large demand increases. Government spending would have to be a major source of these demand increases. Thus, government demand growth and economic growth had become inextricably linked in the new mixed economy after the war.

These great structural shifts may be described as the net outcome of aggregate decisions by the pertinent sectors of society. This is another way of stating, as above, that the shifts had "social endorsement." The business community was always free to increase its rate of investment. Unemployed resources that could be used to produce additional capital goods were almost always available. In booms, I_f rose, in depressions it fell, but the long-run trend of I_f/GNP is remarkably stable at 10 percent.

As for consumption, the outcome of the spending decisions by the household sector was to sacrifice a considerable amount of traditional "private" consumer goods in favor of collective consumption in the form of government purchases of military and civilian goods and the services of public employees. Indeed, "private" consumption became thoroughly permeated with public budget influences. Even if a bit of this great shift be attributed to some aggregate of government agency decisions, as it might well be in the case of foreign policy spending effects, an acquiescent net consensus by business and householders had to develop to make those decisions operative.

The shift to government spending responsibilities after the war went far beyond purchases of goods and services. Government transfer payments are not included in purchases. As previously observed, transfer payments to persons from all levels of government leaped upwards, not only because of big increases in veterans' payments but also because of Social Security benefits, one of the primary welfare state components of the mixed economy. The growth of the budgetary effects of the Social Security Act, including the effects of increased coverage over the postwar years, greatly increased the ratio of Social Security benefit transfers to federal purchases of goods and services. That ratio stood at 13.7 percent in 1940, but by 1949 it had already climbed to 16.6 percent. Following a temporary slowdown during the Korean War, the ratio took off, rising to 19.4 percent in 1956 and a whopping 30.8 percent as early in the era as 1960.

Since G plus all kinds of transfers (including transfers "in-kind") equals government *expenditures,* we have here an additional measure of government size. To see at a glance the relative expenditure advance, as recorded in the national income accounts, from laissez-faire to the immediate postwar mixed economy, we have, for example, the percentage of all-government total expenditures to GNP (in current dollars) as follows:

1929	9.9
1940	18.4
1948–49	21.1

Insofar as the over 100 percent rise in the percentage by 1948–49 represented, as it indeed does, the long-run socially acceptable trend, the rise had become institutionalized, never to be reversed.

The objectives of the historic 1946 Employment Act appeared at first to be frighteningly threatened by the collapse of real all-government purchases in that year. The big increases in transfer income in 1945 and especially 1946 were too small in amount to be an effective counteraction. Yet the unemployment rate increase was held down to less than 4 percent in both 1947 and 1948. What prevented any appeal to the act in those precarious initial years after the war was, in addition to the withdrawal of 2.6 million women from the labor force, an enormous one-year jump in gross private domestic investment in crucial 1946 together with a steady 4 percent annual increase in household consumption spanning the years 1945–49. This surprised the Keynesians, with the exception of FDR's "brain truster" Gardiner Means, because their consumption function depended exclusively on income. It turned out that consumer spending drew heavily on the liquidation of assets like war bonds and drawing upon accumulated deposit accounts. Strong increases in real state and local purchases also gave additional support from 1945 through 1950, before the Korean War spending took over. Unemployment rose from 2 percent in 1945 to only about 4 percent through 1948 and 5.9 percent in "slump year" 1949. The net result of these turbulent demand changes and moderate unemployment rates was such that there arose no public clamor or government inducement for federal action to maintain "maximum employment and purchasing power" from the war's end through the year of the Korean War's terminus in 1953. The act was not put to the test before the Korean War, and that war's huge spending jump forestalled any discretionary activation of it.

The greatest long-term effect of World War II on the government's role was the transformation in the international position of the United States, in the attitude of the public toward "foreign entanglements," and in general on foreign policy. The greatest of all modern world wars destroyed the isolationist current in American public thinking that had prevailed for two decades after World War I.

There were several reasons for this, and they all heightened the federal government's activity during the postwar era. One was the sudden recognition that the USSR was a mighty economic and military power. That changed awareness was soon intensified by the fact that it had brought almost all of Eastern Europe and a large part of Germany into its sphere of influence. Also, almost immediately China added another vast population to the world's "social property" sphere. The history of Western anti-Sovietism before the war readily reveals that a giant global confrontation between a coalition of societies based on the institution of private property and those social property countries, now vastly intensified by Soviet power, could come to dominate international economic and political relations for decades to come.

The confrontation, made ominously official from the American side by the March 1947 Truman Doctrine and generalized by the establishment of the North Atlantic Treaty Organization in April 1949, produced the incredibly and interminably costly Cold War, numerous more localized hot wars, and continual conflicts to shape the internal regimes of many far-flung lands. The confrontation also placed the United States under constraint to try to make itself an international showpiece of democracy, freedom, and economic progress. This too had its public costs.

A second reason for reorienting and augmenting the U.S. foreign policy establishment, partly connected with the first reason, was the assumption of hegemony ("leadership") in the Western sphere by the United States. This hegemonic role of presumed responsibility, prefaced by the European Recovery Program of 1948–51, lasted for about a quarter-century, during which period the enormous economic gap between the size of the American Goliath and the initially prostrate, chronically dollar-hungry Western allies and former enemies was gradually closed.

During that quarter-century, when the world was on a de facto international dollar standard, the United States enjoyed a noble-sounding "free trade" stance made feasible primarily by its superior technology and productivity. Its protectionist position was much milder than had been the case during the pre–World War II era.[65] Furtherance of trade expansion, international monetary cooperation, balance of payments equilibria, and foreign exchange stability were projected through the establishment of, and U.S. participation in, the International Monetary Fund (IMF). Under the mantle of that 1945 Bretton Woods institution, a de facto dollar standard was instituted that lasted for a quarter-century. Participation in the IMF augmented the federal government's role designed to strengthen America's supremacy in world markets. The United States was able to sustain a positive balance on merchandise accounts for every year from 1946 through 1970.[66] That export balance was made possible not only by virtue of its productivity performance but also by its foreign loans, grants, and export subsidies and strong growth on the part of its trading partners. The net exports supported domestic employment and thus helped keep the Employment Act in limbo.

The Bretton Woods, New Hampshire, meeting also produced the International Bank for Reconstruction and Development (IBRD), or World Bank, designed in affiliation with the United Nations (chartered 1945) to lend for Third World development. The latter objective was congruent with a third reason for augmented U.S. foreign policy commitments: the rise to prominence of the Third World of former colonies and dependencies. World War II had doomed the old-style western colonial system.[67] These "underdeveloped" countries became active participants in international affairs and were continuing claimants for economic and military aid. Such aid became highly politicized as it was caught up in the Cold War.[68] It was Cold War strategy, for example, that led to the U.S. Point Four program in 1949 and the launching of the Alliance for Progress in 1961 to counteract with aid the influence in Latin America of Castro's Cuba.[69] The Alliance aid was supplemented by the Agency for International Development, farm export surpluses under Public Law 480, and the Inter-American Development Bank chartered by the U.S.–inspired Organization of American States. But foreign aid, always to some degree humanitarian in purpose, was not necessarily in every case primarily a part of Cold War strategy. The very large program for Israel, for example, was mostly an expression of (1) domestic interest-group pressures and (2) power strategy in Middle East confrontations that were only loosely connected with the U.S.–Soviet antagonism.

The new postwar international power and assertiveness of the United States, shown by all the developments outlined above, enormously increased the size of the federal government. Measuring size by number of employees, the staff of the Department of State, for example, expanded from some 6,300 in 1939 to over 21,000 ten years later, and to 36,000 in 1959. The total civilian personnel of the Department of Defense jumped from an already quite sizable 196,000 in 1939 to become a veritable empire of 880,000 in 1949. And the armed forces on active duty likewise exploded from 458,000 in 1940 to 1,615,000 at the end of the 1940s. The politically powerful, almost sacrosanct veterans population, with lobbies almost completely insulated from criticism, had also increased enormously. Servicing that population raised the total employees of the Veterans Administration from a substantial 39,000 in 1939 to an army of 196,000 ten years later.

Considering the State Department, the "civilian" Defense Department, and the Veterans Administration as a single entity reflecting America's international position and policy as of 1949, we can fruitfully observe that the sum of the personnel in those three agencies accounted for well over one-half of all federal civilian employment. They had accounted for only one-fourth in 1939. If the half million postal workers are excluded from the federal total on grounds that they are an incontrovertible appendage to a growing economy and society, our threesome accounted for well over two-thirds of all the remaining civilian employment in 1949. Such numbers and percentages are the minimum staff reflection of the new postwar, global reorientation, for they take no account of several other relevant agencies, including the Federal Security Agency, the weapons sector of the Atomic Energy Commission, and the Central Intelligence Agency. But we know that during the forties there was at least an additional 850,000-employee response to the new international administrative responsibilities assumed by the federal government. No theory of the long-run rise of big government, no treatment of the fiscal revolution, can hold water unless it fully acknowledges the enormous repercussions of the war and the effects of the ensuing globalization of all national economies on their domestic and foreign public commitments.

One spinoff of both short- and long-run significance coming out of the war was the expected quadrupling in the number of veterans in civilian life. The actual increase as of 1947 was 14 million above the 1941 number of 4.3 million. The Congress, in anticipation of some such surge, passed the Serviceman's Readjustment Act ("G.I. Bill of Rights") in June 1944. The act was designed to serve two major goals: to help prevent uncompensated, war's end mass unemployment, and to help finance veterans' continued education. Accordingly, it provided for a year of $20 per week unemployment allowances (and certain housing subsidies), which pulled about a million veterans off the labor market in both 1946 and 1947. The educational subsidies, which also removed about a million from the market in 1946–48, converted those highly motivated veterans into mostly higher education students. Indeed, they constituted between 40 and 50 percent of total higher education enrollment in those years.[70] The long-run effects were most significant:

> The World War II G.I. Bill had set a veterans' education precedent possessing a momentum no longer derived from the short-run motivations that underlay the original bill. . . . Of 15.6 million eligible veterans, fully one-half participated in education and training programs of all types, at a cost of $14.5 billion . . . .
>
> The inundation of veterans enjoying the privilege of up to four years of college enrollment contributed immensely to the dissemination and democratization of higher education and the advance of technology.[71]

While the federal government continued its educational subsidies as a result of the additional veteran flow from the Korean, Vietnam, and Cold Wars, the financial impact of the G.I. Bill and the supplemental Veterans' Readjustment Act of 1966 fell heavily on the state governments in the form of construction outlays and the operating costs of the greatly enlarged higher education network. For example, between 1941–42 and 1953–54, real current general expenses for publicly controlled higher education institutions, overwhelmingly borne by the states and to a lesser extent by local governments, surged at a 6.4 percent annual rate; and real outlays for plant and equipment soared annually at 16.4 percent—mainly in the short span after 1945.[72] To be sure, this phenomenal acceleration was due also to other influences. But without doubt the rising higher education component of state and local long-run growth was powerfully driven by the G.I. Bill's ramifications.

The respondent flood of newly built city campuses by the states overthrew forever the elitist, rural pattern of college location. The new locational accessibility contributed to a democratic upsurge in nonveteran attendance, doubling the enrolled percentage of all eighteen- to twenty-four-year-olds from a mere 10 percent in 1946 to 20 percent in 1960, and tripling it by 1970 to 30.6 percent.[73]

Then there was the baby boom. Out of the war's suppression of new family formation came the psychologically complex catching-up period from 1946 to its peak rate in 1956. Here again, the governmental responsibilities for the attendant problems fell primarily on the state and local governments because the major impact for years to come was on the educational needs of the suddenly enlarged school-age population. Educational provision at public expense for that influx was as unquestionable as the assumption of government responsibilities of all sorts for the veterans. It was a big-ticket item for state and local governments. Public elementary and secondary school expenditures responded by jumping from 26 percent of all state and local general expenditures in 1949–50 to 31 percent in 1959–60 and 33.4 percent in 1965–66.[74] Both real general expenditures and capital outlays for schools rose at a vigorous 6 percent annually between 1949–50 and 1965–66. The war's long-run effects were therefore continuing to proliferate by raising the size of state and local government. That accommodation to the baby boom generation also gave strong support from the demand side to the overall growth of the economy.

The explosion of state and local government educational expenditures driven by the baby boom highlights a difference between government and market provision of services. In a simple market case, a large increase in the demand for grade and high school education would drive the price of education up, forcing some people to accept lesser quantities of education. In the public service system, on the other hand, all children are expected to have the opportunity to learn, so the supply of educational services expands by as much as the demand. The price increase is through taxes, but it does not ration the children out of school. For social necessities, the nonmarket system is obviously superior. If the United States had allocated education by a market process during the baby boom, a large number of the boomers—much of the current middle class—would now be undereducated in a society increasingly dependent on human capital.

There remains one final governmental step of long-run impact that came out of the wartime experience. That interventionist move was the passage of the 1947 Taft-Hartley amendment to the National Labor Relations Act, a pro-business "correction" to the New Deal measure. Taft-Hartley has already been touched on in connection with the wartime strengthening of the business public image and business influence on government at all levels. The National Association of Manufacturers' pressure for passage of the Taft-Hartley bill received public anti-union support prompted partly by the public's adverse reaction to a big strike wave in 1945–46, with almost 5,000 work stoppages involving about 5 million workers in 1946 alone. The business pressure also profited politically from Republican successes in the 1946 mid-term elections. While labor union membership had more than doubled since 1939 to over 14 million in 1946, "neither the AFL nor the CIO had taken fully into account the extent of public concern over what was considered labor irresponsibility . . . and more important, labor presented no alternative to the Taft-Hartley Act."[75]

What is significant about Taft-Hartley for the long-run role of government is the fact that the act inspired and paralleled many restrictive state laws and very much expanded federal administrative management in the sphere of industrial relations. The government's responsibility for balancing labor's rights under the National Labor Relations Act and employers' rights under Taft-Hartley was to require continual and intimate monitoring of industrial disputes. That "third party" intrusion by government under Republican Party leadership into a vital part of the market system was destined to expand even more.

Subsequently the federal government took it on itself, with some trade union support, to purge unions such as the Teamsters of corruption, racketeering and autocratic governance in the 1959 Landrum-Griffin Act. This "labor-management reporting and disclosure act" rounded out the increasing administrative participation of government in industrial relations that had begun with the National Labor Relations Act and the Taft-Hartley Act. Among other provisions, Landrum-Griffin stipulated procedures for union elections, required filing of union financial statements, made the misuse of union funds a federal offense, extended protection to unions in construction and the garment trade against nonunion subcontracting, and authorized the states "to exercise jurisdiction over categories of cases not dealt with by the N.L.R.B."[76] It also empowered the secretary of labor to seek court remedy for denial of members' rights and to investigate violations of the statute.[77] The resolution of industrial disputes and the internal activities of unions were being molded into a "quasi-public institution" under government surveillance.[78]

Here is one more instance pointing to the gradual displacement of the old private-public dichotomy, to the evolving fusion of those two sectors, generated everywhere and inexorably in the unfolding mixed economy. The three prominent pieces of legislation taken as a whole did not make a major contribution to government's administrative growth. But they were significant nevertheless because they are archetypical. They were the institutionalized incarnation of group pressures demanding more public intrusion into "private" affairs in order to better serve what those groups thought was in their own interest. Labor and government elements cooperated against business resistance to get the National Labor Relations Act. It was chiefly business groups that enlisted government elements against labor resistance to get Taft-Hartley and Landrum-Griffin. Government elements, some public opinion, and labor groups themselves pushed for the two years of Senate hearings that culminated in Landrum-Griffin. As ever, it was organized pressures generated by the evolving social fabric and the changing market nexus that produced the additional interventionist measures.

This survey of the main relevant long-run outcomes of World War II is completed. It shows that the war decade greatly escalated the multifaceted surge in public budgets, government personnel, and administrative management that had begun with the New Deal. By 1949 the mixed economy of big government, fused with the private sector, had already crystallized inevitably in a number of important respects. This has been indicated in connection with the review of major old-line federal agencies, using employees as measure. Of course, some important agencies were not to emerge until later.

A glance at federal expenditure patterns shows that certain long-run features of the mixed economy at that level of government, using the expenditure and employment measure of size, had clearly appeared. In the context of a yearly increase of almost 10 percent in total real federal expenditures during the war decade, the shifts in the component expenditure shares that were of lasting relative significance were as follows:

- National defense far outpaced all other components, rising from 24 percent of total nominal expenditures in 1940 to a substantial 36 percent in 1950.
- The national defense expenditure share of purchases by 1949 greatly exceeded nondefense.
- The nondefense purchases share had fallen far below its 1939 level, and was destined to become a small proportion of total federal purchases and a very small proportion of expenditures.
- The share of transfer payments to persons in current dollars had risen from 14 percent in 1939 to 21 percent in 1949, and were destined to become a rising percentage of total expenditures as the federal contribution to the welfare component of the mixed economy developed in later decades.

As the all-government pattern unfolds after the World War II decade, it will be revealing to examine, particularly in Chapter 4, the more moderate relative shifts in the federal spending components and the reasons therefore. At the same time, the shifting relative shares of the total federal compared with the total state and local governments, together with the evolving state and local component expenditures, will reveal the ebb and flow of pressures on expenditures emanating from the changing societal, market, and government sources. That long-run review will also require for completeness an examination of the institutional forces operating on the revenue side of government's fiscal totality.

Notes

1. For a discussion of the historic break in the long-run growth trend, see Harold G. Vatter, John F. Walker, and Gar Alperovitz, "The Onset and Persistence of Secular Stagnation in the U.S. Economy: 1910–1988," *Journal of Economic Issues,* 24, no. 2 (June 1995), pp. 591–601.

2. Robert H. Zieger, *American Workers, American Unions, 1920–1985* (Baltimore: Johns Hopkins University Press, 1986), p. 23.

3. See Herbert Stein, *The Fiscal Revolution in America* (Chicago: University of Chicago Press, 1969), p. 471, n. 43.

4. Cited in Broadus Mitchell, *Depression Decade* (Rinehart & Company, 1947), p. 88.

5. Ibid.

6. Paul Studenski and Herman E. Krooss, *Financial History of the United States,* 2nd ed. (New York: McGraw Hill, 1963), p. 359.

7. Ibid.

8. The insightful phrase is Edwin E. Witte's in his *Social Security Perspectives* (Madison: University of Wisconsin Press, 1962), p. 87.

9. Milton Friedman and Anna Jacobson Schwartz, *A Monetary History of the United States, 1867–1960* (Princeton: Princeton University Press, 1963), p. 434.

10. Arthur M. Schlesinger Jr., *The Coming of the New Deal* (Boston: Houghton Mifflin, 1958), p. 443.

11. Carter H. Golembe, "The Deposit Insurance Legislation of 1933," *Political Science Quarterly,* 75, pp. 181–182.

12. Friedman and Schwartz, *Monetary History,* p. 435, n. 13.

13. Schlesinger, *Coming of the New Deal,* p. 443.

14. Friedman and Schwartz, *Monetary History,* p. 435, n. 14.

15. *Historical Statistics,* Part 2, p. 1038, Series 742.

16. Schlesinger, *Coming of the New Deal,* p. 91.

17. Cited in Foster Rhea Dulles, *Labor in America,* 2nd ed. (New York: Thomas Y. Crowell, 1960), p. 274.

18. Raymond Wolters, *Negroes and the Great Depression* (Westport, Conn: Greenwood, 1970), p. 185.

19. Ibid., p. 187.

20. The title of a book by Friedrich von Hayek, freely distributed in all physicians offices, etc., in abbreviated form, by *Reader's Digest.*

21. Roy Lubove, *The Struggle for Social Security, 1900–1935* (Cambridge, Mass.: Harvard University Press, 1968), p. 126.

22. Ibid., p. 125.

23. Ibid., p. 171.

24. See Eli Ginsberg and Robert M. Solow (eds.), *The Great Society* (New York: Basic Books, 1974), p. 49.

25. See the discussion of this provision in James Leiby, *A History of Social Welfare and Social Work in the United States* (New York: Columbia University Press, 1978), pp. 203–233.

26. Lubove, *Struggle for Social Security,* p. 120.

27. June Axinn and Herman Levin, *Social Welfare: A History of the American Response to Need* (New York: Harper & Row, 1982), p. 199.

28. Dixon Wecter, *The Age of the Great Depression* (New York: Macmillan, 1948), p. 118.

29. It is hard to reconcile the 26 percent annual expansion rate of real fixed nonresidential investment from 1933 to 1937 with business's Schumpeterian accusation that the New Deal was destroying its "animal spirits."

30. Robert Higgs, *Crisis and Leviathan* (New York: Oxford University Press, 1987), p. 190. The quotation is from Arthur S. Link and William B. Catton, *American Epoch: A History of the United States Since 1900,* 4th ed. (New York: Knopf, 1973), II, p. 148.

31. Ibid., p. 193. The quotation is apparently from Frank H. Knight, *Freedom and Reform: Essays in Economic and Social Philosophy* (Indianapolis: Liberty Press, 1982), p. 73.

32. Quoted in Wecter, *Age of Great Depression,* p. 119.

33. Edwin E. Witte, *Social Security Perspectives* (Madison: University of Wisconsin Press, 1962), p. 85.

34. Frances Perkins, Foreword to Edwin E. Witte, *Development of the Social Security Act* (Madison: University of Wisconsin Press, 1962), p. viii.

35. Wecter, *Age of Depression,* p. 275.

36. Witte, *Social Security Perspectives,* p. 375.

37. See E. Cary Brown, "Fiscal Policy in the Thirties: A Reappraisal," *American Economic Review,* 46, no. 5 (December 1956), pp. 857–879.

38. The military totals for 1929 and 1933 are from Studenski and Krooss, *Financial History,* and refer to the sum of "military establishments" and "Navy establishments" for fiscal 1929 (p. 304) and "national defense" for fiscal 1933 (p. 406). Total FG and the ratio for 1939 are from the *Economic Report of the President* (Washington, D.C.: USGPO, 1990), p. 295.

39. The labels in quotes are actually the titles of books by a non-Marxist, Seymour Melman.

40. Calculated from *Economic Report of the President,* 1990, pp. 295, 383, and 1995, pp. 275, 365.

41. So stressed Ernest Hemingway in his famous novel of the thirties, *To Have and To Have Not.*

42. The quoted phrase is from A.V. Dicy, cited in R. Titmuss, *Commitment to Welfare* (New York: Pantheon, 1968), p. 189.

43. The outstanding exception was provided by the stagnation thesis of the leading American Keynesian, Alvin Hansen.

44. Harold G. Vatter and John F. Walker, *The Inevitability of Government Growth* (New York: Columbia University Press, 1990), p. 31.

45. James Q. Wilson, "The Rise of the Bureaucratic State," in Francis E. Rourke (ed.), *Bureaucratic Power in National Politics,* 3rd ed. (Boston: Little, Brown, 1978), p. 67. Reference is of course to *civilian* federal domestic expenditures.

46. Eveline M. Burns, *Health Services for Tomorrow* (New York: Dunellen, 1973), p. 43.

47. See the 1936 *World Almanac* (New York: New York World Telegram), p. 480.

48. For example, the committee researched the subject in a number of studies, such as Marshall E. Dimock and Howard K. Hyde, *Bureaucracy and Trusteeship in the Large Corporation,* TNEC Research Monograph no. 11 (Washington: GPO, 1940).

49. H.W. Arndt, *The Rise and Fall of Economic Growth* (Chicago: University of Chicago Press, 1984), p. 13.

50. Note that pump priming via G increases assumes investment is a function of demand, at least in the short run.

51. See, for example, Tim Weiner, "Military Is Accused of Lying on Arms for Decade," *New York Times,* June 28, 1993, p. A8.

52. The administrative component of growing government was already well chronicled in the early 1960s by Michael D. Reagan in his *The Managed Economy* (New York: Oxford University Press, 1963), particularly chapter 8.

53. For an able illustrative attempt to measure the economic effects of, for example, "price and entry" and "health and safety" regulation, see Paul W. MacAvoy, *The Regulated Industries and the Economy* (New York: W.W. Norton, 1979), chaps. 2 and 3, pp. 31–104.

54. This concept is developed in Lawrence C. Dodd and Richard Schott, *Congress and the Administrative State* (New York: John Wiley and Sons, 1979).

55. See, for example, Jeffrey M. Berry, *The Interest Group Society* (Boston: Little Brown, 1984).

56. A brief presentation of the public and private interest theories may be found in Michael C. Keeley and Frederick T. Furlong, "Bank Regulation and the Public Interest," *Economic Review,* Federal Reserve Bank of San Francisco, Spring 1986, pp. 55–60.

57. For applications of this taxonomy, see, for example, William Lilley III and James C. Miller III, "The New Social Regulation," *The Public Interest* 47 (Spring 1977), pp. 49–61.

58. Stein, *Fiscal Revolution,* pp. 197–198.

59. Ibid., p. 199.

60. Gerald D. Nash, *The Great Depression and World War II* (New York: St. Martin's, 1979), p. 118.

61. See Studenski and Krooss, *Financial History,* p. 450.

62. See Harold G. Vatter, *The U. S. Economy in World War II* (New York: Columbia University Press, 1985), pp. 147–148.

63. See Reagan, *Managed Economy,* pp. 163–164. Such changes are one of his three reasons for the expanding role of government. The other two are "circumstantial development," such as urbanization, and increased knowledge of how the economy functions.

64. See Friedrich Klemm, *A History of Western Technology* (Cambridge, Mass.: MIT Press, 1964), p. 374.

65. For example, the average of the ratio of tariff duties collected to free and dutiable imports in that quarter-century was only about one half the average level of the ratio from 1922 to 1939. See *Historical Statistics,* Part 2, p. 888, Series u211.

66. See the *Economic Report of the President,* February 1990, p. 410, Table C102.

67. See William P. Bundy, "The 1950s Versus the 1990s," in Edward K. Hamilton (ed.), *America's Global Interests* (New York: W.W. Norton, 1989), pp. 47–48.

68. See John D. Montgomery, *Foreign Aid in International Politics* (Englewood Cliffs, N.J.: Prentice Hall, 1967), p. 39.

69. See Harry N. Scheiber, Harold G. Vatter, and Harold Underwood Faulkner, *American Economic History* (New York: Harper & Row, 1976), p. 431.

70. Vatter, *U.S. Economy in World War II,* p. 137.

71. Ibid., p. 137.

72. Data taken from Tax Foundation, *Facts and Figures on Government Finance,* 1973, p. 153, and 1983, p. 216. Nominal magnitudes converted to real using GNP implicit price deflators, *Economic Report of the President,* January 1973, as follows: For general expenses the state and local deflator (p. 197) and for plant and equipment outlays the fixed nonresidential investment deflator (p. 196).

73. The twenty- to twenty-four-year-old population declined absolutely between 1950 and 1960, and only barely increased during the sixties.

74. *Facts and Figures on Government Finance,* 1973, p. 256, #206. Appropriate GNP deflators, as previously, are applied to get the real data referred to in the following sentence.

75. Foster Rhea Dulles, *Labor in America* (New York: Thomas Y. Crowell, 1960), p. 375.

76. See Henry Pelling, *American Labor* (Chicago: University of Chicago Press, 1968), p. 206.

77. See Philip Taft, *Organized Labor in American History* (New York: Harper & Row, 1964), p. 705.

78. The quoted phrase is from Charles H. Hession and Hyman Sardy, *Ascent to Affluence* (Boston: Allyn and Bacon, 1969), p. 841.

CHAPTER THREE

The Postwar Economy and Government Growth

We know that the main contours of large government characterizing the mixed economy were already pretty well shaped by the end of the World War II decade. What now needs to be discovered is how postwar economic, social, and political evolution developed, modified, and insinuated new elements into those basic governmental contours.

As previously emphasized, the contours of the public sector's growing role are best revealed by examination of three main measures: budgets, employees, and administrative management of the economy and society. The relevant postwar history thus becomes those developments that were connected with the changes in the three measures.

Economic Growth

Whatever large cultural forces may be at work to expand government's role, the long-run growth of real gross product and gross product per capita are linked with the contours and size of the public sector. There are three major links that need to be explored. The first is that output growth provides material support for government's long-run growth. The second connection is that GNP rise and its composition induces a demand from a heterogeneous public for larger government. Finally, public-sector growth causes and shapes the increase of total output and its pattern.

Real gross product, or income, rose at an average compound annual rate of slightly over 3 percent between 1950 and the early 1990s. With population growing at 1.24 percent a year, real income per capita rose at a moderate 1.76 percent average rate. So ignoring distributional matters for the moment, society was producing quite a bit faster than it was growing. Hence, a potential dividend of material support for the resources requisite to a growing government was clearly generated. And we know that potential was in fact realized in the sense that an absolutely rising portion of the material product dividend was allocated to the public sector by the tumult of human decisions.

As for the second link, the overall demand to enlarge government was not a passive accompaniment of total output growth. Allocation of resources and managerial authority to the public sector of some of the fruits of economic growth resulted from the exercise of human discretion. The elements in society's discretionary decisions that are independent of economic change must not be lost sight of simply because those decisions are in turn prompted in varying degrees by economic and other "objective" changes. This fact of discretionary autonomy has been noted earlier, for example, with regard to the historical rise of humanism and also the abiding social preference for expanding institutionalized education.

As for the power of government growth to influence overall economic growth, we must rely upon inference to a large extent. However, the plausibility of such inference is enhanced by some striking features of the postwar experience. One of the most striking, as will be spelled out soon in more detail, is the fact that *both* the real GNP rate and the rate for standard measures of government's size, such as spending, exhibit two quite distinct, lengthy periods within the whole postwar era.

The watershed year that separates the two intermediate periods is the cycle peak 1973. While that year is strictly speaking approximate, almost all of the postwar era's data show 1973 as an appropriate terminal for the first quarter-century after conversion from the war, and for the initial step preceding the basic configurations of the next two decades or so. The first period is one of rapid growth, the second, one of slowdown.

Let us take as initial hallmarks for the two periods the real total product growth rate and some standard measures of the all-government growth rate. Thus for the first period, 1948–73 (using three-year averages centered on those dates), the average annual compound rate of growth for real GNP was 3.67 percent. This was substantially higher than the rate for the whole postwar era previously mentioned. It was a period of excellent output performance that was also well above the twentieth-century average of about 3.0 percent.

The enlargement of the government establishment in that period was equally, if not more, impressive. For example, to take a nonpecuniary criterion, all-government payroll employment increased by 3.62 percent annually from 1948 to 1973. This was twice the average yearly growth rate of the civilian labor force of 1.57 percent.

But we are at the moment concerned with the third link: that between pecuniary measures of government enlargement and GNP as stimulated by those measures. We should therefore note that real all-government purchases of goods and services grew at a vigorous 4.24 percent a year from 1948 to 1973. Since such outlays constituted the second largest demand stream, one largely autonomous with respect to consumption and private investment spending, it is reasonable to infer that GNP in that period grew as strongly as it did partly because the big-government spending component of aggregate demand grew rapidly.

The plausibility of a functional link between the government demand pace and the total demand growth rate, or GNP, is enhanced by the contrasting slow-down record after 1973. From that year until the early nineties, real gross domestic product rose annually at only 2.36 percent. That miserable performance —stagflation in the seventies, constant total output from 1979 through 1982, thirteen years of stagnation in residential construction between 1972 and 1985, tempered by the "Reagan expansion" of the mid-eighties—was paralleled by a corresponding drop in government purchases growth.

The increase in the number of all-government employees also dropped to only some 1.8 percent a year—*slower* than the civilian labor force rate of about 2 percent annually. On the more relevant pecuniary side, the real all-government purchases rate similarly collapsed to only 1.80 percent annually from 1973 to 1993. A similar drop occurs in the case of real all-government expenditures (which include transfer payments). The drop hit both the federal and the much larger state and local demand streams. The interpretation that a change in government purchases can *cause* a change in total spending in the same direction also has support from the fact that it embodies Keynesian theory, the only general theory since Thomas Malthus that has addressed itself systematically to that relationship.

To appraise the possible functional connections between the three great domestic demand streams—consumption, investment, and all-government purchases (G)—it needs to be borne in mind that G amounted to about 20 percent of gross domestic product and averaged about 40 percent larger than gross private domestic investment. That is one good reason for the fact that "there have been no extended periods of rapid economic growth in this century without rapid growth in government purchases."[1]

The concern with the general connections between government spending and total demand should not lead us to ignore the fact that, on the standard measures of size, the "big government" express train of 1948–73 clearly ran onto a siding after the latter year. This is the case for both the number of employees constituting the total government bureaucracy and total purchases, although it certainly was not true of the government's administrative management and guidance activities. This last measure remains to be examined.

But from the standpoint of big government (all levels) viewed as a Leviathan, that bureaucracy explanation of government's growth will have to deal with the awkward fact that the presumed bureaucratic engine was unable to sustain anything like its 1948–73 employee expansion rate, particularly at the federal level. Indeed, its rate suffered a "membership" drop after 1973 of over 50 percent and two whole percentage points in that growth rate during the slowdown decades.

At the federal level, the customary bureaucratic culprit, total civilian payroll employee growth rate collapsed to a minuscule 0.26 percent yearly between 1973 and 1995.[2] Indeed, at the end of 1995 the number was approximately the same as it had been in 1979! By comparison, state and local total payroll employment grew 1.82 percent a year over the same period.[3] If the record suggested bureaucratic enlargement, it would therefore have to have been at the more popularly favored grass-roots state and local level. In any case, the seven-to-one contrast in growth rates is so revealing that it will warrant careful probing in the following discussion.

The Ramifications of Population Change

Population changes after World War II were notable and brought with them certain public pressures for government responses augmenting both the size and the managerial activity of the public sector. The major changes are well known: the baby boom between 1945 and the early 1960s, the rise in the number and proportion of elderly people, and the increase in urban populations. All these socioeconomic developments generated public activism directed at government policy.

The baby boom had little effect on government response in the case of pre-school child care in general. That indifference was in sharp contrast to the public policies in most Western European countries and the Soviet Union. But as pointed out in Chapter 2, the response in the case of public primary and second-ary schooling was a very different matter. The unquestioned community determi-nation in the United States, powerfully expressed by a Supreme Court holding that "providing public schools ranks at the very apex of the function of the states" was that children had a right to public education at least through high school. The result of that consensus, given the baby boom, was an enormous rise in public school enrollment, construction, maintenance, and staff over the first and only great government postwar growth period, 1948–50 to the early 1970s.

State and local governments' major growth contribution, stemming from that public school drive, is clearly revealed by the expenditure record during the years of rapid, conventionally measured, all-government expansion. For exam-ple, real expenditures for public elementary and secondary education between 1950 and 1970, under the concentrated impact of the baby boom generation, rose at an average annual rate of 5.35 percent. That huge rate of increase slightly outpaced the very large 5.23 percent for state and local full-time equivalent (FTE) employees engaged in education. Such educational expenditures advanced as a proportion of all fast-growing state and local real expenditures from 22 to 29 percent over the same two decades.

Further in employment terms, while all state and local FTE employees were vastly outpacing the growth rates of both the civilian labor force and federal civilian workers between 1950 and 1973, those engaged in state and local educa-tion grew even faster. They accounted for 55 percent of the huge rise in the state and local total. As early as 1960 they outnumbered all federal civilian workers, even if the hundreds of thousands of FTE Department of Defense civilian work-ers are included. By 1973 they were 2 million more numerous. This excess grew after 1973, since state and local educational employees continued to rise, albeit much more slowly. The baby boom impact was by then exhausted. The excess over the federal was augmented after 1973 by the fact that federal civilian employment hardly rose at all.

The Ascension of Higher Education

There was more to education's role in the growth of big government than the state and local response to the baby boom. Reference was made in Chapter 2, for example, to the G.I. Bill's higher education route for discharged World War II veterans. The vast numbers could not be turned loose in the private market without an attendant mass unemployment whose sociopolitical threat would be frighteningly reminiscent of the Great Depression. The G.I. Bill was comprehensive and long lasting. It took the form it did to a great extent because it readily latched on to a larger emerging cultural upsurge that was demanding the expansion of higher education opportunity for youth in general. That demand did not yet call for higher education as a universal right, as with society's consensus about children. But it did express a growing recognition that America's vaunted advocacy of "equality of opportunity" was a farce in the context of a 9 percent higher education enrollment on the part of the population aged eighteen to twenty-four.

The higher education upsurge may have been given its initial postwar boost by the G.I. Bill. But powerful coincidental stimuli emanated over postwar time from smaller veterans' educational assistance connected with the Korean and Vietnam wars. They came chiefly from the developing feminist movement, the minority rights movement, the occupational requisites of a technologically advancing urban economy, and the intellectual expectations of many baby-boom high school graduates.

Permeating and extending beyond all those developing specifics were two additional and more general sources prompting a demand for more higher education. The first was an upsurge in educational aspirations within the community at large. The second was an expanded emphasis on human well-being. Both received support from the high and rising level of per capita income with its accompanying growth in the middle class and upper echelons of the blue-collar stratum.

Hence, the resulting diffusion of higher education, largely public, paralleled the public school explosion and persisted after it. Concurrently there was a revolution in college locations as new state university campuses were constructed in the cities and a vast public community college network was created. Such urban accessibility, together with the increasing social participation of women, brought females by new millions into the academic fold.

But the rapid higher education growth period was again approximately the first quarter-century after the war. The initial leap came in the late forties:

enrollment in both public and private institutions of higher education, about equally divided between the two at that time, was 1.50 million in 1940 and 2.66 million in 1950. Thereafter growth of the publicly controlled institutions greatly outpaced growth of the private. Enrollment in them soared from 1.36 million in 1950 to 5.11 million in 1970. This was a whopper of an annual increase of 6.84 percent, a rate much exceeding the vigorous 2.94 percent yearly enrollment rise in public primary and secondary schools.[4] Whereas the enrollment rate in the latter peaked in the early seventies, the number of students in public higher educational institutions continued to drift very slowly upward into the nineties.

During the years of great expansion in women's demand for higher education their college degree-credit enrollment in both private and public institutions increased much faster than men's. The female/male ratio jumped from a low of .46 in 1950 during the heyday of the G.I. Bill (the ratio had been .73 in 1940) to .70 in 1970 and over 1 by 1980. This was a gender revolution powerfully impacting government expenditures for colleges since it was the publicly controlled institutions that absorbed the bulk of the increase.

In general, the growth of government was thus much indebted to the postwar higher education revolution during the first postwar quarter-century. As in other spheres, the fast growth experience, on the basis of measurement by conventional pecuniary criteria, was about exhausted by the early 1970s. But while it lasted, all-government higher education expenditures rose faster than total government outlays, thereby pushing up that total. For example, public higher education expenditures rose from about 2 percent of all-government expenditures (purchases plus transfer payments) in 1950 to 5 percent in the mid-seventies. In ratio to all-government purchases of goods and services they rose from 3 percent to 8 percent over the same years. Thereafter they just about kept pace with the slowed total government rise.

If the sum of the baby boom pressures and the impact of the rising demand for higher education is represented by all-government expenditures for all levels of education, then the contribution of education's rapid increase to all-government growth is seen to be very large. For example, education relative to all-government general expenditures was 22 percent by the early seventies, and relative to total government purchases of goods and services it was 29 percent.

Health

It may come as a surprise that the growth of total public health care in a country that failed to follow the universal compulsory health insurance model of the other advanced market economies contributed significantly to the rise of big government. Public health expenditures in the United States rose from only 2 percent of GNP in 1970 to almost 6 percent in 1992. Moreover, as a share of all-government expenditures they doubled from 8.5 percent to 17 percent over the same period. They also increased much faster than private national health expenditures, which but slightly outpaced real long-run GNP growth. As a result, public national health outlays rose from 57 percent of total private health expenditures to 77 percent over 1970–93.[5] The federal share of the total public increased rapidly up to 1970, but thereafter its relative rise was modest.

The time pattern for public expenditure growth was greatly shaped by the adoption of Medicare and Medicaid in the mid-sixties. The two programs gave a big boost to the real public total outlays for health research, hospital construction, and patient care, which jumped from an annual rate of increase averaging a strong 4.2 percent between 1950 and 1965 to 13 percent yearly during the following eight years. That jump ended in 1973; thereafter the yearly rise was only 3.4 percent, but it nonetheless exceeded the real GNP growth by a whole percentage point because of the sluggish performance of the latter in the slowdown years. At the same time, it should be noted that the public health growth slowdown *followed the pattern of general government growth abatement after 1973.*

The checkered and frustrated career of the public's demand for government provision of some kind of health care for the general population, including socially insured care, seriously got under way early in the twentieth century. Some of that advocacy record before World War II was surveyed in Chapter 2. We present briefly here some additions to that history, but mainly review advocacy developments after the 1940s.

The provision of public health care for the poor only, as distinguished from social insurance for the general community, had been addressed by local governments from very far back in history. But the Progressive movement during the first two decades of the twentieth century brought into focus the more controversial demand for non–means-tested government provision—that is, social insurance. The National Conference of Charities and Corrections, for example, in 1912 called for social insurance to cover occupational disease, sickness, old age, and unemployment.[6]

The National Consumers' League in 1917 resolved to press for state-level compulsory health insurance.[7] The Women's Trade Union League in 1919 advanced a demand for a system of "social insurance . . . against sickness . . . and invalidity pensions"[8] The progressive, welfare-oriented American Association for Labor Legislation (AALL) at the end of World War I embraced a stepped-up campaign for social security protection against sickness, unemployment, and old age.[9] This program was seconded at the same time by the influential Federal Council of Churches of Christ in America. The AALL continued to pursue its crusade for compulsory health insurance throughout the 1920s. Despite the opposition of Samuel Gompers and the other official leaders of the AFL, numerous member unions and state union federations endorsed social health insurance.[10]

While the Great Depression brought the health insurance issue very much into the limelight, the powerful opposition, led as usual by the American Medical Association (AMA) forced deletion of health insurance from the Social Security bill of 1935. The AMA persistently viewed social health insurance as "the most deadly challenge ever faced by the medical profession."[11] The enormous clout of the AMA down through the decades stemmed from its tight-knit organizational expertise, from its widely venerated professional membership (the public's "medicine man" syndrome), and above all from the fact that its members would be crucial, indispensable practitioners in any actual social health program.

Nevertheless, advocates of compulsory health insurance, backed by somewhat ambiguous public opinion polls favoring federal involvement in such a system, were able to continue to get universal compulsory health insurance bills introduced (in vain) into the congressional hopper every year during the 1940s. And in the 1952 report of President Truman's Commission on the Health Needs of the Nation it was stated that "access to the means of attainment and preservation of health" was "a basic human right."[12] But opposition to "socialized medicine" by the AMA and the American Hospital Association along with others stymied the public health insurance effort at every turn.

However, the proponents of public involvement, including at last an organization of the elderly and stepped-up support from the 14-million-member AFL-CIO beginning in early 1957,[13] finally engineered in 1965 a successful entering wedge trick by linking tax-financed, compulsory health insurance to the elderly through extension of the Social Security Act in the form of Medicare. Means-tested Medicaid for the poor, implementing the War on Poverty of the fourth president devoted to social health insurance, was pushed through for the poor at the same time. That is why public health expenditures took a big jump soon after. Medicare expanded the entitlement component of the welfare state; Medicaid expanded the modern version of the "poor law" safety net.

The point of this selective recount of community demand for both public health insurance and means-tested assistance in the "poor law" tradition is to stress the interpretation that the limited achievements were chiefly the product of precisely such community pressures. The organizations mentioned in the recount supplement and in part overlap the extensive list of organized pension advocates enumerated in Chapter 2.

The pressures for public health provision had to presume the recognition that the private market system was not equipped to fulfill the people's health demands adequately. While social reformers in government were always prominent in the advocacy of health assistance and insurance, the actual programmatic achievements were not those of an overweening governmental reform bureaucracy augmenting its empire. Indeed, the opposition's defensive insistence on private medical care generated a vast private bureaucratic health care Leviathan made up of physicians, hospitals, pharmaceutical firms, insurance companies, and consulting claims reviewers that continued to balloon in the 1990s, even as it greatly inflated the entire matrix of long-run health care costs.[14] Thus the end result by the 1990s was the institutionally evolving conflict between private market inadequacies in the health care field and private market solutions to the problem. In the early nineties, more than 30 million Americans still lacked minimal health coverage and employers were diluting employee health care fringe benefits.[15]

In labeling Medicare as a welfare state institution and Medicaid a modern "poor law" arrangement we follow in general A. Dale Tussing's concept of a "dual welfare system."[16] If the program is socially insured, compulsory, contribution financed, and applicable to all income levels within a given group, it will be considered in this work a part of the American welfare state. If it is means tested, voluntary, and not linked with specific contributions by beneficiaries, it will be treated as part of the "poor peoples' system," following Tussing's terminology. The latter class of public programs, such as general public assistance, Aid to Families with Dependent Children (AFDC), Supplementary Security Income (e.g., old-age assistance, aid to the blind and/or permanent disabled), Medicaid, the food stamp plan, and public housing, are thus considered herein as updated "poor law" institutions.

The contemporary upsurge in pressures from the poor is by no means a complete explanation for the extension of poverty programs or President Johnson's War on Poverty. To be sure, there was social and political turmoil particularly in the 1960s. The expulsion of black southern sharecroppers and their mass migration to the urban ghettos alone provided a major base for upsurge of protests and demands. That public aid revolt and the encouraging response it got from the federal government's Great Society program has been well reviewed by Frances Fox Piven and Richard A. Cloward; for example,

> in the 1960s as in the 1930s, poor people banded together to attack the relief system. Just as unemployed groups sprang up during the Depression and eventually banded together in the Workers' Alliance, so in the late 1960s welfare rights groups began to appear and then banded together in a National Welfare Rights Organization. . . . Each arose in a period of widespread social and political upheaval occasioned by profound economic dislocation, and each flourished by capitalizing on disorder to obtain public aid for masses of families in financial distress.[17]

Social activism, along with other factors, is also acknowledged by another careful scholar:

> Political forces further contributed to the rise in social welfare spending. Passage of Medicare revealed the role of these forces in the area of aid to the aged. They accounted also for the unheralded but vitally important liberalization of food stamp legislation, a liberalization that began in 1968, when a TV documentary on hunger in America dramatized the problem of malnutrition. The following year Senator George McGovern of South Dakota picked up the attack in an investigation of hunger and malnutrition. President Nixon, anxious not be outflanked, in August 1969 called for a vast expansion of the food stamp program, a change that appealed not only to liberals but also to conservatives, who preferred to give food instead of cash to the poor and who

recognized that the program could be administered locally, thus simplifying and decentralizing welfare administration. The food stamp program also received important political support from well-organized producers and retailers. For all these reasons it developed great momentum in both parties, and Congress gave Nixon what he wanted in December 1970. Its response showed that certain kinds of welfare spending had become part of a bipartisan consensus, in spite of the rhetorical flourishes of conservatives. By 1974 food stamps were available to all poor families that passed certain means tests, not just to those on welfare.[18]

But a more complete explanation lies equally in the combination of the enabling long-run rise in per capita income, the humiliating paradox of poverty amid plenty, and the continued growth of an ancient humanitarian sentiment, mixed with a fear of social turmoil and the spread of epidemic disease. Deep-rooted in the culture was the awareness that

> the interests of the poorer classes of society are so interwoven with those of every part of the community, that there is no subject more deserving of attention [therefore] let the labours of the industrious–the talents of the wise–the influence of the powerful–and the leisure of the many, be directed to this important subject.[19]

It is appropriate to bring reference to our English eighteenth-century cultural roots forward on the matter. The January 1964 *Economic Report of the President,* for example, in speaking of President Johnson's War on Poverty, emphasized the fact that "poverty is costly not only to the poor but to the whole society. Its ugly by-products include ignorance, disease, delinquency, crime, irresponsibility, immorality, indifference. . . . Poverty is no purely private or local concern. It is a social and national problem."[20] FDR's "one-third of a nation, ill-housed, ill-clothed, ill-fed" thus reappeared three decades later. But the war on poverty continued, un-won.

The career of Medicare and Medicaid reveals the two facets of social welfare policy and their relation to government's growth. Medicare is an entitlement program providing uniform benefits, including hospital care, financed through Social Security taxes. Benefits have been subject to inflation increments, and taxes more or less coordinately raised. However, *real* Medicare expenditures increased at a strong 4.5 percent annual rate between 1970 and 1993. Their undeflated share of total federal expenditures jumped from 3.6 percent to 8 percent over those twenty-three years. The Medicare real annual growth rate was a percentage point above the yearly rate of increase for total real federal expenditures. It therefore contributed in a modest degree to the rise of all federal outlays.

Medicaid was set up at the same time as Medicare, but was a joint federal-state financial program making roughly equivalent payments directly to suppliers of medical care to the "categorically needy." The coverage of the poverty population varies a lot among the different states. For the country as a whole, Medicaid served 30 million low-income people in 1993, but covered less than one-half those below the official poverty level.[21]

In toto, real Medicaid expenditures rose annually by more than a percentage less than the Medicare rate, bringing them up to somewhat less than 5 percent of all-government expenditures in 1993. While they soared in the seventies, driven particularly by payments for nursing home services, they suffered an enormous rate drop in real terms to only 2 percent a year in the eighties as the Reagan and Bush administrations shunted fiscal responsibility for services to the vulnerable poor more and more onto the shoulders of private charity.[22] The welfare state in health care, as predominantly represented by Medicare, while slowing down in that decade, did much better than the "poor peoples' system."

The slowdown, as measured in outlays, in all public health provision after the early seventies holds similarly for public employment. For example, the big state and local bureaucracy of over 1 million persons (FTE) engaged in health and hospital work rose a moderate 3.14 percent annually between 1970 and 1980, but only 0.38 percent in the eighties.[23] At the federal level, personnel in the big Department of Health and Human Services, totaling 156,000 in 1980, gives us a rough clue: growth at 3.72 percent a year in the seventies followed by an absolute annual rate drop in the eighties to minus 2.25 percent.[24] It was down to about 128,000 in 1994. The public health bureaucracy was staff-wise faring very poorly.

So far, two programs have been surveyed that were important contributors to the rise and subsequent slowdown of the public sector: education and health. If the two programs are summed and the expenditures criterion of size is used, they jointly accounted for about 20 percent of all-government expenditures in the 1950s. They then took a big jump in the sixties, ending that decade with a 27 percent contribution. Thereafter, the relative rise was sluggish, accounting for about 34 percent in 1993. This provides us with a rough appreciation of the fact that the public's demands for education and health together were very significant for understanding the growth of government. In saying public "demand," it is of course necessary to recognize that the career of relative prices in the two sectors affected their size compared with all-government expenditures. Nevertheless, even in real terms, they were jointly still relatively very large.[25]

Government Transfer Payments

The largest single contributor to government's expenditure growth was transfer payments under social insurance programs, composed primarily at the federal level of Social Security payments, Old Age, Survivors and Disability Insurance (OASDI). These are the prime hallmarks of the welfare state. In addition to OASDI and Medicare, the social insurance program encompasses all-government employee retirement (including military), railroad workers' unemployment and retirement, unemployment insurance and employment services, cash and medical benefits for temporary disability, and workers' compensation. It does not include veterans' programs, a large commitment on the borderline between welfare state and time-honored "poor law." Nor does it include other updated "poor law" programs such as public assistance (including Medicaid) at all levels of government, Supplemental Security Income payments, the 1946/1962 National School Lunch Program, food stamps, and work-experience training under the 1973 Comprehensive Employment and Training Act.

The distinction between updated "poor law" type programs and the welfare state proper is underscored by, among other criteria, the fact that the social insurance hallmark of the welfare state is not only mandatory and non–means-tested, but it also connects earmarked tax exactions and benefits. In this fiscal respect the United States is by no means unique among the world's mixed economies. However, the worship of self-help and antipathy for governmental intrusion in American culture insisted at the outset in the 1930s that "contributions" (a euphemism for taxes) and benefits be linked. If Social Security had been financed out of general revenues, its beneficiaries would not, so ideology demanded, be "entitled" to payment as a basic human "right." In consequence, the United States provides "far less for welfare out of general government revenues than virtually any other market-oriented economy. . . . One could even argue that . . . government merely administers . . . social security."[26] Indeed, it is not unlike a pay-as-you-go private program that happens to be administered by government.[27] The community consensus that constructed this so-called social insurance institution is thus in sharp contrast with the forces behind both Tussing's "poor peoples' system" and military expenditures, which accept almost complete financing out of general revenues. At the federal level, earmarked employment taxes for the old-age, disability, and unemployment programs, strongly propelled by inflation increments to both taxes and benefits, jumped from 19 percent of total internal revenue collections in 1970 to 35 percent twenty years later.

Based largely on the institutional foundations constructed in the New Deal's Social Security Act, social insurance after World War II built a giant edifice of welfare payments. Expressing in particular the vigorous activism of the expanding elderly population with its increasing life expectancy, together with intergenerational friction over support for elderly family members, social insurance raised its share of all-government current expenditures from about 8 percent in 1950 to 30 percent in 1992. (Incidentally, no conceivable estimate of government employees devoted to administration of the program, as a percentage of government civilian employment, can even remotely approach this 27 percent. If it was a self-aggrandizing bureaucracy, it was a very efficient one.)

In real, price-deflated terms, social insurance including Medicare payments rose almost 8 percent a year between 1950 and 1990. This was much, much faster than any relevant measure of the economy's real growth rate and about three-and-a-half times as fast as the rising elderly population. Real social insurance payments in ratio to real GNP jumped from less than 2 percent in 1950 to 10 percent in 1992. Their big contribution to government's growth is obvious.

As usual, the yearly real payments growth rate of social insurance was much higher between 1950 and 1973—over 10 percent—than afterwards. Indeed, it was well over twice as fast. It is remarkable that in the country's most inflation-ridden years, the seventies, the real rise in payments dropped to 5.34 percent a year (1973–80), although this rate was nonetheless noteworthy. The annual rate fell drastically again in the eighties—to 3.4 percent. Accompanying that rate decline, the number of employees in the Social Security Administration began to fall absolutely after 1983, just as was the case with employees in the Department of Health and Human Services as a whole. Both the federal welfare bureaucracy and the federal welfare state component of the mixed economy seemed to be faltering. So far as federal social insurance employment is concerned, the languishing welfare staff is perhaps not too shocking relative to the total number of federal civilian employees, which rose by only 90,000 in the quarter-century from 1970 to 1995.

The growing elderly population was partially responsible for the social insurance component of the enlarging welfare state. This interpretation is in full accord with one of the outstanding scholarly studies of recent times.[28] On the basis of their international comparative analysis, Pampel and Williamson conclude that "the major influence on the rise of social welfare spending from 1950 to 1980 . . . is age structure—primarily the rise of the aged population." But they appropriately add that "the aged, as both a demographic and a political force, are not the only influence on welfare spending. Economic growth, unemployment, and inflation contribute to the upward trend in spending."[29] An additional influence was the rise in per capita income accompanying economic growth. This more adequately points to the link between the mixed market system's development and the relatively aging population. It was higher incomes and the accompanying improved health care for the elderly that contributed much to the large relative growth of the elderly population itself. Thus, life expectancy for white males at age sixty-five jumped 21 percent between 1950 and 1992; for white females it jumped 25 percent. The economic link is unquestionable.

Sociopolitical activism was also a major part of the explanation for the social insurance explosion, not only in the United States but internationally. Pampel and Williamson concur:

> Our results support a view of the aged as an active political force in advanced democracies. Their political power may come normatively and structurally. The aged may have normative legitimacy to their claims on the welfare state that is denied to most other groups. . . . The aged gain political power structurally through large numbers, effective organization, and common interests in higher benefits. The aged do not need candidates who specialize in aged issues alone, but may use their symbolic and organizational power to pressure candidates from all political parties for support of their demands.[30]

Normative legitimacy is a splendid term also for the special status always enjoyed by the veteran populations, a status we have noted earlier. The same goes for the veterans' favorable *structural* position in society after any period of hot (or cold) wars. But that status and position goes so far back in history that it should not be connected with the welfare state component of advanced mixed economies.

At this juncture it seems appropriate to take stock of the relative contributions to all-government growth of the major programs so far reviewed. For this purpose only the expenditures criterion will be used. Three public-sector expenditure components that were large and growing strongly have been surveyed. By 1995 they accounted for the following shares of all-government current expenditures:

Education	16.4%
Public health other than Medicare	10.9%
Social insurance (Contributions) and	
Medicare (Expenditures)	<u>34.8%</u>
TOTAL	62.1%

Hence, over 62 percent of total government current outlays in 1993 is explicable by reference to these three human welfare developments. Between 1970 and 1993, all-government expenditures rose by $1,854 billion, whereas under the three programs increased by $1,190 billion. Hence the programs accounted for a huge 64 percent of all-government expenditures increase.

The greater part of these programs was administered by state and local government personnel. Therefore they help to explain the fact that state and local employees rose relatively fast compared with federal civilian employees. They were roughly twice the number of federal workers in 1948, but had risen to almost six times the federal by 1995. Jeffersonian "localism" apparently has deep roots in American culture.

But much civilian expenditure is not yet accounted for. Humanism plus social agitation for "poor law" commitments helped fill the programmatic gap. For those commitments focus should be on the category known as public aid—Medicaid, food stamps, Supplemental Security Income payments, Aid to Families with Dependent Children, plus miscellaneous social services. The fund sources for these have been mainly federal, but their administration again largely state and local. As a share of total government current outlays, public aids amounted to about 4 percent in 1950; but by 1973 they, like so many others, had risen greatly to 7.2 percent, remaining higher thereafter and reaching 10 percent by the early nineties. There were 14 million recipients of AFDC benefits in 1993 and 27 million food stamp recipients in 1993. Hence, when public aid is added to the previous total 62 percent share of expenditures for the three big programs previously tallied for 1993, we get 72 percent.

From that level of proportionate contributions to government's rise we can now move to education's rival for second place in relative importance: the official military budget. For clarification of the jump in that source of government expansion—all federal, of course—one must go back to the contrasting 1930s. As noted in Chapter 2, New Deal–style intervention in the economy was overwhelmingly civilian in character. Therefore the great leap upward in American defense and related outlays is to be located in the years from the end of the thirties to the inauguration of the Cold and not-so-cold wars after World War II. "Thereafter . . . the United States never converted to a peacetime economy."[31]

The New Deal year 1939 was the last clearly peacetime one. In that year, the officially delineated national defense outlays amounted to 7.4 percent of all-government expenditures. In the first full year after demobilization—1947—the ratio had leaped up to well over one-fourth. This was the most auspicious beginning of the era of "Pentagon capitalism." Unlike the other surveyed contributors to government growth, the national defense ratio fell at times, except for the Korean and Vietnam war years; it was down to 19.3 percent of all-government expenditures in the year 1973 that has been used as a benchmark for other programs. It reached a "low" of 17 percent in the mid-1970s, rose to 19.3 under the Reagan military buildup, then dropped to 16 percent, following the Soviet breakup in 1994.

Using that last named percentage as a base for government growth stock-taking purposes, when added to the previous all-welfare plus education percentage, we now have about 88 percent of the government expenditures accounted for.

Civilian employees of the War and Navy departments, together renamed Department of Defense after 1947, reached their lowest absolute postwar total of 753,000 in 1950, when they nevertheless accounted for a quite high 38 percent of all federal employees. The renaming was more than the substitution of the more readily embraced term "defense" for "war." This interpretation is aptly pinpointed by one writer who calls our attention to the fact that during the war:

> Another military objective was postwar unification of the services. During the winter of 1941–42 the Joint Chiefs of Staff was established; during the war they effectively bypassed the civilian Secretaries of War and the Navy. . . . Beginning in 1945 the Army and Navy fought this issue in the Congress, and in the summer of 1947, within weeks after the adoption of the Marshall Plan and the Truman doctrine for intervention in Greece and Turkey, Congress established a new Department of Defense, formalized the Joint Chiefs of Staff, established the National Security Council, and set up the Central Intelligence Agency.[32]

Thereafter for over four decades Pentagon civilians consistently averaged rather over 1 million, accounting for higher percentages than 1950 until after Korea and Vietnam, when they settled at about one-third of total federal "civilian" employment. As for national defense outlays, they amounted on the average after the early 1970s to between two-thirds and three-fourths of all federal purchases of goods and services.

Explanations have been offered previously here for other contributory programs making up government's growth. Military outlays and employment also deserve explanation for their very substantial additional contribution to that growth after the 1930s. While other programs burgeoned overwhelmingly from a combination of private market derelictions and a therewith connected sociopolitical activism, the growth of the military component of the evolving mixed economy rather stemmed chiefly from the influence of a powerful government-industry coalition that was inaugurated during World War II and thrived on the ensuing Cold War. Here we have Leviathan indeed, "a blending of private economic power and public political power."[33] As Robert Higgs has therefore so well expressed it:

> The military-industrial complex denotes the institutionalized arrangements whereby the military procurement authorities, certain large corporations, and certain executive and legislative officials of the federal government cooperate in an enormous, ongoing program to develop, produce and deploy weapons and related products. (Some writers include the labor unions, research organizations, universities, and others involved in the programs). Operating in peacetime as well as in wartime, it has no significant antecedents before 1940. . . .
>
> After 1945 the Cold War, the development of ever more-sophisticated weapons systems, and the great migration of retired military officers into corporate employment in the defense industries well-nigh insured that the military-industrial complex would not only survive but prosper, as indeed it has to an almost unbelievable degree during the past four decades.[34]

The new, institutionalized coalition of government and the market drew support in good part from its own sales promotion of a presumed external threat and the newly assumed "global leadership" responsibilities after the war, as noted in Chapter 2. It also gleaned support by its encouragement of the abiding culture current of patriotism that surfaced again with the concurrent extinction of the isolationism that had dominated the interwar years. It derived further support by activating the heritage of traditional, "classical" ideology embodying Adam Smith's legitimation of the national defense function of government. No formal conspiracy between the Pentagon and the Congress was required.

Practically all aspects of the Cold War's military industrial program was made sacrosanct. Democratic principles were repeatedly punished in the name of secrecy. Humans were brutally afflicted as the price of the noble cause. The environment was systemically outraged because the supposedly sacred benefits far outweighed the ignored or belittled costs. Beginning in the late 1970s right-wing circles began successfully to enhance the defense budget by adding to the general arms race a more specific focus: a spending race with the USSR. The allegation was that "if the United States began spending like crazy on defense, the Soviet, with an inferior economy, would ultimately be forced to accept that they could never keep up. . . . The Soviet Union, a backward nation . . . would find its economy shattered by an arms-spending race."[35] And the very costly Strategic Defense Initiative ("Star Wars" program) would fit well into such a bigger spending contest.

As the military program evolved, hundreds of communities acquired a vested stake in the jobs and income provided by the defense contracts and military bases. Proposed contract cancellations and base closings when the Cold War wound down drove home this fact as they elicited piteous and humiliating displays of community retention efforts. Those "local," congressionally supported efforts typically exhibited a combination of remarkable global military expertise, sometimes flaunting the Pentagon's recommendations, along with wailing and gnashing of teeth over the enormous human costs to the local economy that such dismantling would entail.

Thus over the decades the Employment Act of 1946 was being implicitly, haphazardly, inadvertently, and almost deceitfully implemented through substantially fabricated fears and an aroused devotion to national patriotic values. Sustained congressional patriotic appropriations became a matter of course. The military appropriations helped greatly to sustain the economy, but they hardly constituted a fiscal policy or a deliberate growth policy. Nor were they implementations of a consistent, short-run stabilization policy. Indeed, the right to employment and the public planning of investment embodied in the original Full Employment Bill of 1945 was sidetracked not only by the emasculation of the bill in the 1946 Act, but also by the episodic character of the large defense outlays together with the evolving substitution of social welfare, antipoverty, and other supply-side, public assistance–type policies. Legislative examples of this last named policy group are to be found in such labor market measures as the 1962 Manpower Training and Development Act, the 1964 Equal Opportunity Act, the 1973 Comprehensive Employment and Training Act, and the 1982 Job Training Partnership Act.[36]

All the public programs so far discussed, along with others, obviously compete with one another for resources and appropriations. Each claimant in the perennial contest can be said to crowd out the others. This is the essential, institutionalized character of "the turbulent, conflict-ridden pluralistic process" typifying the democratic mixed market systems of the Western nations.[37]

If we classify the government programs as either welfare/"poor law" or military, then on an international comparison the United States devoted a much higher share of its resources to the military than the other mixed economies of the West in the post–World War II era. Insofar as increased public spending was necessary to sustain satisfactory economic growth in the mixed market systems, it can be averred that the people in the other Western systems faced up to implementation of their growth goals through a greater relative emphasis on their welfare state expenditures. From such perspective, Americans, on the other hand, rejected a similar emphasis because they chose rather to limit welfare/"poor law" in favor of a greater relative reliance on their defense budget.

This perspective is particularly useful for appraising the post–Cold War economic growth requirement from the demand side in the United States. Meeting that requirement in all likelihood will necessitate a continued rise in all-government public spending, in the context of a presumed contraction of the military budget and a withering of exclusive U.S. "global leadership." Assuming a commitment to growth and high employment, Americans for the first time in postwar history may have to face up to a relative welfare state (and other civilian) component that is historically larger—that is, similar to that of the other mixed economies. This is one of the great covert issues of the 1990s and after. The standard American pragmatic focus on short-run specifics will not fend off that policy challenge.

This survey of the major contributors to government's growth, as measured by resources absorbed, has left over some 20 percent of the total escalating components untreated. For some clues to those residual programs, and the forces inducing them, one can turn to an examination of government *agencies'* expansion as measured, for example, by their number of employees.

Agency Expansions

Many agencies at the various levels of government, though not all by any means, have of course increased in size *absolutely* as population and socioeconomic requirements expanded. But the concern here is rather with *relative* growth.

Some public agencies, like the General Services Administration, have experienced absolute decline, or even practical disappearance, and not merely through absorption by some other agency. The Reconstruction Finance Corporation went out of existence. Declines occurred widely during the years of the Reagan presidency in particular. For example, even the Department of Energy lost 18 percent of its employees between 1980 and 1990; Housing and Urban Development lost 20 percent (the former expanded after 1990 and the latter stopped contracting).

New social, environmental, and/or military-strategic activities brought into existence several new smaller federal agencies during the post–World War II era that were designed to implement either the government's administrative guidance of the economy or its entrepreneurial function. Prominent examples, in addition to the previously mentioned Central Intelligence Agency (CIA), are the Environmental Protection Agency, the National Aeronautics and Space Administration, the Equal Employment Opportunity Commission, and the Nuclear Regulatory Commission (the older Atomic Energy Commission). These totaled (without the CIA) about 48,000 employees in 1994, only a tiny fraction of federal civilian employment. A number of other, fast-growing or new agencies like the Alcohol, Drug Abuse and Mental Health Administration and the FDIC are too small to make much difference.

However, there were a number of relatively sizable agencies that made growth contributions by expanding comparatively fast during some extended period of the postwar era. As criterion of relative growth for an agency, comparison may be made in three selected approximate periods of agency employee rise with total civilian labor force increase. The average annual compound rates for the civilian labor force were as follows:[38]

1950–1990   1.8%

1950–1973   1.6%

1973–1995   2.3%

Using these rates for comparison, approximate data sources permitting, one can find several government agency personnel numbers that exhibited faster annual growth rates than these within certain of the three periods or subperiods. These were:

1.	Federal Treasury Department,	2.4%	1973–90
	within which is the Internal Revenue Service (IRS)	4.4%	1980–88
2.	Federal Department of Justice	2.6%	1950–90
		3.5%	1973–94
3.	Federal Deposit Insurance Corporation[39]	6.1%	1952–89
		4.7%	1952–73
		9.7%	1973–94
4.	State and local police and fire	2.6%	1952–90
		3.7%	1952–73
5.	City governments, sanitation, and sewers	3.3%	1952–74

All of the listed agencies are comparatively large in terms of employee numbers, except for the FDIC. The Treasury Department embracing the IRS alone, however, had a staff of 156,000 in 1994 (it had 130,000 in 1985).

The Treasury Department's expansion was almost entirely due to IRS growth. The rapid expansion of the IRS must surely be viewed as primarily a governmental general service and monitoring response to the dictates of burgeoning total federal tax returns and receipts, and the factors in society and the market responsible for the congressional tax policy underlying those receipts. Since the volume of receipts handling (outputs) was growing much faster than the IRS staff, the indication would seem to be that the staff was getting more productive (with the help of computers, no doubt) as time passed. Alternatively put, the IRS bureaucracy growth was lagging behind the volume of services it was performing.

Of course, the Treasury Department had many other responsibilities, not the least of which was supervision of the Resolution Trust Corporation, the bailout and cleanup agency dealing with the savings and loan debacle of the 1980s.

The factors behind the rising volume of federal receipts handling have been treated already in connection with the examination of expenditure growth, except for the federal government's greatly rising (until the Reagan administration) flow of grants to the state and local governments. Such grants reached 15 percent of all federal budget outlays by 1994.[40] They helped finance such familiar state and local outlays as those for public welfare, highways, and education.

A good part of the IRS staff of the Treasury Department had to be occupied not only with tax receipts but also with negotiating and administering the enormous and growing volume of *tax expenditures*. The gerrymandered structure of tax concessions was of course the product of multitudes of pressures from lobbyists and pressure groups generally. Dealing with that structure was a part of government administrative guidance of the economy and society, as previously noted. Estimated federal tax expenditures alone totaled over $400 billion in fiscal 1993—a fantastic sum that approximated probably as much as a third of all federal receipts. It should be noted, however, that totaling to some extent exaggerates because of the interdependence of different types of tax expenditure.[41] The trend of tax expenditures/tax receipts was rising in the 1980s until the Tax Reform Act of 1986 brought tax expenditures down after 1987. In any case, staff productivity (i.e., output over labor alone) was rising even more if tax expenditure handling is added to tax receipts handling.

The moderately sized federal Department of Justice staff growth was extremely modest over the 1950s and 1960s—about 1.2 percent a year. But subsequently there occurred two remarkably accelerated staff expansion periods. The first spanned roughly the period 1970–76, when departmental employment rose 5 percent annually. The second occurred from 1985 to 1994, with a very strong yearly expansion rate of 4.8 percent. These two periods were approximately matched by acceleration of the department's real budget outlays at 12.8 and 9.4 percent a year, respectively. Significantly, the larger overall federal commitment for the "administration of justice" in all spheres generally exhibited the same temporal pattern, as did also the real expenditures for, and employment in, the federal criminal justice system as a whole. The point of noting these parallels between the Justice Department expansions and the federal crime-control system in general is to suggest the explanation that the department's growth reflected, not antitrust activity or such new additions to the department as the Civil Rights Division (established in 1957), but mainly the growth of crime in society.

The first half of the seventies stands out starkly from the preceding and immediately following years as a period marked by an epidemically high rate of increase in both violent crime and property crime.[42] For example, the steadily rising homicide victim rate per 100,000 population, which had averaged about 6 in the sixties, jumped to an average of 9.5 in the first half of the seventies. In addition to a vigorous state and local institutional response, the federal criminal justice system was impelled to expand, with FTE system employment jumping over 10 percent a year, from 59,000 in 1970 to 96,000 only five years later. The system's expenditures leaped accordingly, from $978 million in 1970 to $2.8 billion in 1977, a real annual rise of 7 percent. Concurrently, the number of persons indicted at federal instigation by the department's criminal division for corruption in public office soared 300 percent between 1970 and 1975. At the same time, the number of federal prisoners rose from 20,000 in 1970 to 27,000 in mid-decade. This amounted to a yearly increase of over 5 percent. It was clearly a half-decade of surging criminality. Thus, while Justice Department employment increased by 6,000 between 1965 and 1970, it rose by twice that number in the next five years. As of 1976 the department had 54,000 employees.

This crime upheaval of the early part of the seventies was repeated in the last half-decade of the eighties. A much more prevalent incidence of narcotic offenses marked this later period, however. By that time the criminal drug business had illicitly entered the market system with a vengeance. Narcotic drug arrest rates per 100,000 inhabitants zoomed for the whole decade of the eighties, from 256 at the beginning to 346 in 1985 and 527 in 1989.[43] The department's Drug Enforcement Administration (DEA) had been created in 1973 by absorbing the domestic and international drug enforcement duties of a formerly loosely coordinated interdepartmental alliance of five agencies.[44]

While some crime rates were constant, or even fell somewhat between 1985 and 1990, others jumped up. In general, 1985–90, like 1970–76, stood out as a half-decade with a high rate of increase in the number and rate per 100,000 population of both violent and property crime offenses. The same was true of drug removals, laboratory seizures, and persons indicted by the DEA. Particularly striking and pertinent to the work of the Justice Department's Bureau of Prisons was the enormous rise in the number of prisoners held under federal correctional authorities from 40,223 in 1985 to 67,432 in 1990—a yearly leap averaging 11 percent![45] The number leaped again to 80,259 in 1992.[46] And over 60 percent of all federal prison inmates in 1993 had been convicted of drug offenses.[47]

It is not the intent to use the growth of crime to explain practically all of the expansion in Justice Department employment from 31,000 in 1960 to 98,000 in 1994. The department has many divisions, some but loosely connected with the criminal upsurges of the types referred to here. There is, for example, the Antitrust Division, the Civil Rights Division, the Tax Division, the Land and Natural Resources Division, the Immigration and Naturalization Service (INS), and the Community Relations Service. However, it is reasonable to presume that the chief work of the department, including activities of some of the units just mentioned (e.g., the INS, which faced an estimated $25 billion a year in the 1990s to prevent illegal entry[48]) is a response to crime growth as delineated here.

The plausibility of this presumption is enhanced by a glance at what was concurrently taking place in social spheres ordinarily falling under the criminal justice jurisdiction of the state and local governments. Aside from the general crime data already presented, the 1985–92 period, for example, continued to rack up big increases in robberies, motor vehicle theft, and especially drug arrests. The pervasiveness of criminality at the state and local level is indicated by the number of state prisoners, which jumped from 448,000 in 1985 to 836,000 in 1993—despite federal restrictions on prison overcrowding. For the country as a whole, the combination of rising criminality and the specifics of the criminal justice system "made corrections a one-million-inmate, $25-billion-a-year industry—the world's largest and costliest prison system" in 1993.[49] The United States had the highest per capita imprisonment rate in the world. Prisons and their operation absorbed over 85 percent of the nation's criminal justice resources.[50] In the early 1990s, corrections, along with health care, was the fastest growing budget area for the states.[51]

As in the federal Justice Department experience, the first half of the seventies was another period of big increases in state and local employees concerned with crime. For example, state and local police protection FTE employment rose from 450,000 in 1970 to 557,000 in 1976, a yearly rate of 3.6 percent.[52] For the whole decade of the seventies, state FTE employment for police protection rose a vigorous 35 percent, while local police staffs increased 28 percent. It was a notorious decade for a surge in youth (eighteen to twenty-four years of age) arrests in particular.[53]

The central objective here is to submit the interpretation that a modest part of all-government growth, as represented in certain administrative departments on the different levels of government, is and will probably continue to be a response to the upsurge of criminality in recent times. The interpretation is well supported by the judgment of a member of the Senate subcommittee on Commerce, Justice, State and Judiciary, Senator Phil Gramm, Republican of Texas, who has declared that "with the end of the Cold War, domestic crime is now the greatest threat to the safety and well-being of Americans."[54]

It is not the intent to embark here on the formidable task of tracing the sources of the crime upsurge, however. While that sinister rise is no doubt connected in part with market-related factors such as unemployment, poverty, urban malaise, and occupational dead ends, there are many other determinants, some not clearly identified, some located but not yet appraised to the point of agreement by social theorists.

There has developed no organized anticrime movement within the community that is comparable, for example, to the environmental movement. In the environmental case, interest groups and their political lobbies carried their message to the public authorities and won public environmental regulatory agencies and policies. Generally in the crime-control case, however, government agencies were left to themselves to treat the problems without noteworthy pressure-group initiative or support and with inadequate financial resources. As a result, while the criminal justice system has added to the governmental apparatus, that apparatus has been understaffed, underequipped, and unable either to adequately enforce the law or to tackle the prevention aspect of crime. The combined all-government judicial and enforcement institution, with 1.7 million FTE employees in 1990, has indeed gotten absolutely and relatively bigger, amounting perhaps to almost 10 percent of all-government civilian employment. The $74 billion spent by the total criminal justice system in 1990 also amounted to 10 percent of all-government civilian purchases of goods and services.[55] But that was not big enough to effectively reduce the crime epidemic.

This brief excursion into the domain of government agency employment growth clearly does not explain much of the unaccounted-for residual of all-government growth that remained after our analysis of various expenditure increases. But it must be remembered that the expenditure and agency employment growth, although they provide considerable information about governmental guidance of resources in the economy, do not specifically address the vast rise in the totality of public administrative guidance and management. That institutional sphere is a big part of government growth in the mixed market system, and remains to be treated. It is therefore to that phenomenon that we now turn.

Administrative Guidance and Management Since the New Deal

The big extension of government management of the economy during the New Deal years was touched upon in Chapter 2. The three main types of management illustrated there were, it may be recalled, guidance of resource allocation, the provision of direct services, and manipulative regulation. Those government functions continued and expanded in the post–World War II era.

It is clear that growth in public expenditures itself generated direct service provision, resource allocation effects, and regulatory impacts. But at the moment we are concerned rather with those influences on the economy and society that emanate mainly from government's administrative manipulation as such.

Unlike expenditure magnitudes and patterns, administrative guidance defies clear measurement. It is all very well to say it is growing, but there is no *numeraire*. Furthermore, the variety and coverage of administrative instrumentalities and managerial activities are enormous. This means that we must rely on a selection of examples to show the postwar expansion of the administrative element in the "managed economy."[56] Of the many new and augmented older managerial functions marking and contributing to the government's postwar growth at all levels, we select here, without necessarily excluding other functions, the following:

- Consumer direct services and protection, broadly conceived
- Environmental policies
- Housing support
- Energy management
- Transportation support and controls
- Major federal tax expenditures
- Employees Retirement Income Security Act

The Consumer: Protection and Direct Services

Since everyone is a consumer, *the entire scope of the growing government controls and direct-service apparatus is in some way pertinent to consumer policy.* For example, the long-run expansion of certain public infrastructures and their operation directly serves consumer needs (and does the same for business and government itself). Also, there is necessarily a large amount of consumer overlap in many specific, growing public policy instrumentalities as a glance at the above list of managerial functions clearly suggests.

It follows that consumer programs are unique by virtue of their diversity and comprehensiveness. Consumers relate to society, the economy, and government in a multitude of capacities. Consumers are buyers, workers, homeowners, borrowers, depositors, stockholders, environmentalists, pensioners, minorities, taxpayers, patients, commuters, travelers, recreationers. There is lots of overlap. For example, an energy-gluttonous society needs and has demanded consumer consideration in every major aspect of the energy industry's operation: natural resource use, the mix of energy types, production efficiency and costs, safety research, and environmental impacts. As a consumer coalition of eleven national environmental and energy organizations, the Safe Energy Communication Council testifies, storage of nuclear wastes from civilian reactors and military ordnance under the federal Nuclear Waste Policy Act, another responsibility of the Energy Department, is very much a consumer policy program.[57] Millions of consumers function in an employee capacity. Hence, public employment and occupational oversight by federal and state governments impact the consumer. The same goes for consumers as pensioners or stockholders.

State and local utilities provide direct services to consumers as well as to businesses. So do public school systems, as well as public parks and recreation facilities at all governmental levels. The provision of public passenger transportation and the regulation by governments of privately owned passenger transportation are consumer services. For some of the direct services we fortunately have crude *numeraires*, although they do not separate households from business. For example, state and local real expenditures and capital outlays for utilities (including interest) rose annually at a 4 percent rate from 1960 to 1990, of which electric and transit increased over 5 percent; sanitation and sewerage rose 3.7 percent. Real housing and urban development expenditures exceeded a 4 percent rate, as did outlays for parks and recreation. All these annual growth rates exceeded the real GNP rate.

The expansion of the government's consumer apparatus involved both the reaction of new "independent" agencies with explicit consumer responsibilities, like the Consumer Product Safety Commission (CPSC), established in 1972, and the assignment of new consumer responsibilities to older agencies or departments, such as pesticides monitoring and enforcement of the Wholesale Meat Act of 1967. One has to but name a public policy or its governmental instrumentality, and nine chances out of ten there is some consumer involvement.

In consequence of the market system's development of a mass-consumption society with its enormously augmented number, variety, and complexity of goods and services in the household market basket, the rising consumer movement in the postwar world had to add greatly to its traditional bundle of products to be brought under public controls. The result was an ever larger body of consumer goods legislation with its attendant government research, standards specification, and (we hope) enforcement apparatus.

The postwar proliferation of administrative apparatuses has been a much more evident historical development than has been the provision of appropriations and dedicated staffs adequate to carry out their pro-consumer mission. Furthermore, at every step of the way, from the agency creation or augmentation process to subsequent operation, the attendant restraints have all too frequently been fought, usually by organized business. And undermining from within the apparatus has often been the operational response to the continued opposition from the outside. This has to be expected from the comparative weaknesses characterizing the historically jejune and relatively fragmented consumer movement.

The economic and political coagulation of the consumer interest has been slow to develop in the United States. The achievements of the muckrakers and Progressives, expressed for example in the Pure Food and Drug Act and the Meat Inspection Act (1906–1907) was but little more than an isolated precursor of the later developments in consumerism and that citizen movement's public regulatory victories. In a recent list of twenty-five major consumer protection laws through 1980 in the *Dictionary of Business and Economics,* there is nothing after those two acts until the Sea Food Act in 1934; and nineteen of the total were passed after World War II.[58]

Certain precursor books of wide circulation, showing victimization of consumers by business, began to stir the household millions, raising somewhat their level of consumer consciousness in the decades before the New Deal. In the tradition of Upton Sinclair's *The Jungle* about the scandalous practices of the meat packers, there came *Your Money's Worth* in 1927 by Stuart Chase and Frederick Schlink. There followed *100,000,000 Guinea Pigs* by Frederick Schlink and Arthur Kallet in 1933. But publication in 1965 of *Unsafe At Any Speed* by Ralph Nader, the outstanding leader of post–World War II consumerism and founder of the influential advocacy organization Public Citizen, was a tonic needed to further propel a movement already gaining significant momentum.[59] In addition, Rachel Carson's 1962 *Silent Spring* contributed much to coalesce the environmental and consumer movements. Some scholars have suggested that the enthusiastic reception accorded Nader's book and his subsequent testimony on the subject before Congress were largely responsible for the creation in 1970 of the Federal National Highway Traffic Safety Administration, an agency within the Department of Transportation.[60]

The Great Depression with its New Deal was able to generate only a few mild measures of response to a still inchoate consumer effort. One historian of the New Deal has pointed out, for example, that

> causes which were not sustained by powerful interest groups frequently made little headway. Those which relied on a mythical "consumer interest" fared poorly, as the history of the NRA Consumers' Advisory Board and the sad saga of Tugwell's futile attempt to get an effective pure food and drugs bill amply demonstrated.[61]

He adds, "When the pure food and drugs bill, first introduced in 1933, was finally passed as the Wheeler-Lea Act of 1938, it was a toothless crone."[62] That act, by the way, was one of only four listed in the previously cited *Dictionary of Business and Economics* for the New Deal years, and indeed for the entire period from 1907 to 1951.

One student of the citizen public-interest movement finds a period of stalemate following the passage of the Wheeler-Lea Act, a time during which "a congressional minority was able to put ... crucial issues on the back burner. Dedicated to preserving the status quo, it postponed dealing with national problems and correcting glaring inequities."[63] This judgment seems basically correct.

The postwar period, up to the time of the Reagan administration, was a different story. That period brought forth an "advocacy explosion," as Jeffrey Berry has called the upsurge of interest groups and their influence on government.[64] That advocacy phenomenon included a consumer movement that blended with the proliferation of other liberal, citizen public-interest organizations dedicated to goals that overlapped consumer concerns, like the environment and labor conditions. Berry points out that the postwar citizen groups should be distinguished from earlier reform movements "by the breadth and durability of their lobbying organizations" which "collectively ... have helped to change the political environment of this country."[65] The consumer components of the citizen action groups have raised the level of accountability of both business and government.

As noted previously, new consumer advocacy organizations mushroomed in the 1960s and 1970s. Along with the older organizations, they add up to many more than can be recorded here. But a short listing will give some appreciation of the variety and scope of the causes to which they are devoted:

Consumers Union, Consumer Policy Institute
Consumer Federation of America
National Consumer's League
National Consumers' Week (begun 1981)
Society of Consumer Affairs Professionals in Business
Food Research and Action Center
Public Voice for Food and Health Policy

Public Citizen, Congress Watch (Nader)
Americans for a Clean Environment
Environmental Action Foundation
Environmental Policy Institute
Center for Clean Air Policy
Natural Resources Defense Council
U.S. Public Interest Research Group
National Coalition Against Misuse of Pesticides
National Citizens Coalition for Nursing Home Reform
National Rifle Association
Bank Card Holders of America
(Local) Citizens' Utility Boards (utility rates)
United Shareholders' Association
National Insurance Consumer Organization
Consumer Insurance Interest Group
Center for Science in the Public Interest
United States Privacy Council
Union of Concerned Scientists

This modest sample of organizations conveys diversity well enough. But it bypasses hundreds of state and local bodies that over the years have pursued, with varying degrees of effectiveness, programs furthering consumer interests. Also, business itself, usually the target of consumer activity designed to restrict business practices or control its products, has often taken the initiative. For example, it has done so in the case of energy conservation, nuclear energy safety, and the search for energy alternatives. In addition, there have been many spontaneous local or regional consumer actions in response to specific occurrences—actions often calling for governmental intervention that may never have crystallized in law or the establishment of an enduring public agency.

Spontaneous, widespread public outrage produced consumer advocacy that was responsible for the creation of lasting manipulative regulation. Prominent among such types was the surge of demand for control of certain prescription drugs. For example, public reaction to the deaths of some seventy-five people who had taken a new drug, elixir of sulfanilamide, stimulated passage of the 1938 federal Food, Drug and Cosmetic Act. Similarly, much later, after discovery that deformed infants were being born of mothers who had taken a new sleeping pill (Thalidomide), the consequent scandal was used by Senator Estes Kefauver to secure passage in 1962 of effective amendments to the 1938 Act that added at least two years to the period required for the testing of new drugs.[66] Outrage was, to be sure, an extreme form of the advocacy impulse. But much consumer organization did crystallize a strong resentment, especially toward business suppliers and to a lesser degree toward government inaction or weak enforcement of existing regulations.

In view of the citizen advocacy groundswell from the late fifties to the beginning of the eighties, it is not surprising that there occurred a concurrent responsive tidal wave of consumer and related consumer and environmental legislation at all governmental levels, setting up a greatly augmented administrative apparatus. To represent that expansion it may be helpful to scan the following short selective list of major agencies having pro-consumer responsibilities. The sample is designed to convey some appreciation of the diversity and broad scope of government consumer interventionism:

Numerous Congressional Committees
Executive Office of the President
    Office of Consumer Affairs
    Consumer Advisory Council
Federal Government Departments
    Agriculture (Extension Home Economist; with Food & Drug
        Administration on pesticides)
Health and Human Services:
    Food & Drug Administration (FDA)
    Public Health Service
    National Institute of Health (NIH)
    National Institute of Mental Health (NIMH)
    Office of Consumer Affairs
Justice
    Drug Enforcement Administration
Energy
Labor
    Pension Welfare Benefits Administration
    Occupational Safety and Health Administration
    Employment and Training Administration
    Mine Safety and Health Administration
Housing and Urban Development
Transportation
    Federal Highway Administration
    National Highway Traffic Safety Administration
    Federal Aviation Administration
    Urban Mass Transportation Administration
    Federal Independent Agencies
    Federal Communications Commission
    Interstate Commerce Commission
    Consumer Product Safety Commission
    Environmental Protection Agency (EPA)
    Federal Trade Commission
    Equal Employment Opportunity Commission

Federal Deposit Insurance Corporation
National Transportation Safety Board
Nuclear Regulatory Commission
Occupational Safety and Health Review Commission
Pension Benefit Guaranty Corporation
Securities and Exchange Commission
State and Local Agencies
Consumer Protection Agencies
State Citizens Utility Boards
State departments of food and agriculture
Pennsylvania Insurance Commission

It is pointless to attempt to list even a sample of the state, county, and city consumer instrumentalities. As noted in one consumer policy study, the increase in their numbers

> was one of the most significant developments in consumer affairs in the 1970s. ... In all states, there is a consumer-fraud or consumer-protection agency or bureau as part of the Office of Attorney General ... more than 100 counties and nearly 100 cities have established consumer offices.[67]

The selective list of agencies fails to do justice to the rash of legislation that the agencies became responsible to administer. A legislation list would be much more extensive and would reveal even greater diversity of issues dealt with. But since the focus here is on the growth of administrative guidance, the agency sample is more pertinent.

The establishment of a public consumer agency or departmental division is an addition to government's administrative management functions, reflecting either consumer demands or government's acknowledgment of some consumer need. Most of such governmental programs operate in the tradition of the Interstate Commerce Commission, which is to prevent "the occurrence of objectionable deeds in the future."[68]

But it should be recognized that program opponents usually continue their pressure to undermine the exercise or enforcement of an agency's functions by getting its appropriations cut or influencing its staff to water down activities or simply do nothing. Representatives of industries subject to regulation make up the overwhelming proportion of persons appearing at federal regulatory agency proceedings, and it is hence no accident that agency decisions commonly reflect their views.[69]

Agency ineffectiveness owing to incompetent staff or inadequate appropriations may be compounded by sabotage of the mission on the part of the staff. For example, the FDA, a most prominent consumer agency, has had primary responsibilities for ensuring water purity, particularly the safety of bottled water. But it did not even adopt for that purpose all of the public drinking water standards established by the EPA and "repeatedly failed to set adequate safety standards for chemical contamination of bottled water and . . . neglected any responsibility for bottled-water testing.[70] Even the industry trade group favored tighter regulation of bottled water.

However, underfunding and adverse pressures from outside are no doubt more important factors undermining the work of consumer instrumentalities. The EPA, for example, is commissioned to safeguard the purity of the nation's drinking water under the Clean Water Act and the Safe Drinking Water Act of the early 1970s. But the consumer-advocacy Center for Resource Economics found as of 1993 that the EPA was unable to perform its basic regulatory functions precisely for such undermining reasons.[71] Inadequacies in mission performance unquestionably qualifies, although it by no means erases, the growth impression presented by the brute proliferation of consumer protection agencies.

With the election of Ronald Reagan in 1980, the federal consumer support apparatus, along with much of the federal administrative machinery, came under a wholesale deregulation attack designed to dismantle as much of big government as politically possible (except for the military).[72] Ralph Nader's Public Citizen organization found that already by 1984 there had been a severe retreat from safety enforcement at both the Occupational Safety and Health Agency (OSHA, created by Act in 1970) and the FDA.[73] The organization's publication adds:

> At the FDA there was a 49 percent decline in enforcement actions. . . . At OSHA, the number of workers covered by inspections dropped by 45 percent, citations for willful violations dropped 67 percent, and citations for repeat violations dropped 58 percent. . . . In October 1984 Ralph Nader obtained copies of studies conducted by the National Institute of Occupational Safety and Health showing that the government knew of over 200,000 workers who had been exposed to hazardous chemicals, placing them at increased risk of developing cancer, lung disease, heart disease and other health problems. . . . The administration had turned down a budget request of $4 million to notify those workers.[74]

Government protective standards for workers and consumers are of little significance for the understanding of government's growth unless they are enforced.

But dilution of consumer programs in the eighties involved more than the enfeebling of enforcement. The weakening process also affected staff and brought budget cuts in agencies and departments having some new consumer responsibilities that had mushroomed in the sixties and seventies. Many of the state consumer protection laws were likewise weakened or even eliminated.[75] At the federal level between 1980 and 1988, in addition to the 21 percent staff cut in the Department of Health and Human Services, the Labor Department staff decline was from 23,000 to 18,000, the Housing and Urban Development Department decrease was 21 percent, the Transportation Department lost 9,000 employees (a 12 percent drop), the Energy Department's staff (established in 1977 to bring together four agencies devoted to assuring safe and continuous supplies of electricity and national gas to consumers and businesses) dropped by 21 percent, and the Education Department lost a whopping 38 percent of its staff.

Some agencies escaped cuts, but like the Nuclear Regulatory Commission (with a fast-growing staff from 1975 to 1980) and the very strategic Environmental Protection Agency (with a staff growth of 7 percent a year between 1975 and 1980), barely held their own. The latter actually managed to get a 4 percent staff growth during the Reagan presidency. Employment in the small Nuclear Regulatory Commission rose 2 percent! In some of the cases cited, the declines over 1980–88 were moderately reversed between 1988 and 1994, although their staffs remained well below 1980 levels. However, by the end of the eighties the federal and state consumer apparatus was still historically large compared, for example, with the structure in 1947. Its long-run role in a growing government had been, and still was, notable.

Environmental Management

Programs devoted to assuring a livable environment overlap consumer protection, just as they do energy policy. But they nevertheless have been assigned to relatively distinct administrative bodies within the governmental structure. The development is partly attributable to difference in the tasks to be performed and, related thereto, differences in the character of the demands advanced by discrete organizations that constitute the explosive post–World War II citizens' environmental movement.

While that spectacular movement was primarily a citizen effort, it succeeded in enlisting surprisingly widespread cooperation from certain business groups as well as support from government bodies. A prominent example of such cooperation was the industry and government common response to scientific revelation of ozone destruction.[76] The household sector, as consumer, is inclined to confront the business sector, but we all share much the same environmental conditions. Public relations alone underscores this fact of life, especially urban life. Given such communality, we cannot possibly explain the growing societal acceptance of the environmental ethic on the basis of such distortive generalizations, as many of these groups (for example, the Environmental Defense Fund, the National Resources Defense Council, and the Union of Concerned Scientists) have a pro-environment perspective and may therefore rightly be accused of representing only a particular sector of the public. Energy conservation and efficient use of energy in particular have considerable acceptance *as a social objective* by environmentalists in almost all walks of life.

The link between the emergence of the community's concern with the condition of its environment and economic development is too obvious to require extensive analysis. It is a striking historical fact that, with the exception of wanton natural resource exploitation, deficiencies in urban sanitation, and a paucity of urban parks, Americans generally ignored for decades the accretion of damage to themselves being generated by such developments as uncontrolled technological advances, the concentration of ever larger urban poverty populations, adverse externalities from a rising per capita output, and the 60,000 different chemicals in that output.[77] Both business and households thought only of private costs and gains. It was a laissez-faire world. Because of a veritable worship of unfettered, market-driven economic growth with its material compensations, such concepts as social costs, externalities, discommodities, and disamenities were not in the lexicon of the nineteenth- and early twentieth-century populations. Social costs were definitively insinuated into the literature of political economy for the first time only with the publication of A.C. Pigou's works on welfare in 1912 and 1920.

The New Deal record was also noteworthy for a general lack of attention to the accretion of environmental damage. Of course, it had more immediately pressing problems. In other words, the socioeconomic conditions necessary for a massive environmental movement were not yet ripe prior to World War II. But about that time they did ripen—gradual quantitative and qualitative change produced a major historical discontinuity in society's relation to its environment.

The empirical record makes it possible for us to identify in general the emergence of a powerful environmental movement with the post–World War II era of general government growth, the mixed economy. That movement concurrently very much influenced government managerial expansion into the field of environmental policy. Popular concern about deterioration in environmental conditions surged especially during the 1950s and 1960s and peaked at approximately the end of that second decade.[78] The record of legislative and governmental administrative organization reflects this advocacy timing. The President's Council on Environmental Quality and the crucial Environmental Protection Agency, for example, were both created in 1970. The EPA brought under more centralized administrative control the earlier programs of the Department of the Interior and those that had been gradually transferred to the Department of Health, Education and Welfare.[79] The major federal laws under the aegis of the EPA dot the decadal landscape of the fifties and sixties:[80]

Water Pollution Control Act, 1956, with major amendments in
    1961, 1965, and 1972
Clean Air Act, 1963, amended in 1965 and 1970
Solid Waste Disposal Act, 1965
Resource Recovery Act (for materials reuse), 1970
National Environmental Policy Act, 1970
Consumer/Environmental-type amendments to the Drug and Cosmetic
    Act of 1938:

Pesticide Chemicals, 1954
Food Additives (Delaney Clause), 1958
Color Additives, 1960
Hazardous Substances Labeling, 1960
Labor/Environmental-type laws:
    Federal Coal Mine Health and Safety, 1969
    Occupational Safety and Health, 1970

Some additional legislative steps were taken later—for example, the federal Superfund program, created in 1980 by the Comprehensive Environmental Response, Compensation, and Liability Act for cleanup of the worst toxic-waste sites, and the federal Resource Conservation and Recovery Act (1984), an amendment to the hazardous-waste law designed to recycle such wastes by burning them as fuel.

Of course, there were numerous state departments of natural resources, water inspection agencies, and so on, as well as local government agencies and the like for solid-waste disposal. Historically, responsibility for clean water supply, sewage treatment and disposal, waste treatment and trash collection (e.g., city dumps) lay with local governments. But a prominent feature of the post–World War II era is the transfer of pollution supervision and general environmental policies more and more to the federal government.[81] As the multiple environmental repercussions of business policies and affluent household economic decisions mounted quantitatively over the years, they increasingly spilled over into interstate areas, becoming federal matters. Local governments are too small to set environmental policies in the United States.[82]

The federal EPA may be taken to represent the central government's response to the environmental upheaval. It can be considered a proxy for the larger network of environmental programs including other departments and independent agencies such as the Energy Department, Interior, Health and Human Services, and the Nuclear Regulatory Commission. Indeed, we may even more simplistically take the EPA as proxy for environment programs at all governmental levels.

Staff size can be used as a major indicator of the EPA career and therefore the environmental policy contribution to government administrative management. For such comparative purpose the EPA staff growth may be set against that for certain other agencies and departments in the federal administrative hierarchy. For example, in 1978, eight years after its origin, EPA employees already equaled 58 percent of the staff size of the new Energy Department, 52 percent of the Labor Department's staff, and 64 percent of the number of employees in the Housing and Urban Development Department. Only fourteen years of environmental policy later, in 1992, the staff proportions for EPA were as follows:

Energy	87 percent
Labor Dept.	102 percent
Housing and Urban Dev.	133 percent

The EPA also made remarkable relative gains on the very large Department of Transportation staff, averaging 70,000 over the period. Its staff size was only 14 percent of Transportation in 1975, but by 1992 it was one-fourth as large. This was partly because the EPA proved relatively impervious to the Reagan regime's attack on federal civilian employment in general. The EPA's annual percentage staff increase between 1975 and 1992 greatly exceeded that for all federal civilian employees and all state and local government employment.

What is more significant for direct comparison with long-run expansion in the economy, the EPA staff grew 3.13 percent a year between 1975 and 1992, while the civilian labor force as a whole grew annually at only 1.80 percent—well over a percentage point faster.

The EPA thus comes off quite well on these growth rate comparisons, and also regarding its expansion as quantitative contributor to government's administrative growth. But there can be no question that a staff of 18,000 in 1994 could hardly cope with the enormity of its burgeoning assignments. It was most fortunate for the agency that it was able to secure some assistance from the business community and from state and local bodies. It was unfortunate, however, that jurisdictional differences with state and local instrumentalities as well as state and local resistance to federal standards in some cases almost nullified task fulfillment.

So far as the future is concerned, environmental management by government will without any doubt experience very great expansion. At the very least, the different governmental management levels will have to deal with vastly expansive nuclear-waste cleanups, nonnuclear toxic-waste disposal from many of the 33,000 sites pinpointed by the EPA under the 1980 SuperFund program, runoff from land, loss of threatening amounts of the country's topsoil, pesticide use, application of the Omnibus Water Act of 1992, city water pollution, sewerage contamination, the ramifications of urban blight, the chemical content of products, support for pollution control technology, acid rain, deforestation, and even ocean fisheries depletion.[83]

Housing Support

If American idealogy and public policy have romanticized the vanishing small family farm and long accepted agriculture's political lobbies, profound devotion to home ownership is at least equally time honored. Resource allocation favoring a sector that accounts for 29 percent of the gross stock of fixed reproducible tangible wealth of the country has been a top priority of government administrative management throughout the history of the mixed economy.

There was more to housing policy development than the abiding home ownership ideology, however. Certain changes in the economy accentuated and brought to maturation the community's belief that all Americans were entitled to decent shelter. The relevant economic changes were (1) the enormous growth of housing requirements accompanying urbanization; (2) the comparative un-profitability of the private housing construction market and especially provision for the rising millions of low-income households; (3) the excessive concentration, exacerbated by suburbanization of those housing-deprived lower-income persons, minorities in particular, in the inner-city areas of urban centers; and (4) then aging of the housing stock in the inner cities, the hard core of urban blight. Unaided business refused to meet these challenges, and sociopolitical activism arose to do so. However, the larger poverty phenomenon of the politically inarticulate home-less persisted.

As is the case with much public management, the direction of resources into housing has its contradictory features. The dwelling needs of the millions of homeless and imminently homeless have been most inadequately met. Local governments rely heavily on property taxation that is often discriminatory to-ward residential property as contrasted with business property. Government in the United States, unlike many advanced economies, has abjured public owner-ship of dwellings.

But on the other hand, the federal government in particular has built a vast network of supports for the residential mortgage markets. Beginning in 1932, at the threshold of the New Deal, a Democratic-dominated Congress[84] inaugurated the network by setting up the Federal Home Loan Bank structure to advance emergency loans to thrift institutions. (This was by no means the first occasion in U.S. economic history that emergency claims were used to establish lasting institutions.) Then the New Deal set up the Federal Savings and Loan Insurance Corporation (FSLIC) in 1934. Like the FDIC, the FSLIC insures investor's sav-ings accounts in thrift and home-financing institutions up to $100,000. All fed-eral and qualified state savings and loan associations (S&LA) are covered. A liquid credit reserve for S&LAs is provided by the earlier (1932) system of twelve regional Federal Home Loan banks owned by S&LA, mutual savings banks, and insurance company members. This system of home loan banks is an independent U.S. government agency operating under the supervision of the Federal Home Loan Bank Board.

But there was even more for housing aid. The National Housing Act of 1934 established a Federal Housing Administration (FHA) to bolster the then ailing residential construction industry and underwrite loans by commercial banks, S&LAs, mortgage companies, and similar lending institutions. The FHA sub-sequently became a subagency within the U.S. Department of Housing and Urban Development, an executive department with about 13,000 employees in 1994.

The foundation for the edifice of housing credit was thus firmly grounded by 1934. That foundation was a response to a Depression-driven eruption of de-mands by farm and urban homeowners that government put a stop to the escala-tion of actual and potential foreclosures and evictions by creditor institutions. Some 273,000 homeowners were foreclosed in 1932, for example; and in early

1933 about 1,000 homes were falling into the hands of mortgage holders daily.[85]

A big addition to the growing structure was made with the creation in 1938 of the Federal National Mortgage Association ("Fannie Mae"). The new U.S. government corporation established a *secondary* market for the purchase and sale of FHA and Veterans Administration *insured* home mortgages. (A secondary market is like the stock exchanges, in which extant, non-new financial paper is traded.) As time passed the secondary market for mortgages grew enormously and became almost completely dominated by government agencies.[86] This pervasiveness of public intervention resulted from the federal government's extension of public underwriting to *conventional* (i.e., uninsured) home mortgages. The extension was inaugurated during a new wave of intervention in 1968–70 with the chartering of two government-sponsored enterprises, the Government National Mortgage Association ("Ginnie Mae") and the Federal Home Loan Mortgage Corporation ("Freddie Mac").

Freddie Mac became the world's largest trader in conventional mortgages, although it also deals with government-insured mortgages. Fannie Mae and Freddie Mac are the primary institutions that bolster the secondary market by securitizing home mortgages—that is, underwriting the growing *pools of home mortgages* purchased from their originators that are then financed by the issuance of mortgage-backed securities to investors.[87]

The federal and the state and local governments also incurred very large, direct obligations in support of the diversion of resources to the housing sector. For example, in 1995 the federal government disbursed directly about $27 billion for housing assistance and urban development. The state and local governments in 1992 directly spent over $17 billion for housing and community development. To top it off, federal tax expenditures (revenue losses) for deductibility of mortgage interest and residential property taxes on owner-occupied homes in 1996 totaled a huge $70 billion.[88] All these sums had grown vigorously in real, price-deflated terms over the years since 1960.

It can be concluded that the expansion of government support measures for the channeling of resources into housing since the New Deal has been a major contributor to the long-run propagation of the managerial element in government's growth.

Energy Policy and Resource Allocation

Certain ostensibly private business activities and their publicly owned counterparts have historically been subjected to public controls because they provide some essential service. For that reason they may be judged by the community and by government to be affected with a public interest. Examples include the provision of roads, sewerage, community water, and electricity. They constitute infrastructure, necessary for the functioning of the market system. This bundle of characteristics, among others, makes the activities public utilities.

The provision of energy, or power, is endowed with infrastructure characteristics. It is usually defined to encompass a collection of economic activities that include both power generation and the fuels required for it. With the exception of a small proportion of electric power from hydro and nuclear sources, the fuels used for power generation are overwhelmingly fossil in character: coal, oil, and manufactured or natural gas.

Government intrusion into the energy provision package has historically taken the form of public utility regulation for electricity and natural resource policy for fossil fuels. The latter policy included the notoriously generous depletion allowances for petroleum extraction and expensing of capital costs under the federal tax law. Electric power generation and the production of manufactured gas from coal were made public utilities because in addition to their essential service character they exhibited, like rail transportation, natural monopoly characteristics. Since their markets were local or narrowly regional in scope, government regulatory intrusion was almost exclusively at the state and local level.

The production and distribution of natural gas from petroleum was regulated by state boards such as the Texas Railroad Commission. Such regulatory management was very power-company supportive, committed to pricing that yielded a fair return on a fair valuation of a firm's property.

The director of the Institute of Public Utilities at Michigan State University in East Lansing has called attention to the passive posture of regulation, pointing to Professor Warren Samuels's generalization that the traditional commission regulation was not only a partial means to curb business power but also subject to capture by business and hence a means for establishing, concentrating, and maintaining economic power.[89] This was all very much in the spirit of laissez-faire and has continued throughout the twentieth century. More broadly, with respect to governmental management in the energy field, one authority has generalized regarding policy:

> The United States had neither energy policy nor energy politics, as these are understood today, before the Arab embargo of 1973. Decisions about energy were handled by separate regimes, each of which was the product of a long process of historical evolution. In each, free market forces had been attenuated to some degree: in the coal and petroleum regimes to assure stability and higher profits to private participants, and in the natural gas and electric power regimes to do this and to protect consumers. The government was involved but not in a manner that permitted public authorities to treat energy affairs in a unified manner.[90]

In brief, there was no overall, integrated energy policy, but there was policy of some sort for the separate energy regimes. The major move to correct this dispersiveness at the federal level was the creation in 1977 of the Energy Department (DOE).

There is no clearer case of energy regulation in the service of the regulated than petroleum. For example, when the Mideast and certain states other than Texas, Oklahoma, and Louisiana became important sources of additional crude supply in the late 1950s, the government jumped to the aid of the domestic majors in the industry by instituting mandatory federal import quotas in 1959. (Prices on domestic old—i.e., previously discovered—crude were already controlled.) This supply restriction effort, designed to support prices and thus let the consumer pay the additional costs, lasted until the OPEC embargo beginning in the fall of 1973. One writer in the mid-seventies has judged this quota policy the most important instance of federal intervention in the petroleum industry.[91]

The coal industry did not receive the government protection and support for prices or supply restriction that was extended to petroleum. Coal was a slow-growing industry marked by unruly competition and excess capacity in the service of the electric power market, as well as outright captive to big electric power and steel companies. Federal belated efforts by the Interior Department to institute minimum prices and restricted output under the Bituminous Coal Acts of 1935 and 1937 (Guffey Act) were a failure. A subsequent market control attempt, lasting from the end of World War II to the early 1970s, took the form of an equally unsuccessful, private, labor-management alliance.[92]

Nor was government coal policy thereafter a significant contributor to the expansion of administrative management. Federal concerns with the environmental effects of coal burning, miners' safety, strip mining, and leasing of portions of its large coal reserve holdings were not able to generate an increase of its administrative involvement sufficient to overcome the constraining effects of the Reagan regime's deregulation drive.

In the case of energy policy more generally, the federal government had begun to break out of its passive posture with the coming of the New Deal. Trebing summarizes in part the policy awakening by reference, among other matters, to the previously discussed establishment of public power projects such as the 1933 Tennessee Valley Authority (TVA) and the Bonneville Power Administration (BPA) in the Northwest, together with the Rural Electrification Administration (REA) under the Department of Agriculture in 1935.[93] The TVA had an enormous developmental impact on a vast region. The BPA contributed to the institutionalization of coexisting private and public power systems. The REA greatly advanced the technological base of rural America by bringing that backward sector both electricity and telephone service. Trebing emphasizes also the fact that these New Deal energy policy measures "revealed the inability of the commission system to come to grips with broader social problems or to anticipate the future."[94] Technological change by the 1930s had gradually been laying the base for more significant government intervention into the energy regimes at the federal level. The development of high-voltage electric power lines was making interstate transmission increasingly feasible, and the installation of large-capacity pipelines made the movement of natural gas, extracted as a by-product from petroleum, similarly interstate in scope.[95] Natural gas, a fossil fuel, had been replacing the more costly, locally regulated manufactured gas. A New Deal Congress responded in 1938 to these technological changes and to consumer concerns by giving broad authority under a 1935 Federal Power Act to the act's commission (FPC) to "supervise the construction of natural gas pipelines from wells in the Southwest and to regulate the rates the pipelines charged big city utilities that bought natural gas for distribution to consumers."[96] Thus the historically moderate and local, pro-business management of the fossil fuels was beginning to take on some also modest consumer complexion, even as it shifted upward toward the federal level.

There were big subsequent additions after the Depression decade to the breakthrough in energy policies inaugurated by the New Deal. One was due to the rise of nuclear power, both civilian and military. Another was the influences on energy fuels policy of a surging environmental movement, also after World War II like nuclear power, that went programmatically far beyond the old conservation movement. A third addition to energy programs, particularly regarding petroleum, came with the energy crisis of the seventies—President Carter's moral equivalent of war. The 1973–74 OPEC embargo and subsequent price explosion firmly established the fact that oil was profoundly connected to the public interest. The impact was not only domestic. It also penetrated foreign policy, particularly the national security aspect. Important legislative results included the creation of the International Energy Agency in 1974, the Emergency Petroleum Allocation Act of 1973, and the strategic petroleum reserve under the Energy Policy and Conservation Act (EPCA) of 1975. On the administrative level there was the establishment of the DOE. These were followed in 1980 with the Energy Security Act, with its Synthetic Fuels Corporation devoted to research into, and lending for, fuel production from coal, shale, and tar sands.

The EPCA fostered a state energy conservation program and related efforts to cut energy use by 5 percent through both voluntary and mandated programs.[97] It also stipulated increased auto miles-per-gallon targets. Additional federal measures passed in the last half of the seventies created a number of programs to be implemented by the states, a surge that lasted until oil prices collapsed and the Reagan administration undermined them in the early eighties. The programs included audits of home utility use, weatherization assistance, matching grants to schools and hospitals for energy-efficient equipment, a Solar Energy and Energy Conservation Bank (loan subsidies), and commercial/apartment audits.[98]

Underlying all these crisis policy developments, such as they were, there were certain relevant, long-run changes in the economy, including per capita output growth, technological innovations, an increase in crude oil imports in excess of 7 percent a year between 1950 and 1972, and phenomenal expansion rates in urban automobile transportation, the motor truck industry, and the airline industry. Some of these were obviously particularly pertinent to petroleum, the key fuel in energy policy.

So far as petroleum policy was concerned, there was more political ado from the cross-currents of interest groups than there was creation of enlarged, lasting administrative agencies at any level of government. The government and private businesses interact and interfere in each other's responsibilities quite regularly. Motor fuels are an extreme example of this joint development. The oil industry, recognizing the enormous increases in demand for gasoline that accompanied the adoption of the motor car, had written a model gasoline tax that it then lobbied through the state legislatures. The distinctive feature of the American gasoline tax is that the government can use the revenues derived from the tax only to construct and maintain roads. Every state in the union adopted the tax and tied it to road construction between 1919 and 1929. The federal government added a federal motor fuel tax, again tied to the construction of roads, in 1932.

In the 1920s a common argument in favor of building paved roads throughout the country was that (1) the people were going to drive from New York to Chicago, (2) driving on paved smooth roads took less gasoline than driving on dirty rutted roads, and consequently (3) taxing gasoline sales to build good roads conserved the scarce natural resource petroleum. In fact, building good roads made cars much more useful and pleasant, increased their use substantially, and greatly increased the use of gasoline. The various state highway departments in effect became sales agents for the gasoline industry.

Over the longer run, the oil industry has developed an amazing policy. It regularly runs advertisements decrying government spending. It posts notices announcing how unreasonably high gasoline taxes are on every gas pump. Yet higher highway spending helped build their industry and American gasoline taxes are the lowest of any developed country. In most other countries gasoline taxes are measured in dollars per gallon while in the United States they are measured in cents per gallon. In other countries gasoline taxes are part of the general revenue of government while in the United States they are tied to road construction and maintainence—that is, to increasing the demand for gasoline.

As the petroleum industry has acted to create whole departments of government, so government has acted to change the structure and behavior of oil companies. The government restricted, then prohibited the use of tetraethyl lead in gasoline; required the adoption of elaborate and expensive gasoline fume recapture devices; changed the size of the fuel filler nozzle; wrote elaborate rules to restrict the conditions of transport of oil, gasoline, and other petrochemicals to reduce the costs and dangers of accidents and spills; and so on. In some periods the government has restricted the importation of oil to hold the domestic price up—that is, to force Americans to use only American petroleum. In other periods it has encouraged the use of U.S. oil at the expense of foreign oil in the name of energy independence.

In the famous 1954 change of government in Iran, the United States acted to restore the shah, and then Iran signed oil production and development contracts with American oil companies at the expense of the British, who had done almost all the oil development in Iran up to 1954. The Persian Gulf War of 1992 can be viewed as befriending some OPEC members at the expense of other OPEC members and increasing the U.S. ability to get cheap foreign oil. Quite simply, viewing petroleum as a private industry is benighted. It is and always has been significantly connected to the public interest. The government has been used as a tool by the industry on occasion. The government has forced unwanted changes on the industry on occasion. The two have acted together against both foreign and domestic enemies on occasion.

The oil price inflation of the seventies collapsed in the eighties. Alaskan oil had begun to flow into the domestic economy in the early seventies. Also, possible policy concern over the considerable rise of crude oil imports from 1970 to 1990, concurrently with the downward drift of domestic production, was dampened by the almost constant petroleum product consumption. It is true that transportation demand was rising. But the oil price rise of the seventies had prompted householders to make a big shift away from residential consumption of oil toward electricity (which raised coal consumption). The same shift occurred in the case of commercial buildings. Hence the increase in petroleum policy's contribution to governmental administrative management growth peaked in the seventies.

Much the same may be said of energy policy in general. Except for environmental concerns about fossil fuels and nuclear wastes, economic trends were undermining increases in governmental administrative involvement. Per capita domestic energy production fell from 304 million Btu in 1970 to 255 in 1993. Per capita energy consumption was the same in 1993 as it had been in 1970. And energy consumption per dollar of real GDP fell notably over the same period.[99]

The national security aspects of petroleum were a sideshow compared to the considerations regarding nuclear power. While the federal government played a major entrepreneurial and subsidizing role in channeling resources into the development of nuclear facilities after World War II, its considerable civilian focus was swamped by its almost frantic nuclear weapons program, including the construction of a large nuclear powered and armed undersea naval armada.

Atomic energy was a significant postwar addition to the production of electricity and to governmental administrative management. On the civilian front, the federal government in particular promoted, researched, and subsidized in a multitude of ways nuclear power generation through the mid-seventies and into the early eighties. Largely because of the bomb, the 1946 Atomic Energy Act gave the federal government a monopoly of nuclear power development under the administration of the Atomic Energy Commission (AEC) together with the Congressional Joint Committee on Atomic Energy. The AEC was commissioned to encourage and regulate nuclear power development. But progress was slow, and it was not until the 1960s that such a power source came into operation to a significant degree.

The Price-Anderson Act of 1957 gave new stimulation to private commercial development of nuclear power plants for generating electricity by limiting company liability in case of accidents through the provision of government bailout in excess of insurance coverage. The problems of safety and accidents were given scant attention by the AEC and the commercial firms. Practically no consideration, as to cost or otherwise, was given by anybody to the enormous decommissioning and long-run radioactive waste disposal costs.

The future public works outlays of all types for nuclear garbage disposal boggle the mind and will continue to boost that upcoming but amorphously publicized component of the public budgets. Cases in point are the DOE's Pantex plant near Amarillo, Texas; the Hanford, Washington, cleanup and disposal; and the costs of shipping and storing all plutonium-contaminated bomb wastes. The DOE's *exploratory* project to develop a storage place in New Mexico had already as of 1993 "cost $1.5 billion, and will cost that much more again by the year 2000."[100] To these must be added the large costs of dismantling and recycling Cold War overkill weapons and other ordnance that are partly nuclear in character.[101] Peaceful public works, yes, but hardly infrastructure building.

Public concern about nuclear power plant safety was aroused early and reached clamor levels in the late 1960s and the 1970s. In fact, environmentalists' activities, including state pollution control bodies conscious of the nuclear safety issue, were largely responsible for essentially putting a stop to the excessive growth of civilian nuclear power facilities by the early 1980s. Ironically, this was just the time when the oil crisis came to an end. Nevertheless, as Franklin Tugwell has aptly summarized,

> without government promotion and subsidy, there would have been no civilian nuclear power industry. Furthermore, the government's involvement was critical in shaping the character of the industry that did emerge. Federal policies assured the transition from public monopoly to private oligopoly, determined the character of the technology that was eventually deployed, and promoted the growth of the industry long before economic conditions made it attractive to private investors.[102]

Of the total energy consumption in 1993, nuclear power accounted for 7.5 percent, a growth from two-tenths of 1 percent in 1970.[103] The Nuclear Regulatory Commission's (NRC) staff (descendant of the AEC) of 3,336 in 1994 had grown from its initial 2,247 in 1975 and had, like the DOE, survived almost intact the deregulation attacks of the eighties. Defense-connected nuclear matters continued to absorb the bulk of the Energy Department's $16 billion 1995 budget. Atomic energy defense activities accounted for $11 billion of federal outlays in 1994.

With regard to overall energy policy since the New Deal, the available data cannot possibly give us a good quantitative appreciation of the growth of administrative management in that field. In the first place, state and local data for the energy policy category and its impact on the direction of resource use are almost entirely absent. They are, for example, buried in more comprehensive categories such as state expenditures for natural resources, state and local total expenditures for utilities, similar outlays by cities, and state and local outlays on capital (which increased in real terms at a strong annual rate of 4.3 percent from 1970 to 1990). And since there are no aggregate data on tax concessions or grants by state and local governments to implement energy behavior of the private sector, we cannot appreciate fully what must have constituted an enormous set of influences on the pattern of resource use.

At the federal level there are only spotty staff data, for example for the TVA (18,846 in 1994), for components of what became the DOE in 1977, and for the DOE thereafter (19,899 in 1994). We have total employee data for the NRC. Bonneville Power had about 4,000 employees in 1990. We know that energy work is buried in the aggregates for the Departments of Interior and Agriculture, to say nothing of the Defense Department. Most cabinet departments and the Congressional Office of Technology Assessment are to some extent concerned with energy issues.[104] Additionally, we have federal outlays for energy that drop drastically in the eighties and for atomic energy defense activities that surge upward over the same decade. All these are proxies that tell us all too little, however. So we have to make do with the qualitative information such as reviewed herein. Unfortunately, even that information is confined primarily to actions on the federal level.

We must conclude on such qualitative grounds, nevertheless, that there was sufficient growth in the parts of the energy policy collection to engineer considerable resource allocations in the private (and public) economy. The contributing parts may be listed by way of summary and conclusion: increased public electric power coupled with regional development, including TVA and BPA; major support for electrification and communication in the rural economy; nuclear power development, military and civilian; support for restraints on the human and environmental damages from nuclear power and weaponry; R&D support for the development of alternative fuels; policies at all levels of government, which elicited cooperation from the private sector, that helped curb the aggregate demand for energy; price and subsidy policies in support of the domestic petroleum and natural gas industry; policies (even Gulf Wars) to assure the supply of petroleum imports; a program to stockpile a domestic supply of crude petroleum; and continued growth in state and local government regulatory policies to ensure the provision of electric power at rates that, it is hoped, minimize interest-group conflicts. Quite a package!

Management of Transport Infrastructure

Underwriting the development and operation of the for-hire passenger and freight transportation sector represents one of government's greatest contributions to support of the private market system. In both the canal era before the

Civil War and the railroadization era afterwards, private entrepreneurs and creditors in transportation enjoyed the widespread governmental encouragement necessary to create that part of the system's infrastructure.

During the era of railroads' transportation dominance from the 1870s to the late 1920s, federal government management under the 1887 Interstate Commerce Act and its commission (the ICC) was much concerned both to ensure the quasi-monopolistic railroads a fair return and at the same time to protect shippers and their customers against extreme discriminatory practices.

Lesser forms of transport were not neglected. The Army Corps of Engineers, the Congress, and the maritime agencies of the federal government provided internationally competitive and national security subsidies for U.S. merchant shipyards and haulage. Financial and operational support was extended to intercoastal, coastal, Great Lakes, and the oceangoing carrying trade. Local public port authorities managed the capital programs and operations of waterborne and connected transport in the nation's seaports and inland waterway terminals.

The market's development gave birth in the early twentieth century to a revolutionary technological innovation. The motor vehicle destroyed the even tenor of the ICC's simplistic administrative task, permanently augmenting its responsibilities. The spread of the motor truck forced the commission to make a place for truck haulage in the publicly supported sphere and to address itself increasingly to the new rivalry over freight traffic share.

But the public intervention prompted by the motor vehicle extended far beyond ICC regulatory surveillance. All levels of government again rose to the occasion. In particular, government built the roadbed for automobiles and trucks with a vigor that put to shame the roadbed subsidies formerly granted to the railroads. Paved public streets, roads, and interstate highways became the new, indispensable transport infrastructure underlying the market system. Congress approved funding in 1956 for a 41,000-mile system of interstate and defense express highways.

Fifty billion 1950 dollars was the initial high-cost projection for the system. Special taxes were instituted to build the necessary trust fund, and the federal government thereby permanently enlarged its responsibility to facilitate the longturn growth of the automobile and, more strategic freightwise, the trucking industry. About three-quarters of the system was already completed by 1970. Total federal investment in highways between the program's inception in 1956 and 1990 amounted to $436 billion (in 1990 dollars).[105] By thus underwriting interstate trucking, the federal government, and to a lesser extent the states, generated the ominous conditions for the later government railroad rescue operations.

The ICC's high value of service railroad rates and its insistence on maintaining the growing number of unprofitable freight routes in the face of truck competition brought the agency under attack after World War II by the Association of American Railroads itself. The railroads knew that cost-oriented rates were essential to save the rail freight market. The organized trucking industry, which

Congress had brought under ICC regulation in 1935, found the ICC's standard railroad policies congenial to its own ability to compete. It also resisted during the deregulation wave of the 1970s the congressional and presidential efforts to deregulate it: The leading carriers correctly feared both destructive fare and services competition and the ease of entry into the industry. Deregulation was ultimately accepted with great reluctance. After all, the industry had enjoyed, like the railroads and barge lines, effective exemption from the antitrust rate-fixing laws after the 1948 Reed-Bulwinkle Act; and the ICC had widely restricted new entry into trucking, as well as fostered trucking rates high enough to cover the costs of less efficient carriers.[106]

By the early 1990s, the ICC's slashed staff of approximately 600 employees, the Transportation Department's 70,000 workers, and the total federal outlays for transportation of $35 billion substantially managed national commercial transport. Among the tasks was a stabilization of the rail/truck competitive shares of intercity ton-miles of freight traffic at some 37 percent for railroads and 28 percent for trucks. Helped by cost-based rail freight rates and innovations such as the piggyback—the trailer-on-flatcar—the long-run rail retardation had apparently been arrested.

But the long-run decline in rail freight was apparently irreversible. Railroads had accounted for over 57 percent of the volume of domestic intercity freight traffic in 1950. While some technological innovations helped, others hurt. For example, advances in high-tension electrical transmission cut into the railroads' important long-distance coal haulage monopoly. Perhaps the most shocking single occurrence was the bankruptcy of the Penn Central in 1970—ironically, on the eve of the deregulation drive. Simultaneously, the collapse of private railroad passenger traffic was acknowledged.

What then happened is a vivid reminder of the fact that there is much more to government administrative management than regulation. There is government *assumption of responsibility* whenever any basic underpinning of the market system is seriously threatened. Penn Central was bailed out (shades of the later savings and loan fiasco).

The Penn Central had brought together in 1966 the former Pennsylvania Railroad and the New York Central, both giants among the giants. The vast Penn Central system was in terms of assets the largest merger in U.S. history. But it became an infamous financial fiasco, going bankrupt only four years after its creation, owing in part to indifferent, incompetent, and even destructive private management.[107] The Penn Central was by no means the only member of the railroad bankruptcy club, however, and six other smaller lines in the Northeast filed bankruptcy papers during the early seventies. The seven roads taken together suffered annual deficits in those years ranging from $100 million to $250 million.[108] Stubbornly resisting nationalization and recognizing the economic indispensability of the rails, the federal government expended hundreds of millions in subsidies, mostly in the form of loans and loan guarantees, to these and other roads. The seven bankrupt eastern railroads, including the Penn Central, were merged in April 1976 into the Consolidated Rail Corporation (Conrail) under authority of the federal Regional Rail Reorganization Act of 1974. Conrail was the largest merger of transportation companies ever effected in the United States. The new consolidation stretched from St. Louis to the Eastern Seaboard.

The bailout (through loans, outright subsidies, or acquisition) is close to the extreme of administrative management. The ultimate bailout is nationalization, and that is exactly what was done with Conrail's creation and also with railroad passenger equipment and service. The automobile, with significant assistance from the airlines after World War II, had almost destroyed intercity rail passenger service by 1970. Consequently in that same Conrail year, a federally owned and operated (and subsidized) National Railroad Passenger Corporation (Amtrak) was created, implementing the Rail Passenger Service Act of 1970. A great and modern nation without railroad passenger service was unthinkable, although the traffic volume barely held its own in absolute terms in the following quarter-century.

Federal funding for Conrail, like the passenger road Amtrak, was in the hundreds of millions. Chronically unprofitable interest rates below market constituted an additional partial subsidy. The federal government, after the manner of the British nationalization technique, obligated itself to pay the former owners of the bankrupt rail properties. The amount, equal to the court-adjudicated differences between the properties transferred to Conrail and the common or preferred stock awarded in exchange plus some federally guaranteed certificates of value issued by the U.S. Railroad Association (a federal agency set up to oversee Conrail), could total billions of dollars.[109] By 1979, not long before it began to show a profit, the federal investment in Conrail had already totaled $3.3 billion, only a portion of the federal freight railroad involvement.[110] Amtrak had received by 1993 some $13 billion in federal subsidies.[111]

The automobile also dealt a body blow to urban mass passenger transit. Suburbanization, which continued after World War II, did further damage to municipal transit; it could easily be handled by the automobile. Buses fought a rearguard action. But the number of revenue passengers riding public transit dropped from 17.3 billion in 1948 to 5.9 billion in 1970. Nevertheless, the market system's operation demanded some urban mass transit, particularly for the lower rungs of the labor supply ladder. The outcome was a large transfer of privately owned transit lines to public ownership and to local-state-federal cooperative management support and subsidy for what was left.

Concurrently with these long-run developments, consumer market developments brought an increase in passenger vehicle miles of travel, more passenger car registrations per adult population, more costly traffic congestion (that began to interfere with the efficiency of trucking), more commutation delays, more motor vehicle pollution, and a high (though falling) rate of accidents. The outcomes involved more than just traffic management, increased gasoline taxes, and motor vehicle license fees. The public demanded safety and environmental protection by the government. Those developments, conjoined with growing community efforts to get greater mass transit ridership, were pregnant with sustained public management. For example, at the federal level alone, operating grant approvals for mass transportation totaled over $13 billion between 1977 and 1991, and capital grants approvals for the same purpose totaled $38 billion.[112] Real all-government spending for mass transit rose at a vigorous 4.7 percent a year in the decade of the eighties.[113] However, the late 1970s saw the highest levels of federal assistance for urban mass transit.[114]

Airlines

By far the biggest contributor to general government administrative growth emanating from the transportation sphere after World War II was airline management. As ever, the roadbed—supply, maintenance, and even operation of terminals—was publicly provided. In addition, air traffic control, passenger safety, airport access routes, procurement rules, hiring regulations, and more recently, negotiations in disputes between airlines and airports over landing fees[115] were under different levels of government direction. All of these management responsibilities survived the Airline Deregulation Act of 1978. Also as ever, substantial resource diversion into the sector was vigorously fostered by government. Private aircraft design and production was also much assisted by Pentagon R&D and military aircraft procurement.

The public developmental efforts were eminently successful in building a vast new passenger transport industry. For example, persons employed in scheduled domestic and international air transportation zoomed from 83,000 in 1950 to 537,000 in 1993—an annual rate increase of almost 5 percent. The 1993 total was almost three times the number of employees in Class 1 railroads. Express and freight ton miles flown, though very small in the national freight total, exploded from 213 million to 12 billion over the same period. Private travel agencies proliferated. The Federal Aviation Administration, which was formed in 1958 by combining several previously existing agencies, had a very large staff of some 43,000 when it was transferred to the newly created Department of Transportation (DOT) in 1967.

The DOT became a giant among federal instrumentalities. By 1994 its staff was much larger than that of the Department of Commerce, almost twice the size of the entire legislative branch, and almost 2.5 times that of the State Department. By that year it embraced the Federal Aviation Administration, the Federal Highway Administration, the Federal Railroad Administration, the National Highway Safety Traffic Administration, and the Urban Mass Transportation Administration.

Civilian commercial airlines, while privately owned, were and are today treated much like public infrastructure generally. They are subject to government's safety and environmental regulations and their labor relationships are subject to presidential declaration of a transportation emergency. That type of administrative dependency was dramatically demonstrated when President Reagan fired all air traffic controllers en masse in 1981. Administrative management also had important international dimensions in the case of airlines, as bilateral agreements with over eighty other countries had to be governmentally supervised.

The bold, brash Deregulation Act of 1978 provided for the dissolution of the old Civil Aeronautics Board (CAB) of the 1930s within six years and the usual removal of fare stipulations, as well as opening up entry for competing airlines. The CAB had already eased route and fare restrictions in 1936 despite prophetic resistance by the airline companies and unions.[116] Although passenger traffic and freight/express ton miles continued to drift upward for a while after deregulation, and an oliogopolistic core in the industry persisted in the face of numerous competing new nonhub carriers, the annual net profit aggregates for the sector in the eighties were modest and became erratic and frequently negative, especially when the economy slowed after 1989.[117] Excess capacity and fare wars plagued the industry through the eighties and into the nineties. In short, deregulation had opened the door to a competitive shambles in an infrastructure industry that was affected with a public interest.

Small wonder that in consequence, after three consecutive years of frightening losses, President Clinton and the Congress set up a National Commission to Ensure a Strong Competitive (*sic*) Airline Industry in May 1993.[118] The commission's report in August of that same year pointed towards what might well be described as the reinstitution of much federal management: encouraging more multinational agreements to open additional international markets, tightening up the air traffic control system, and increasing the involvement of the DOT in the airlines' financial decision making.[119]

Indeed, it was announced in early 1994 that the Clinton administration planned to ask Congress to create "a government-owned corporation like Amtrak to operate the nation's air traffic control system."[120] The rationale for the proposal included the usual antiregulation arguments, but of course it was not noted that government subsidies provided about a third of Amtrak's annual financing. It would indeed appear that there can be too much free market for a major transport sector serving long-distance business travelers, the tourist market, and vacationers, particularly in an economy with a lamentable rail passenger network.

Conclusion: Government and the Responsibilities for Transport

The importance of growing governmental management influence over the economy in the case of for-hire passenger and freight transportation resides first of all in the fact that a healthy transport industry is an absolute essential for the functioning of the private market order. In the second place, the transport sector is of noteworthy size. While of slowly declining relative long-term importance on standard measures up to the early 1990s, employees in the sector accounted for 3.34 percent, on average, of all employers on nonagricultural payrolls, 1970–90, and 4.2 percent of employees in the service-producing sector of the economy. Outlays for freight and for-hire passenger service totaled, on average, 8.7 percent in ratio to gross domestic product from 1970 to 1990.

The career of both commercial transportation activity and government involvement in it paralleled in general the growth pattern of the economy: vigorous from 1950 to about 1970, sluggish from 1970 through about 1990. For example, the crucial category—the volume of total intercity freight traffic—increased by almost 3 percent a year between 1950 and 1970, but the annual growth rate dropped a whole percentage point in the following twenty years. Again, real expenditures of all governments for highway transportation rose steadily and strongly until 1970, falling off sharply thereafter until the later 1980s. Exceptions to that general pattern were real mass transit and aviation outlays at all government levels, which rose steadily over the very long run.

The deregulation programs, more significant for airlines, railroads, and trucking than for pipelines, urban transit, and water shipping,[121] more or less coincided with the sluggish growth phase in the economy. Deregulation was thus superimposed upon, and tended to accentuate, the long pause in administrative management and its influence that accompanied the retardation in the growth of the major transport types.

However, it would be a mistake to conclude that government responsibility eroded with the post-1970 slowdowns in total freight traffic in general and railroad retardation in particular. Less rail freight in itself, for example, did not bring about an equal percentage retardation in the ICC's manifold responsibilities for that traffic. The ICC still had to guide the decisions regarding continuance or discontinuance of money-losing lines, to mediate in the rivalry between the railroads and the trucking industry, to resolve policy conflicts with the DOT, to handle railroad shipper contracts that had to be filed with it under the deregulatory 1980 Staggan Rail Act, to control rates where certain roads were judged able to exercise market dominance, to regulate coal-for-export shipments, to grant exemption from regulation of certain selected products, to police safety and environmental regulations, and to manage Conrail until it reverted to private ownership in 1987. As for the catastrophic private railroad passenger demise, we have seen that the assumption of total responsibility by government through Amtrak continued public administrative management in a new and more stringent form.

Furthermore, deregulation aside for a moment, government responsibility for strongly growing freight traffic by truck (over 4 percent a year, 1950–70; almost 3 percent a year, 1970–90) and passenger traffic by airline (10 percent annually, 1950–90!) also tended to compensate significantly for any public managerial slowdown connected with the railroad declines. Also, real all-government expenditures for highways, which rose vigorously at over 5 percent a year from 1950 to 1970, still increased in excess of 3 percent annually between 1980 and 1990 (real gross domestic product in the eighties rose at only 2.5 percent a year). Real all-government spending (using the all-government implicit price deflator) for airport transportation increased 3.4 percent annually in the deregulated eighties, and for mass transit, as noted earlier, 4.7 percent.[122] These evidences of government involvement should be appreciated in making any attempt at the difficult task of quantifying the public management accompaniments of the transportation growth record, as well as the impact of deregulation on public management.

The deregulation sweep created some accompanying oversights that ensured private market infrastructure deterioration in the longer run within parts of the transport sector. The attendant accumulation of rehabilitation costs and a necessary matching increase in future government involvement was the long-run consequence. For example, by the end of the 1980s there was a national highway crisis.[123] Deregulation policy had allowed aggregate user taxes, tolls, and fees to increasingly fall short of public disbursements. The awkward turn to government general funds to try to fill the gap proved quite inadequate. Forecasts of the capital needs for the highway system for the nineties called for much larger public outlays than was currently being committed. That shortfall in capital commitments was exacerbated by a growing drain of capital funds for highway maintenance alone.

Attempts to turn over the infrastructure to market forces have historically always been hazardous ventures because of the free-rider impulse on the part of each individual benefiting from the service and maintenance of the infrastructure. What trucking company is going to volunteer payments for its contribution to pavement damage? What private airline is going to volunteer to pay its debatable share of the necessary costs of maintaining the city of Los Angeles's international airport?

This examination of government management of the commercial transportation sector has proved particularly useful methodologically because it has shown that the different task of quantifying the size of government cannot be understood by simply looking at standard criteria, such as agency staff size or budget. It is true that for adequate appraisal of size we need to know the human financial and physical resources committed by government to the administrative tasks. If possible, we also need to determine staff efficiency in performance—for example, devotion to agency purpose and irrelevant interagency cooperation or conflict.

But public managerial *influence* also depends on such matters as the nature and scope of the applicable controls and/or aids that pertain to the affected activity. The regulatory network is an important component of those policies. Where bailout occurs, influence at once becomes more comprehensive. The sheer size of the supervised and/or supported sector is also to be incorporated into quantification of managerial influence. The sector's growth rate, as was noted in the case of the airline industry, is likewise pertinent. And, of course, in cases of outright government acquisition the control of resources is complete, and there is direct public dispensation of the services of the resources. The commercial transportation sector has evinced several examples of such direct dispensation: municipal mass transit, city street and intercity highway mainte-nance, Amtrak, and the operation of airports and port authorities.

In the post–World War II decades marked by the rise of big government, the transport management duties assumed by government bodies continued to sup-port long-run relative expansion of government up to about 1970. After that growth turning point the duties no longer stimulated relative expansion, but only absolute expansion. In other words, after 1970 the pace of transportation man-agement continued to contribute positively to government's growth in its admin-istrative management sphere.

Federal Government Resource Guidance Through Tax Expenditures

The federal government, through its tax policies, (1) directs, supports, or inhibits the allocation of human and other resources to various sectors of the economy and (2) influences the material status of the different socioeconomic groups, business firms, and state and local governments. The impact of tax policies on material status indirectly allocates resources, so the two impact categories inter-act. Also, tax policies and conventionally defined subsidies overlap. For exam-ple, it was estimated in 1993 that the tariff (a tax) on textiles and apparel amounted to a $46 billion subsidy to the domestic industry by reducing cheaper imports.[124] Since consumers had to pay higher prices, the tariff was the government's vehicle for engineering a consumer-financial subsidy for the in-dustry. This was what might be called an indirect subsidy.

Some subsidies are engineered *directly* through budget outlays rather than through tax receipts. These fit the popular sense of the term "subsidy." Such is the case, for example, with the previously discussed federal transportation outlay subsidies of $36 billion in fiscal 1993, and the farm income stabilization pay-ments of $19 billion in that same year. Resources were thus channeled directly into transportation and agriculture. *Indirect* channeling of resources is widely accomplished through outlay subsidies to socioeconomic groups such as cash or in-kind assistance to the poor and to children for housing, food, and nutrition. Humans get the subsidy's direct material benefits, the housing and agriculture industries get the indirect resource allocation supports.

We are here concerned, however, with similar general policy objectives by the federal government that are engineered through the tax system. The vehicle is estimated tax revenues *waived,* called tax expenditures (TE). The term "expen-ditures" expresses the fact that they have the same effect as government pay-ments to favored taxpayers. Rather turgidly defined by the U.S. Office of

Management and Budget, TEs are predicted revenue losses attributable to provisions of the federal tax laws that allow a special exclusion, exemption, or deduction from gross income or that provide a special credit, a preferential rate of tax, or a deferral of liability.

We unfortunately do not have compendia of TEs by state and local governments, perhaps because of the enormity of the task that would be required to compile them. Indeed, the federal government did not construct its first comprehensive list of TEs until 1967.[125] The first publication in the *Statistical Abstract* of detailed TEs was in 1975 (see p. 231 therein). Therein, separated from traditionally defined budgetary outlay subsidies, TEs are presented and totaled at $40 billion, and conventional subsidies (by calculation, Table No. 380) at about $25 billion. The TE tally shows thirty-nine items for 1970—for example, exemptions for students, expensing mineral exploration and development, and expensing of R & D. It is from this tally that the selected items in Table 3.1 are presented, a selection which in most cases appears in later years, so that we can get a record over time.

The list of all TEs for fiscal 1994 has fifty-one items totaling $478 billion.[126] This sum amounted to an impressive 42 percent of the fiscal 1993 total of all federal receipts![127] All TE items cannot be discussed here, of course. Our more limited purpose is chiefly to illustrate briefly and selectively the career of a representative and economically significant group of TEs over time.[128] The group will indicate, it is hoped, how this form of administrative management works and how in its totality it impacts people and resource allocation in major ways.

Table 3.1 shows the totals for the chosen items for each selected year. Strictly speaking, totaling is risky because of the interrelationships among the estimated components. Changes in some TEs could cause concurrent alteration in others.[129] But allowing for strict nonadditivity, the aggregate picture is approximately satisfactory.

This record in current dollars can be deceptive, however. If the totals are adjusted for price change, using the gross domestic product deflator (1987 = 100), we get, in billions of constant dollars for the TE totals,

1970	79.4
1976	105.4
1983	227.2
1988	210.6
1993	250.7

This more appropriate record looks rather different. The rise in the seventies is but moderately strong since it is lessened by an almost 7 percent yearly rise in the deflator: the real TE rise is 4.8 percent annually. From 1976 to 1983 the jump is very great at 11.6 percent a year despite an even higher inflation rate than obtained in the preceding period.

Table 3.1

Federal Tax Expenditures, Selected Fiscal Years (millions of current dollars)

Type of tax expenditure	1970	1976	1983	1988	1993
Investment credit	2,630	9,495	21,245	9,150	3,130
Accelerated depreciation on machinery and equipment	NA	NA	10,920	23,700	19,505
Exclusion of interest on life insurance savings	1,050	1,655	4,335	5,410	10,460
Exclusion of pension contributions	3,310	8,350	56,900	54,655	82,470
Excess of percentage over cost depletion, oil and gas	1,470	1,295	1,280	NA	1,450
Deduction of mortgage interest and property taxes on owner-occupied homes	5,400	8,900	28,810	43,775	58,245
Exemption of interest on state and local debt	2,200	4,365	9,080	10,350	14,505
Deductibility of nonbusiness state and local taxes (excluding owner-occupied homes)	3,842	7,255	18,070	17,250	25,300
Deductibility for medical care	3,150	6,805	18,685	26,650	60,715
Exclusion of Social Security benefits*	1,454	3,700	19,120	17,360	23,390
Deductibility of charitable contributions*	3,450	3,285	9,635	10,515	12,470
TOTAL	27,956	55,105	198,080	218,815	311,640

Sources and Methods: Statistical Abstract, 1993, p. 334, No. 515, 1993.
* Calculated assuming TE/taxes in 1976 apply to 1970.

The mid-eighties, spanning the years that saw the elimination of some major TEs under the Tax Reform Act of 1986,[130] exhibits an absolute fall in spite of a big drop in the inflation rate to less than 4 percent annually. The real total TE decline can even be detected by scanning some of the current dollar totals in particular items in the table. For the five-year span after 1988, despite continued mild inflation, the rise in real TEs is moderated to about 3.5 percent annually. Nevertheless, the sample of tax preferences in the table, which in current dollars totaled about 15 percent of all federal receipts in 1970, had risen to about 27 percent in 1993. Hence, this particular vehicle for intended direction of economic conditions and behavior had expanded notably.

The particular spheres targeted for administrative management through TEs can be sampled and scrutinized by glancing at the list in the table. The investment tax credit, which was gradually phased out, was for new, short-lived business equipment, and was intended to stimulate the economy partly by reducing the cost of capital.[131] The same basic objective was to be implemented by the tax code provision for accelerated capital consumption allowances on machinery and other producers' durable equipment under the Economic Recovery Tax Act of 1981. This was nothing new because a similar accelerated depreciation measure, along with restoration of a 7 percent investment credit, had been instituted in 1971. It was hoped that the investment credit and depreciation concessions would help cope with the severe stagnation of the economy that had begun in 1969 (and lasted until 1993) with a brief respite from 1983 to 1988. The policy goal was economic expansion by favoring more resources for business investment.

The concession for oil and gas depletion speaks clearly for itself as a form of indirect subsidy for that particular industry. Related to the subsidy stimulus, it was expected that petroleum reserves would increase. After pointing out that the depletion allowance was reduced from 27.5 to 22 percent in the Tax Reform Act of 1969, Brookings economists Joseph Pechman and Benjamin Okner commented in 1972 that

> These preferences have been justified . . . on national defense grounds and on the grounds that there are special risks involved in locating and developing natural resources. Economists have generally concluded that the generous provisions lead to overinvestment in the preferred industries and hence tend to result in a serious misallocation of resources.[132]

The point being stressed here is not whether this TE results in misallocation of resources, but simply that it was designed to influence allocation and that a related objective was national defense.

Pechman and Okner also comment on another TE item in Table 3.1: the exclusion of interest on life insurance savings. "This tax incentive and relief from a personal pecuniary burden favors . . . savings invested by individuals in life insurance . . . because interest accumulated on policy reserves is not taxable to the policyholder, while the insurance proceeds are not taxable to the beneficiaries after the death of the insured."[133] Thus this TE, which in price-deflated

measures grew a vigorous 4.6 percent annually between 1970 and 1993, subsidized the insurance industry, relieves individuals who take out life insurance, favors one type of property income, and encourages holding savings in insurance rather than in other forms like bank deposits, bonds, stocks, or mutual funds. The encouragement of savings in any way has the implicit orthodox rationale that savings get invested, and investment is unmitigatedly beneficial to the economy and society.

The deductibility of charitable contributions is designed to bolster non-educational, philanthropic institutions. That TE in the table we are examining was approximately a constant in price-deflated terms over the years covered. In this favored part of the nonprofit sector of the economy, religious institutions particularly score because over half of all private philanthropy funds typically go to their activities. Church and state are conjoined, with the state budget automatically reduced whenever individuals choose to give more to the church.

The distributive effects of this TE are worth noting. One analyst argues that these effects, which violate equity principles, "simply . . . grew up that way without the government or philanthropy really thinking through its implications."[134] The same analytical authority constructs an ironic distributive scenario about the TE on the assumption that the deduction is translated into a direct expenditure program. He thus employs the outlay equivalent approach. He first establishes a governmental Division of Charitable and Educational Assistance. His scenario (in part) then follows:

> Suppose a person calls and says: I am too poor to pay an income tax but I am contributing $15 to my favorite charity. Will the Government also help it? The answer here will be: We appreciate your sacrifice but we cannot use our funds in this situation.
>
> Suppose a person calls and says: I am quite well-off and want to send a check for $3000 to one of my favorite charities. Will the Government also aid it? The answer here will be: We are delighted to be of assistance and are at once sending a Government check for $7000 to that charity.
>
> Suppose a person calls and says: I am really very wealthy with a considerable fortune in various stocks that originally cost me or my family very little. In fact, I will be selling about $2 million of stock to pay my income tax this year and to raise cash for other purposes as well. I think that a particular charitable institution deserves support and while I have decided not to contribute anything myself, I am calling to inquire whether the Government will contribute to it. The answer here will be: We understand the situation and will be delighted to contribute $2 million to that institution. We will of course say it is in your name. And, in appreciation of your suggesting this to us, we are sending you a check for $100,000, tax-exempt of course.[135]

The hypothetical scenario reveals that savings fare well under this TE. And again, when savings and equity clash, savings wins. Thinking through implications is hardly necessary. It is appropriate to add that, while the well-to-do make the bulk of the charitable contributions, they hardly contribute in proportion to their incomes.[136]

The deductions allowed for both mortgage interest (estimated at $48 billion in fiscal 1994) and property taxes ($14 billion) on owner-occupied homes, together with the failure to tax imputed net rent on those homes, clearly are designed to encourage the channeling of resources into the home-building industry. On the all-American ideological level as we have previously noted, a nation of home-owners is a goal on a par with a world of family farmers (who are presumed to be farm owners). Tax expenditure policy serves the farmer ideology, just as direct expenditure policy in the form of farm income-support outlays are supposed to serve the latter. The social benefits of both policies are presumed to more than compensate for any costs connected with the induced resource shifts that are presumed.

We are here concerned mainly to discover such policy goals of TEs, not to explore the effectiveness with which the goals are achieved. However, in view of the enormity of the TE totals in this case, it is tempting to look at the question of effectiveness, if only briefly. The answer seems to be that the TEs have not induced impressive results. Rather, the general career of home ownership seems to have been primarily responsive to the changing vigor of the economy's performance. For example, the proportion of owner-occupied housing units rose over the long run in tandem with the secular rise in real per capita income.

Some 46 percent of all occupied home units were owned in 1920; seventy years later the proportion was about 64 percent.[137] This change amounts to a yearly increase rate of 0.63 percent in the proportion. Shorter period rate changes are revealing of the impact of the economy's performance, given this long-run yearly figure. For example, the ownership proportion rose moderately in the moderately prosperous twenties, before the federal income tax concessions could have had much effect. In the following depression decade the proportion fell absolutely, undoubtedly because of the economy's decline and stagnation. As a consequence, the ownership proportion was absolutely lower in 1940 than it had been twenty years earlier. The depression effect swamped the long-run impact of an annual rise in real per capita income of 1.4 percent during those two decades.

In the 1940s the economy zoomed because of the war, and the ownership proportion also zoomed, from 44 percent to 55 percent. Economic performance scored again. After the war, in the period of strong growth in real GDP at 3.6 percent annually up to 1970, the ownership proportion again jumped upwards to 63 percent in that year. Could this have been due to the relevant federal TEs? It is doubtful, as indicated by the record of the next two decades: while the sum of the price-deflated TEs for the two components of the home ownership tax concessions grew at a strong 5 percent annually, the ownership proportion of all housing units rose only from 62.9 to 64.2 percent; and indeed, it was constant in the eighties. Such a sluggish rise is readily attributable to the drop in the real GDP rate of increase to only 2.9 percent a year between 1970 and 1990. Whatever the economic effects of the pro-ownership TEs might be, they would seem to obtain in other areas.

Partiality toward home ownership in the tax law is discrimination against renters. The latter group is generally on the lower rungs of the income distribution ladder. Therefore, the two deductions, together with exclusion of imputed rent from the income of home owners, are regressive. On this distributional issue, economist Joseph Pechman points out that "homeowner tax preferences provide little benefit to the poor, while housing allowances do," adding the distributional generalization that ". . . most tax credits help only families that pay taxes, while grants help all families."[138]

Wallace Peterson mobilizes the distributional evidence specifically on the mortgage interest deduction, which supports the regressivity interpretation of that TE.[139] Indeed, Peterson's cited evidence indicates that TEs addressed to individuals, as are the great bulk of TEs, are generally regressive.[140] This means that they favor savings over consumption.

Two TEs in Table 3.1 specify state and local government tax concessions. Both show federal partiality toward state and local governments' competition with it for funds, be they tax revenues or borrowings. This partiality represents by implication support for state and local governments' *uses* of the funds—for example, for education, public welfare, hospitals, social infrastructures (including utilities), employee retirement. In particular, as noted by two economists at Clark University, "the exemption of interest on state and local government securities . . . is in its essence a subsidy to state and local government capital formation."[141] They add a further comment on distributional aspects of that particular TE—that is, that the exemption "creates inequities in the federal income tax structure by both reducing the progressivity of the tax system—the vertical equity problems— . . . [and] reduc[ing] the horizontal equity of the tax; that is, it results in taxing people with the same incomes by different amounts."[142] The president of the United Steel Workers of America also testified at the same hearings the day before to the effect that estimates in 1972 showed "the super well-off enjoys 76% of the tax-free benefits gained by individuals who own state and local bonds."[143] The spillover effect is again a related partiality toward savers.

The table's remaining three backdoor expenditures, as Congressman Wilbur Mills once called TEs—that is, medical care, pension contributions, and Social Security benefits—account for about 54 percent of the 1993 total for all the selected items. This group in a loose sense differs somewhat from what may be called "tax incentive" TEs in other parts of the table. Tax incentive concessions, as may be gathered from the preceding discussion, are designed primarily to induce those favored to direct more resources into some particular economic activity. On this classification, related effects of the design are viewed as ancillary. The triad under immediate consideration, however, may be characterized as "designed to provide tax reduction in order to relieve misfortune or hardship—situations involving 'personal hardships,' as contrasted with . . . 'tax hardships.' "[144] Concessions for "tax hardships" are provided chiefly for business activities.[145]

The medical care TE is similar to household consumption of necessities because it relieves the personal individual hardship of deprivation connected with illness. The fact that it underwrites a decision to purchase health care, and therefore the greater use of medical resources, is ancillary to the individual hardship relief design of that TE. Most TEs have more than one effect, as has been shown. It would have been appropriate to use Surrey's classification in the previous discussion of home ownership: renting could be viewed as a personal deprivation in a society that worships ownership. The pro-ownership TE is therefore seen as providing a personal, nonrevenue incentive by the government that helps individuals avoid "renter hardship." Of course, there is some distinction here because home ownership lacks the more necessitous, quasi-involuntary feature of health care.

As for the remaining two exclusions, the design is similar to medical care. The exemption from taxable income of employer contributions to pension funds accomplishes chiefly an escape from the "hardships" of older age. Ancillary effects include an individual incentive to retire and support for the consumption patterns of the elderly.

The exclusion of Social Security benefits is clearly designed not as a tax incentive to direct resources or stimulate particular economic activities. Social Security is practically involuntary on the individual level for the great mass of the population, and primarily helps provide some escape from "misfortune and hardship" in the older years (or in the cases of involuntary unemployment).

A more complete appreciation of the TE managerial vehicle would require awareness of many areas necessarily omitted because of space and time constraints—for example, big, bypassed tax concessions by state and local governments; and at the federal level, international affairs; general science, space and technology; R&D support; community and regional development; credits for child and dependent care expenses; exclusion of the employer share of hospital insurance taxes; exclusion of workers' compensation benefits; and tax credits for corporate income from doing business in U.S. possessions. Clearly, public managerial supervision and direction through TEs penetrates very, very many departments of economic life and human day-to-day experience.

ERISA

As a coda to this record of selected administrative management illustrations, let us look briefly at one other quite significant intrusion by government into the private sector. This intrusion is known as ERISA, which is the acronym for the Employees Retirement Income Security Act of 1974. The act insinuated certain public policy stipulations into some of the existing voluntary, tax-advantaged, private pension and health benefit systems of employer-defined benefit plans.

These plans stemmed historically from the postwar growth of the World War II union-management fringe-benefit contracts originally designed to compensate labor for the restraints exacted by wartime wage ceilings. Additionally from the business side there was a desire to forestall and dampen general labor initiatives in these areas. Business also wanted, as the 1970s and 1980s unfolded, to deflect the gradually mounting threat of a universal national health system. So did the federal government. As the *New York Times* reported on May 19, 1992, "A major goal of President Bush's health policy is to expand the role of private insurance and to fend off demands for national health insurance financed by the government."[146]

Government intervention with respect to the pension and health varieties of welfare problems is clearly a venture into the important socioeconomic interrelationship between the welfare state and the private market's operation. In other words, such intervention shows at once the enormous overlap between "administrative management" and what is typically termed regulation. In the case of ERISA, the welfare areas involved fall under the special rubric of "social regulation."

The pension provisions of ERISA, like the health provision, are a case study in the compromising pattern of much public regulatory management: they tortuously express the ongoing conflict between socially decent objectives and heterogeneous private pecuniary maximization goals. The federal government became heavily involved, in a limited regulatory sense, in the muddle.

One of the purposes of ERISA was to make private pensions more certain for workers. A worker was said to be guaranteed a private pension when it was vested. Before ERISA, vesting and other benefit provisions were extremely uncertain and widely differing in magnitude. The simplest generalization was that private workers did not get pensions, even if the employer nominally had a plan.

After ERISA less than half of workers were covered by private pensions (one-third of women workers, half of men workers).[147] Of the one-half covered, only one-half were vested. So reform significantly improved the pension prospects of some while ignoring major social dilemmas, like more pensions for the relatively short-lived men and fewer pensions for the relatively long-lived women. Reversing this discrimination would, of course, be more expensive for the employers. It became employer practice after the act to vest covered workers, but only those with at least ten years of continuous service.

ERISA "guarantees that employees promised pension benefits after working for an employer a given number of years will actually be paid."[148] It requires funding and uniform fiduciary and disclosure standards for pensions but not health plans, and at least 50 percent survivors benefits.[149]

The government also became fiscally involved in the private pension network through the simultaneous establishment of the Pension Benefit Guarantee Corporation (PBGC), a self-financing, government agency that guarantees the payment of pensions even if the employer terminates the plan with insufficient funds.

PBGC clearly smacks of welfare statism. This additional fiscal involvement shows that ERISA forms an interventionist triad: administrative management, regulation, and the welfare state.

ERISA stipulated nothing about the dollar amounts of pensions or health benefits. No cost-of-living increases were assured by the act. Employers were permitted to cut back or end pension and/or health benefits without any government interference. Plans were often terminated without enough assets to cover benefit commitments. These gaps in ERISA were characterized as an "elaborate shell game" by Thomas B. Stoddard, a former executive director of the Lambda Legal Defense and Education Fund.[150] A defender of the regulatory gap, on the other hand, David G. Ball, assistant secretary of labor for pension and welfare benefits, declared that "employers don't have to offer benefits at all. An employer is much more likely to offer benefits if he has an opportunity to cut them back at a later date."[151]

One of the ugliest elements of the American welfare state is that security elements are tied to the type and behavior of employer. Some workers with responsible employers do have cradle-to-grave income and health security. Others have none. Under ERISA and PBGC an employer who pretends to be responsible and provides services for a time then defaults will leave the government to pay the employees pensions. Other employers who do not feign responsibility will leave employees with no government aid. The question is: Why should government aid needy potential pensioners according to the pretense of their past employer?

One task for federal administrative management is to deal with the relationship between the federal and state and local governments. ERISA did not want private employee benefit plans to be subjected to conflicting state stipulations. Thus, states were not permitted to require employers to help pay for their employees' insurance or to offer insurance at a minimum level. This is a fundamental break in the American tradition that only state governments regulate insurance. Also, they were not permitted to require all employers to offer insurance at some minimum level. Any state seeking to waive these two restrictions had to get special dispensation from Congress. Self-insured employer plans were exempt from state taxes on insurance premiums. In general, the act is punitive toward state initiative. It bars states from regulating the health plans of employers who self-insure. For example, it "effectively blocks many state health care reform programs, including Oregon's effort to require employers to cover their workers."[152] One of the major lobbying arguments generating this intragovernmental clash of social regulatory management was that large multistate business corporations insisted on the right to offer the same benefits to their employees in different states.

The health care commitment embodied in ERISA was but vaguely appreciated in 1974. Governmental legislative and management response to public agitation for pensions superseded and antedated a health care response, even such as

ERISA, in the regulation of private plans. There was no "Health Benefit Guarantee Corporation" accompanying PBGC. It took the buildup of health care agitation and the explosion of health care costs over the ensuing two decades to seriously challenge ERISA's woeful regulatory ineptitude in that sphere.

The smoldering incongruities of ERISA's health interventions finally surfaced eruptively twenty years after the act's passage. In a breakthrough essay in the *New York Times,*[153] it was revealed that the organization of the nation's state insurance commissioners had attacked ERISA for permitting employers to reduce or deny health benefit claims of ostensibly insured employees.

The commissioner's organization asserted that people with voluntary self-insured employer health plans had fewer protections than persons with conventional health insurance. It consequently called for revision of ERISA to allow state regulation preventing employers from "outrageous exclusions" and discontinuance of conventional group health insurance plans (which they already monitor) in favor of unregulated self-insurance. The trade association representing mostly Fortune 500 corporations countered with its standard contention that state regulations made no sense for multistate employers. Correct as this assertion might be, it left unresolved the crucial matter of needed reforms in ERISA. Whatever reforms eventuate from the conflict among the National Association of Insurance Commissioners, Fortune 500 representatives, the courts, the Labor Department's ERISA administration unit, and spokespersons for employees, government at various levels will no doubt continue to be deeply involved in monitoring the so-called private health and pension plans.

In this section of the survey of government growth in the mixed economy a limited sample of the expansion in administrative management since World War II has been reviewed. The review has taken us into a vast sphere of largely immeasurable public intervention that goes beyond the previously treated government activities as measured by such criteria as direct expenditures including direct subsidies, budgets, public employment or administrative agencies per se. The few selected managerial spheres that have thus been added to those more readily measured activities—consumer protection, environmental policies, housing supports, energy policy, transportation encouragement and surveillance, and tax expenditures—have conveyed an appreciation of the enormous extent of this additional type of government influence on the economy and society.

The main reasons for the augmented government sector and its institutionalized fusion with the reshaped market system have been specified in the preceding discussion. Those reasons were found in (1) population developments, (2) community demands for intervention, and (3) perceived changes in the functioning or malfunctioning of the market system.

A number of the chief specific governmental expansion spheres have also been highlighted. They are education, health, poverty, income security, national defense, crime control, public infrastructure, a good portion of administrative management affecting the economy and individual behavior patterns, and government operation itself. However, certain other spheres appear to be worthy of further examination: the peculiar American welfare state; the military element within the domestic economy; management through fiscal, and to a lesser extent, monetary policy; and some other areas of regulatory management. Additionally, the ever-enlarging role of international factors in the mixed economy's evolution needs scrutiny. These three areas of institutional change are uniquely significant for an adequate explanation and understanding of the government growth phenomenon.

Notes

1. Harold G. Vatter and John F. Walker, "Stagnation and Government Purchases," *Challenge* 35, no. 6 (November/December 1992), p. 56.
2. Calculated from *Economic Report of the President,* February 1996, p. 329, Table B-42.
3. Ibid.
4. Rates calculated from the *Statistical Abstract,* 1975, p. 111, No. 175.
5. Ibid., 1995, p. 109, No. 150.
6. Clarke Chambers, *Seedtime of Reform* (Minneapolis: University of Minnesota Press, 1963), p. 88.
7. Ibid., p. 7.
8. Cited in ibid., p. 10.
9. Ibid., pp. 11–12.
10. Roy Lubove, *The Struggle for Social Security, 1900–1935* (Cambridge, Mass.: Harvard University Press, 1968), pp. 85 and 221.
11. Cited in Peter A. Corning, *The Evolution of Medicare,* U.S. Department of Health, Education, and Welfare, Social Security Administration, Office of Research and Statistics (Washington: GPO, 1969), p. 89.
12. Cited in Theodore R. Marmor, *The Politics of Medicare* (Chicago: Aldine, 1973), p. 10.
13. Corning, *Evolution of Medicare,* p. 78.
14. See, for example, in this connection Richard Bartel, "Introduction," *Challenge* 36, no. 1 (January/February 1993), pp. 2–3.
15. The dilution campaign by business is discussed in Robert J. Samuelson, "R.I.P.: The Good Corporation," *Newsweek,* July 5, 1993, p. 41.
16. See A. Dale Tussing, *Poverty in a Dual Economy* (New York: St. Martin's, 1975). The same distinction is made in Michael Reagan's *The Managed Economy* (New York: Oxford University Press, 1963), p. 166.
17. Frances Fox Piven and Richard A. Cloward, *Regulating the Poor: The Functions of Public Welfare* (New York: Random House, Vintage Books, 1971), pp. 320–321.
18. James T. Patterson, *America's Struggle Against Poverty, 1900–1980* (Cambridge, Mass.: Harvard University Press, 1981), p. 168.
19. *The First Report of the Society for Bettering the Condition and Increasing the Comforts of the Poor* (London: W. Budmer and Co., for T. Becket, Bookseller, Pall-Mall, 1797), pp. i, iii.
20. *Economic Report of the President,* January 1964, p. 55.
21. *New York Times,* July 8, 1993, p. C18.
22. Steven Rathgeb Smith and Michael Lipsky, *Non-profits for Hire* (Cambridge: Mass.: Harvard University Press, 1993), p. 71.
23. Calculated from *Statistical Abstract,* 1991, p. 308, No. 502.

24. Ibid., p. 332, No. 537.

25. Calculated from *Statistical Abstract,* 1995, pp. 109, 151, and *Economic Report of the President,* February 1996, p. 371.

26. Philip A. Klein, "Economic Activity and the Public Sector: Is Small Beautiful?" *Journal of Economic Issues,* 14, no. 2 (June 1985), pp. 426–427.

27. Ibid., p. 427.

28. Fred C. Pampel and John B. Williamson, *Age, Class, Politics, and the Welfare State* (New York: Cambridge University Press, 1989).

29. Ibid., pp. 165, 166.

30. Ibid., p. 167.

31. James L. Clayton (ed.), *The Economic Impact of the Cold War* (New York: Harcourt, Brace & World, 1970), p. 3.

32. Carroll W. Pursell Jr., *The Military-Industrial Complex* (New York: Harper & Row, 1972), p. 8.

33. Ibid., p. 85.

34. Robert Higgs, *Crisis and Leviathan* (New York: Oxford University Press, 1987), pp. 212–215, *passim.*

35. Gregg Easterbrook, in *Portland Sunday Oregonian,* June 6, 1993, p. LC1.

36. This point is brought out in a work by Gary Mucciaroni, *The Political Failure of Employment Policy, 1945–1982* (Pittsburgh: University of Pittsburgh Press, 1990), as reported in a review of it by Robert R. Keller, *Journal of Economic History* 53, no. 2 (June 1993), p. 455.

37. The quoted succulent phrase is James O'Toole's, cited in Mortimer J. Adler, *Haves Without Have-Nots* (New York: Macmillan, 1991), p. 60.

38. All data are from various issues of the U.S. *Statistical Abstract.*

39. The rate estimates are terminated in 1989 to avoid possibly exaggerated long-run implications should 1990 be the terminal date used. FDIC personnel, a small agency, jumped from 9,031 in 1989 to 17,641 the next year, no doubt because of the insurance crisis in the thrift industry.

40. *Statistical Abstract,* 1995, p. 337, No. 522; and p. 343, No. 530.

41. Wallace C. Peterson, *Transfer Spending, Taxes, and the American Welfare State* (Boston: Kluwer Academic Press, 1991), p. 76.

42. All data used in this paragraph are from the *Statistical Abstract,* 1979, Sections 6 and 9.

43. *Statistical Astract,* 1992, p. 188, No. 304.

44. Attorney General of the United States, *Annual Report,* 1974, p. 161.

45. *Statistical Abstract,* 1992, p. 198, No. 331.

46. *Statistical Abstract,* 1994, p. 216, No. 342.

47. "Drugs, Crime and Punishment," *New York Times,* July 8, 1993, p. A13. The statistic is cited in an Op-Ed article by Jack B. Weinstein, a judge in Federal District Court in Brooklyn, New York.

48. Cited by Pete Carey and Steve Johnson (Knight-Ridder News Service), *Portland Oregonian,* June 27, 1993, p. A5.

49. Francis X. Clines, *New York Times,* May 28, 1993, pp. A1, B16.

50. Ibid., p. B16.

51. *New York Times,* July 27, 1993, p. A6.

52. *Statistical Abstract,* 1980, p. 193, No. 326.

53. Ibid., p. 181, Figure 6.3.

54. "Judges Set Crooks Free," *New York Times,* July 8, 1993, p. A13.

55. The $74 billion estimate is from Drug Policy Foundation, *Drug Policy Letter,* No. 19, June/July 1993, p. 3.

56. See in this connection the seminal work of this title by Reagan, *Managed Economy*, especially chap. 8.

57. See the article by Matthew Wald, *New York Times,* August 6, 1993, p. A8.

58. Christine Ammer and Dean S. Ammer, *Dictionary of Business and Economics* (New York: The Free Press, 1986), pp. 100–101.

59. These books (except *The Jungle*) are cited with similar interpretive object in Ansel M. Sharp, Charles A. Register, and Richard H. Leftwich, *Economics of Social Issues,* 8th ed. (Plano, Tex: Business Publications, 1988), p. 196.

60. Douglass C. North and Roger LeRoy Miller, *The Economics of Public Issues,* 6th ed. (New York: Harper & Row, 1983), p. 24.

61. William E. Leuchtenburg, *Franklin D. Roosevelt and the New Deal, 1932–1940* (New York: Harper & Row, 1963), p. 88.

62. Ibid., p. 88, n. 72.

63. David Cohen, "The Public-Interest Movement and Citizen Participation," in Stuart Langton (ed.), *Citizen Participation in America* (Lexington, Mass.: D.C. Heath, 1978), p. 58.

64. Jeffrey M. Berry, *The Interest Group Society* (Boston: Little, Brown, 1984), chap. 2, pp. 16–45.

65. Ibid., pp. 29, 23.

66. North and Miller, *Economics of Public Issues,* pp. 56–57.

67. Stewart M. Lee and Mel J. Zelenak, *Personal Finance for Consumers* (Columbus, Ohio: Publishing Horizons, 1987), pp. 440–441.

68. Louis M. Kohlmeier Jr., *The Regulators* (New York: Harper & Row, 1969), p. 13.

69. Barry Checkoway and Jon Van Til, "What Do We Know About Citizen Participation?" in Stuart Langton (ed.),*Citizen Participation in America* (Lexington, Mass.: D.C. Heath, 1978), p. 33.

70. *New York Times,* April 11, 1991, p. A10.

71. *Public Citizen,* July/August 1993, p. 11.

72. Federal civilian employment other than the Defense Department and Postal Service declined slightly between 1980 and 1988, whereas the armed forces rose by 4 percent and Defense Department employment by 9 percent.

73. *Public Citizen, 1984 Year in Review,* p. 23.

74. Ibid. The Department of Health and Human Services, within which FDA is a division, had a staff of 156,000 when Reagan was elected and 123,000 in 1988.

75. Lee and Zelenak, *Personal Finance,* p. 438.

76. *New York Times,* August 26, 1993, p. A1.

77. See the discussion of the urban aspects in Charles N. Glaab and A. Theodore Brown, *A History of Urban America* (New York: Macmillan, 1967), pp. 87–90, 97, 178–180.

78. Edwin S. Mills, *The Economics of Environmental Quality* (New York: W.W. Norton, 1978), pp. 184, 186, 191.

79. Ibid., p. 184.

80. This legislation list is drawn chiefly from ibid., pp. 184–199.

81. Ibid., p. 183.

82. Ibid., p. 219.

83. See the summary discussion "A New Era Unfolds," by Lester R. Brown, *Challenge* 36, no. 3 (May/June 1993), pp. 37–46.

84. In the 72nd Congress, 1931–33, the Democrats had a House majority of 220, with 214 Republicans (but some had publicly bolted); the Republicans had a Senate majority of 48, with 47 Democrats.

85. Dixon Wecter, *The Age of the Great Depression, 1929–1941* (New York: Macmillan, 1948), p. 49.

86. Mei Kohn, *Money, Banking, and Financial Markets,* 2nd ed. (New York: Dryden Press, 1993), p. 406.

87. On this ingenious technique, see Congress of the United States, Congressional Budget Office, *The Federal Home Loan Banks in the Housing Finance System,* July 1993, pp. 3–4.

88. *Statistical Abstract,* 1995, p. 339, No. 523.

89. Harry M. Trebing, "Realism and Relevance in Public Utility Regulation," *Journal of Economic Issues,* 8, no. 2 (June 1974), pp. 212–213.

90. Franklin Tugwell, *The Energy Crisis and the American Political Economy* (Stanford, Calif.: Stanford University Press, 1988), p. 166.

91. Mark W. Nadel, *Corporations and Political Accountability* (Lexington, Mass.: D.C. Heath, 1976), p. 152.

92. Tugwell, *Energy Crisis,* p. 35.

93. Trebing, "Realism and Relevance," p. 213.

94. Ibid.

95. Louis M. Kohlmeier Jr., *The Regulators* (New York: Harper & Row, 1969), p. 188.

96. Ibid. The 1938 measure was called the Natural Gas Act.

97. John C. Sawhill and Richard Cotton (eds.), *Energy Conservation Successes and Failures* (Washington: Brookings Institution, 1986), p. 207.

98. Ibid.

99. See also the trends review in U.S., DOE, Energy Information Administration, *Annual Energy Review 1990,* pp. 3–6.

100. *New York Times,* October 22, 1993, p. A11.

101. Barry Meier, "Breaking Down an Arms Buildup," *New York Times,* October 15, 1993, p. C1.

102. Tugwell, *Energy Crisis,* p. 91.

103. *Statistical Abstract,* 1994, p. 585, No. 920; and 1995, p. 588, No. 935.

104. William A. Vogely, "Federal Government Energy Organization," in Robert J. Kalter and William A. Vogely (eds.), *Energy Supply and Government Policy* (Ithaca: Cornell University Press, 1976), p. 307.

105. U.S. Congress, Congressional Budget Office, *How Federal Spending for Infrastructure and Other Public Investments Affects the Economy,* July 1991, p. 14, Table 1.

106. *Economic Report of the President,* February 1975, p. 153.

107. See Joseph R. Daughen and Peter Binzen, *The Wreck of the Penn Central* (New York: New American Library, 1973).

108. Alexander L. Morton, "How to Revive the Railroads," *Challenge,* 17, no. 6 (November/December 1974), p. 32.

109. National Transportation Policy Study Commission, *National Transportation Policies Through the Year 2000,* Final Report (Washington: GPO, June 1979), p. 181.

110. Ibid., pp. 181–182.

111. *Condé Nast Traveler,* December 1993, p. 27.

112. American Public Transit Association, *1992 Transit Fact Book.*

113. Calculated from 1992 *Statistical Abstract,* p. 281, No. 452, applying the government purchases implicit GOP deflator.

114. U.S. Congress, Congressional Budget Office, *New Directions for the Nation's Public Works,* September 1988, p. 29.

115. *New York Times,* December 2, 1993, p. A11.

116. Mansel G. Blackford and K. Austin Kerr, *Business Enterprise in American History,* 3rd ed. (Boston: Houghton Mifflin, 1994), p. 376.

117. *Statistical Abstract,* 1993, p. 635, No. 1056; and *New York Times,* November 23, 1993, p. C23.

118. Paul W. Bauer and Ian Gale, "Airline Deregulation: Is It Time to Finish the Job?" in Federal Reserve Bank of Cleveland, *Economic Commentary,* September 1, 1993, p. 1.

119. Ibid.

120. *New York Times,* January 6, 1994, p. A10.

121. Clifford Winston, "Economic Deregulation: Days of Reckoning for Microeconomists," *Journal of Economic Literature,* 31 (September 1993), p. 1264.

122. Calculations drawn from the *Statistical Abstract,* 1992, p. 281, No. 452.

123. The immediately following points are taken from a letter by Clifford Winston, Senior Fellow, Brookings Institution, to the *New York Times,* January 16, 1989, p. A12.

124. See Myron E. Ullman 3rd, *New York Times,* December 9, 1993, p. A23.

125. Wallace C. Peterson, *Transfer Spending Taxes and the American Welfare State* (Norwell, Mass.: Kluwer Academic Publishers, 1991), p. 61. Peterson's discussion is one of the best summaries available (pp. 57–92).

126. *Statistical Abstract of the United States* (Washington, D.C.: U.S. Department of Commerce, 1993), p. 334, Table 515.

127. Ibid.

128. Peterson, *Transfer Spending Taxes,* p. 76.

129. See ibid., pp. 76, 78.

130. Ibid., p. 71.

131. *Economic Report of the President,* 1993, p. 274.

132 "Individual Income Tax Erosion by Income Classes," in U.S. Congress, Joint Economic Committee, *The Economics of Federal Subsidy Programs,* Part 1—General Study Papers, May 8, 1972 (Washington: GPO, 1972), p. 18.

133. Ibid.

134. Statement of Stanley S. Surrey, professor of Law, Harvard University, in U.S. Congress, Joint Economic Committee, Subcommittee on Priorities and Economy in Government, *Hearings,* January 14, 1972 (Washington: GPO, 1972), p. 52.

135. Ibid.

136. See, e.g., *Statistical Abstract,* 1995, p. 393, No. 620.

137. The proportions and the ones following are from the *Statistical Abstract* for 1993, p. 724, No. 1235.

138. "Tax Expenditures," in the Brookings Institution, *Setting National Priorities: The 1979 Budget* (Washington: GPO, 1978), pp. 316, 318.

139. Peterson, *Transfer Spending Taxes,* pp. 87–89.

140. Ibid., pp. 83–87, *passim.*

141. Statement of Attiat F. Ott and David J. Ott, in U.S. Congress, Joint Economic Committee, *Hearings on Tax Subsidies and Tax Reform,* July 20, 1972 (Washington: GPO, 1972), p. 114.

142. Ibid.

143. Ibid., July 19, 1972, p. 68.

144. This rather useful classification is offered by Stanley S. Surrey in his study paper for *The Economics of Federal Subsidy Programs,* Part 1, pp. 80–81.

145. Ibid.

146. *New York Times,* May 19, 1992, p. A8.

147. Stephen Crystal, *America's Old Age Crisis* (New York: Basic Books, 1982), p. 117.

148. Robert N. Butler, *Why Survive?* (New York: Harper & Row, 1975), p. 61.

149. Ibid., pp. 61–62.

150. *New York Times,* June 19, 1992, p. A8.

151. Ibid.

152. *The Oregonian,* September 25, 1994, p. B5.

153. Robert Pear, *New York Times,* September 21, 1994, p. A16.

CHAPTER FOUR

Fiscal Policy and Government Growth

Fiscal policy is the purposeful manipulation of the elements of the public budget—spending, taxing, and borrowing—to ameliorate business cycles and change rates of economic growth and unemployment. Increases in welfare and public works programs during severe economic contractions had been practiced for centuries. But classical economic theory taught that if left alone, the economy would automatically return to full employment and produce good economic growth.

The Great Depression did serious damage to the glorious harmony doctrines of classical economics. The fall in output was too large and the return to full employment was too slow for any decent society to accept with a simple nod to laissez-faire. Economists in many countries began to rewrite their equilibrium models to explain less than full employment equilibria and slow responses of and to market signals. The new economics that resulted has come to be called Keynesian economics, after the great English economist who produced a theoretical model that encouraged debate, discussion, and policy toward government manipulation of the economy without significantly changing the nature of the private property, private enterprise system. Fiscal policy is the name for such policies.

The Origins of American Fiscal Policy

Fiscal policy strictly defined attempts to change the short-period or intermediate-period behavior of the economy with the mildest of tools: increases in government spending to increase the work of government suppliers and employees, and tax cuts to increase the spendable income of the workers and the investable funds of businesses. Much of the increase in spending, consumption, and investment, as well as government purchases, would be financed by government borrowing.

When Keynes used the term "fiscal policy" in his book, he was referring to the idea that the tax system affects the distribution of income, which in turn probably affects the rate of saving and the choice of the government to save for capital expenditures or borrow for them.[1]

In the economic journal literature, the first two articles with the term fiscal policy in their titles appeared in the *Papers and Proceedings of the American Economic Review* for March 1938. They were papers given at the annual convention of economists held at the end of 1937. It was acknowledged that Keynes's book *The General Theory of Employment, Interest and Money* was the source of interest in the question: Could government budget policy affect total output?

The acceptance of Keynes's ideas within the United States was reasonably quick but quite turbulent. Alvin Hansen, who came to be known as the American Keynes, wrote a very critical review of *The General Theory,* which includes the following observation

> Mr. Keynes says (in a review of Hobson's *Gold Prices and Wages*): "One comes to a new book by Mr. Hobson with mixed feelings, in hope of some stimulating ideas and of some fruitful criticisms of orthodoxy from an independent and individual standpoint, but expectant also of much sophistry, misunderstanding and perverse thought.... The book is ... made much worse than a really stupid book could be, by exactly those characteristics of cleverness and intermittent reasonableness which have borne good fruit in the past." This characterization by Mr. Keynes himself is not altogether inapplicable, some may perhaps say, to his own book. (ellipsis in the original)[2]

Hansen thought well enough of this criticism to reprint it as the first chapter of his next book, *Full Recovery or Stagnation.*[3] However, that book includes discussion of one of the breakthrough ideas of Keynesian economics: government expenditures can create income. In the classical world of full employment, the only way government can get resources is to take them from the private sector. So an increase in government must be financed by reductions in either consumption or investment. But with unemployment, the government can hire the unemployed resources (both labor and capital) and use them to produce output that otherwise would not exist. However, Hansen still had virtually no discussion of fiscal policy, with only one reference in the index.

At the 1937 convention of the American Economic Association, Arthur Gayer of Columbia University presented data on "federal net income-increasing expenditures" and a detailed explanation of how they were calculated.[4]

> The term "income-increasing" used here in reference to any given transaction means that the money changing hands is either itself a payment for current output, or that the nature of the transaction implies that the money will be used as payment for current output in the near future. ... To say that a transaction is income-decreasing means that the volume of spending on current output is less than it would have been had the transaction not taken place. [5]

In general, tax receipts were treated as income-decreasing since the taxes reduced private activity. An exception was estate tax collections that were assumed to be financed out of the general liquidity of the estates, which like most holders of wealth during the Depression were very liquid. He noted that the assumption would not be correct in an expansion when estates and other wealth holders are less liquid. Most expenditures were considered income creating, but debt retirement was not. Since tax receipts tend to be lumped around the quarterly payment dates, Gayer assumed that the effects would be spread roughly evenly over the year. This is a very early attempt at accrual accounting.

Although the details of Gayer's analysis have been substantially modified by later work, his conclusion stands as correct today as it was in 1937, "From the discussion above it should be clear that any coincidence of the income-increasing deficit and the reported deficit is purely accidental. . . . It is the 'income-increasing deficit' and not the reported deficit which measures the direct impact of federal fiscal policy upon the economic situation."[6] This conclusion has led to continual research and substantial innovation in federal budgeting. There have been several budgets devised to measure the direct impact of federal fiscal policy on the economic situation. Some of these will be discussed below.

The prolific Alvin Hansen was becoming ever more Keynesian. His next book, *Fiscal Policy and Business Cycles,* is almost purely Keynesian.[7] However, Hansen more thoroughly developed the long-run aspects of the theory:

> The high savings economy, barring government intervention, can escape a fall in income and employment only through the continuous development of new outlets for capital expenditures. As far as private investment outlets are concerned, this requires continuous technological progress, the rise of new industries, the discovery of new resources, the growth of population, or a combination of several or all of these developments.[8]

This is a brief statement of the long-run secular stagnation problem that Hansen believed afflicted the developed capitalist economies. It was a recurring theme in his books and articles which led to an intense debate with William Fellner, who believed a largely private capitalism had a more sanguine future.

In the two books already cited Hansen quite completely kills the then popular notion of "pump priming." The conventional belief was that the capitalist economy was essentially benign and would normally act efficiently and at or near full employment. However, when a depression occurred it was a proper role of the federal government to restart the investment pump of capitalism by priming it with a shot of government spending. Then as the private market took off, the pump-priming spending could end and the private expansion would absorb the resources released by the government.

Hansen showed that when the pump-priming expenditures ended, the jobs they created ended with them. He explained that the bigger the government got, the harder it would be to cut it back, because so many jobs and so much income

Table 4.1

GNP, Annual Change in GNP, and Annual Federal Net Income-Increasing Expenditures, 1931–38 (billions of dollars)

Year	(1) GNP	(2) FNP change from previous year	(3) Net federal income- increasing expenditures	2/3 ratio
1930	90.4	−12.7	0.3	—
1931	75.8	−14.6	1.7	—
1932	58.0	−17.8	1.6	—
1933	55.6	−2.4	2.4	1.9
1934	65.1	9.5	3.2	.34
1935	72.2	7.1	3.1	.44
1936	82.5	10.3	4.0	.39
1937	90.4	7.9	0.9	.11
1938	84.7	−5.7	5.7	NA

Sources: Economic Report of the President, 1970, p. 177; Arthur D. Gayer, "Fiscal Policies," *Papers and Proceedings of the American Economic Association*, March 1938, p. 107.

would be lost. The bigger the government cutback, the less likely investment was to expand. Cuts in government spending are lost income to the recipients of that spending. As their income goes down, so does their investment and consumption. With total spending falling, there is no need to invest, since the existing capacity can produced more output than the economy currently demands. *In such a world, government spending and private investment are complements—things that go together rather than substitutes for each other, as the classical economists argued.*

The experience that led to many of the above observations was the severe business contraction of 1937–38. From 1932–33 to 1937 the real economy had expanded very substantially, clearly led by government action, although also helped by private investment. Table 4.1 is a crude demonstration of what was happening.

In the years 1930–33 when the GNP was falling, the federal budget was attempting to expand the economy, but the private and state and local government forces for collapse were overwhelming it. Finally, after the trough in 1933, the economy expanded at a 12.9 percent annual rate through calendar 1937 then contracted again. In the first three expansion years, federal net income-increasing expenditures averaged over 39 percent of all the increase. Gayer's numbers are net expenditures; there is no multiplier applied to them. (Multipliers describe the multiplication of total spending caused by an increase in a particular spending stream.) If there is anything to multiplier analysis, and it was then taken very seriously, most of the expansion of 1933–36 was caused by the federal government. Although the expansion rate was good, the income level was weak. The 1936 GNP was barely 80 percent of the 1929 level.

The conventional wisdom of earlier times was pressing on the minds of the political leadership and the more conservative members of the economics profession. The federal government had run large deficits since 1930. President Roosevelt had campaigned for a balanced budget. The drop in the net federal income-increasing expenditures from 1936 to 1937, shown in Table 4.1, was caused by a small absolute decrease in federal expenditures and a large increase in federal taxes clearly aimed at balancing the budget. The result, of course, was that the private expenditures supported by the public spending collapsed and the economy had another recession within the Great Depression. However, the measured deficit (a meaningless number) fell.

Hansen carefully analyzed the recession of 1937–38. He concluded that many normal forces typical of a market economy were at work to cause it, such as a classic inventory cycle and excessive swings in the stock market from optimism to pessimism and back.[9] Still he concluded that

> if a bold program of federal expenditures had been undertaken in September, 1937, when danger signals were sufficiently in evidence, the precipitous stock market crash of October could have been largely averted, and the recovery pushed forward after a moderate and wholesome (in terms of the cost-price situation) setback.[10]

Hansen concluded that the New Deal had never been extensive enough to end the depression. He divided fiscal policy into two categories: salvaging programs and programs for positive expansion.

Salvaging programs are the programs necessary for the relief of suffering and to increase the rate of economic activity to a level where private investment again makes some sense. From 1929 to 1933 the output of the country halved. But the labor force grew and the capital stock hardly changed. All of the resources for the 1929 output of 103 billion existed in 1933 when GNP was 55. Obviously very little investment would be needed until demand increased substantially. As Hansen observed, "a deep depression requires vast salvaging expenditures before a vigorous expansion process can develop."[11]

On the tax side, Hansen was strongly opposed to the expansion of federal, and particularly state and local, government taxes on consumption. The logic is simple. Taxes on consumption directly reduce private demand. When the governments spend the taxes, that in no way increases total demand; it merely shifts it from the private to the public sector. Taxes on wealth and income may be partially paid with wealth or savings reductions, and consequently when the tax receipts are spent there is a small net demand increase.

E. Cary Brown, one of Hansen's many prominent students, produced the most authoritative statement about federal fiscal policy in the 1930s.[12] Brown's conclusions reaffirmed Hansen: "In brief, then, it took the massive expenditures forced on the nation by the second world war to realize the full potentialities of fiscal policy. Until then, the record fails to show its effective use as a recovery measure. Indeed, the general expansionary policy seems stronger in the early part than in the later part of the decade."[13] Unfortunately, Brown did not address the efficacy of the salvaging expenditures—that is, how much better or worse would the Depression have been without government relief programs? Brown's method parallels that of Gayer, but is twenty years more advanced in its ability to estimate the effects of spending and tax changes on the total level of activity. Like Gayer, the appendix to the article explaining the methodology is almost as long as the article itself.

Most discussants of the impact of fiscal policy debate the effects of different types of public expenditures on the propensity to consume (a change in consumption as a proportion of a change in income) and by implication on the multiplier. Keynes clearly thought the rich saved higher proportions of their income than the poor, so spending on the poor would be promptly and more completely respent by them. Hansen thought public works would be more expansionary than welfare because, although payments of small amounts to many destitute people would be promptly spent again to many small retailers and landlords, the next round of spending after the welfare recipients' would be small, since they all had excess capacity and could absorb the small increases in spending within their current operations. A similar amount of spending on public works would represent a much larger proportion of total receipts to contractors and would thus more likely push them to invest and hire more. Brown discusses these notions but can find no strong evidence to support one kind of spending over another.

Debates over the differential expansion or relief effects of different federal government spending programs continue to this day. Much has been recently written about whether defense spending expands the economy more or less than other kinds of government spending. By 1941, factors identified that might affect the efficacy of fiscal policy included the types, amounts, and duration of spending and taxing; the level of economic activity or the phase of the business cycle; and which individuals and groups received the government benefits. There was no discussion of long-run growth other than Hansen's.

If fiscal policy is defined as budgeting purposefully aimed at salvaging or expansion, the World War II expenditures were not fiscal policy. The goal of the spending was destruction of the enemy, not employment of the domestic population. It can be said, as Brown did, that the war expenditures clearly expanded the economy. But war had been a well-demonstrated expansionary phenomenon since at least the Napoleonic wars. The invention of fiscal policy in the 1930s was aimed directly at using the public budget as a tool to induce economic recovery through salvaging the wasted resources of unemployed workers, underutilization of capital, and the reestablishment of reasonable rates of expansion toward some high level of resource use.

An extension of the time period reference of the notion of fiscal policy was to recognize that simple pump priming was not adequate. The pump of capitalism required continual additional priming to maintain adequate growth rates over the long run, as Hansen argued. A further extension of the notion is that fiscal policy could restrain demand and thus fight inflation. Most principles of economics textbooks describe an inflationary gap, where total demand exceeds total potential output. In such cases it is said that taxes should be increased to cut private demand and government spending reduced to lower public demand. With total demand down, general price increases should be eliminated. With taxes up and spending down, the government might also run a surplus; however, it should not use the surplus to retire the national debt. Since the goal of the surplus is to reduce demand, retiring debt would cause the private economy to exchange bonds for money, which would be likely to increase private spending, the opposite of the goal. Because of this peculiarity, national debt in an anti-inflationary fiscal policy world is a ratchet. There are reasons for it to rise but no reasons for it to fall.

The Struggle for Political Acceptance

Two major endorsements of fiscal policy added to the acceptance of the notion of the federal government's responsibility for the performance of the economy: the Employment Act of 1946 and the publication of the report *Taxes and the Budget* by the Committee for Economic Development (CED) in 1947.[14] The CED advocated deficits in years of weak economic performance and adoption of the cash budget as a measure of the government's effect on the economy. The Employment Act adopted as a policy goal for the federal government the achievement of "maximum employment and purchasing power." As Herbert Stein observed,

> The Employment Act did not create a new American fiscal policy. It and the debate which preceded its enactment confirmed the policy which existed. It recognized the expectation that federal fiscal policy should be used in an attempt to maintain high employment, but high employment is not the only goal of fiscal policy, and fiscal policy is not the only means to high employment.[15]

Stein clearly delineates the debates over what was to be included and excluded from the Employment Act. The phrase "high employment" was an exclusion. The alternative "full employment" was also excluded in favor of the final "maximum employment." There was no clear statement against either deficit spending or inflation in the Employment Act, although both were discussed.[16]

The CED was a private association of senior executives of the very largest businesses dedicated to studying and issuing public policy papers on important social, primarily economic, issues. Beginning in 1944 it studied the connection between the elements of the federal budget and performance of the economy. It rejected the annually balanced budget because it required increased taxes when the economy slowed down to cover the authorized spending and tax cuts to avoid excess revenue when the economy accelerated. Over several years it worked out the notion of balancing over the cycle. Setting the tax code to generate a surplus when the economy was at high employment and a deficit when the economy was at low employment meant that in many years there might be deficits that would at least in part be paid off from the surpluses of the good years. A principal concern of the CED membership was stability in tax rates to make business planning easier.

The CED recognized that the budget used to measure the effect of the government on the economy had to include all of the federal government. That was the cash consolidated budget, sometimes called the cash budget, which had been first developed by Lauchlin Currie in the mid-1930s. It included the receipts and expenditures of the federal trust funds, most importantly Social Security, which were not part of the budget of that time, later called the administrative budget.

Unfortunately, we have no general examples showing the government's use of fiscal policy to restrain inflation. The only inflations with price increases of above 4 percent per year for more than one year have been the inflations associated with wars and oil crises. War inflations were found to be fully controllable with price controls, which is fortunate since restraining government spending during war is a clearly defeatist policy. Inflation caused by foreign cartel pricing of critical inputs cannot be changed by reducing government spending. It might cause a domestic recession, but it would not change the policies of other societies.

There was an interesting application of fiscal policy as a restraint on private demand in World War II. With the huge increase in government and then total demand, employment and personal incomes began to rise very rapidly. However, with the economy at overfull employment and the government taking over 40 percent of gross national product, there was not much increase in consumer goods output to exchange against the huge consumer income increase. The inflationary gap has been estimated below in Table 4.2.

As Table 4.2 shows, there was an enormous increase in personal taxation. The amount increased from $3.3 billion to $20.8 billion and the average rate from 1 percent to 12.2 percent. Even after such enormous tax increases the inflationary gap grew continuously until the war's end.

People were not consuming much more, primarily because there was very little increase in consumer goods for them to consume. The surplus funds of individuals were absorbed in part by the taxes shown above (fiscal policy) and in part by large individual purchases of the national debt (partially fiscal policy, partially coercion by employers who wanted to meet or exceed bond sales quotas), rationing and increased individual holdings of money as measured by M_2 (currency, checkable deposits, and small savings accounts).[17]

Table 4.2

Calculating the Inflationary Gap in Real Consumption in World War II
(1935–39 = 100)

	Personal income	Personal taxes	Disposable income	Personal consumption	Inflationary gap
1941	95.3	3.3	92.0	76.8	15.2
1942	122.4	5.9	116.5	76.1	40.4
1943	150.7	17.8	132.9	80.4	52.5
1944	164.4	18.9	145.5	86.2	59.3
1945	169.8	20.8	149.0	93.1	55.9

Source: Calculated from Harold G. Vatter, *The U.S. Economy in World War II* (New York: Columbia University Press, 1985), Tables 6.1 and 6.2, pp. 103–104.

The Postwar Transition

The large increases in individual holdings of money and national debt are partially credited with the very successful transition from World War II to a high-employment, reasonably expanding economy in the later 1940s. The bonds and other liquid assets of individuals financed a large consumption boom after the war. Table 4.3 illustrates the magnitude of the consumption boom and its remarkable character in the face of an income collapse followed by an investment-arrested expansion.

For the years 1945–49, income was down. Consumption was up every year, state and local government spending was up every year, and investment was up, then down. Obviously, neither consumers nor state and local governments were financing their increased expenditures from increased income; for most there was no increased income. It was consumers' large holdings of cash and government bonds that enabled the rapid, continuous increases in spending to continue for so long. The same was true to an extent for investment, but four years with no increase in total demand (1946 through 1949) was more than business could take, so investment fell 18.9 percent in 1949. The next year it rose 39 percent, and the old business cycle driven by the instability of investment was clearly reestablished.

Consumption spending was probably supported by a plateau in personal taxation in 1945 and a drop in 1948. In Table 4.4, personal taxation is approximated by total federal, state, and local personal taxes and Social Security taxes plus state indirect business taxes. Most of indirect business taxes are property taxes and sales taxes, which are probably substantially paid by persons, although certainly part of both property and sales taxes must be shifted to the sellers rather than the buyers. Of course, some of the sellers are also persons.

Table 4.3

Transition from Total War, Real GNP and Its Principal Components
(1982 = 100)

Year	Gross national product	Personal consumption expenditures	Gross private domestic investment	Total federal purchases	State and local purchases
1945	1,354.8	592.7	76.5	634.0	70.5
1946	1,096.1	655.0	178.1	159.3	77.6
1947	1,066.7	666.6	177.9	91.9	87.9
1948	1,108.7	681.8	208.2	106.1	93.4
1949	1,109.0	695.4	168.8	119.5	106.5
1950	1,230.7	733.2	234.9	116.7	114.2

Source: Economic Report of the President, 1987, pp. 246–247.

Table 4.4

Personal Income and Personal Taxes, 1946–50
(NIPA basis in billions of 1982 dollars)

Year	Personal income	Personal taxes	Average rate
1946	807.3	154.5	19.1
1947	860.6	170.5	19.8
1948	886.4	163.7	18.4
1949	806.3	146.5	18.2
1950	870.6	160.7	18.4

Source: Economic Report of the President, 1970, pp. 177, 253, 259; 1987, pp. 248, 269. The personal consumption deflator is used.

The drop of 1.4 percentage points in the measured average personal tax rate from 1947 to 1948 is the largest such drop in the postwar era. A change in the average rate, so measured, is a combination of policy changes in the tax codes and changes in the economy, which alter the bases the rates are levied against. In the 1948 case, all of the decline in revenues is in federal personal income and Social Security receipts. Since real personal income and real wages and salaries both rose from 1947 to 1948 while federal tax receipts from them fell, we can say the federal taxes acted to expand the economy that year.

The next year total personal taxes fell again, as did the economy. That is a case of salvaging. With the arrested expansion, federal relief expenditures automatically rose, and with falling incomes federal receipts of taxes on incomes (including wages) also automatically fell. Hansen observed,

Fiscal policy played an important role in cushioning the 1949 recession. Government cash payments increased 7 billion dollars from 1948 to 1949, and cash receipts substantially declined. Thus a cash surplus of 7 billion dollars in 1948 was converted into a cash deficit of 3 billion dollars in 1949. The shift-over of 10 billion dollars helped to sustain private spending and played a major role in preventing the recession from turning into a more serious depression.[18]

Stein discusses the tax cut of 1948 in great detail. He begins with the Republican Party control of the 80th Congress, which served in 1947 and 1948. It started with a proposal for an across-the-board 20 percent cut in income taxes. But it was seen as unfair, since almost all of the cuts would go to the high-income groups, so provisions to help lower incomes (bigger personal exemptions) and middle incomes (income splitting for married couples) were added. A problem was that estimates indicated the tax cut would create a deficit, whereas consensus fiscal policy thinking was that during an inflation (in 1946–48 it averaged 10.2 percent per year) there should be a budget surplus.

The postwar inflation was driving up federal revenues so fast that a surplus was being created. Then the estimates of potential expansion began to show signs of a recession—just what the tax cutters needed. After two vetoes, the tax cut was passed over the president's veto on the third try. It cut rates as of January 1948, but it did not cut withholding until May 1, 1948. Consequently there was no effect on fiscal 1948, which ended June 30.[19]

Many contemporary economists were convinced that the tax cut was a mistake. But it took effect almost exactly as a recession started, consequently significantly ameliorating it. Stein has emphasized that the Republican Congress accepted the argument that a recession in the offing was a reason to cut taxes. In 1930 it had been a reason to raise them. All parties agreed that the tax cut would increase the deficit although there were arguments that somehow over the long run less deficit reduction early would lead to more deficit reduction later.

Strangely, this entire episode reproduces arguments made in the 1980s and again in the 1996 election campaign. In 1948 there was nothing like the Laffer curve argument—that a tax cut would raise total revenues. The income tax receipts of 1949 and 1950, from the new lower income tax, were substantially below the receipts in 1948. In calendar 1947, personal income in current dollars was 191.3 billion and federal personal tax collections were 19.6 billion, whereas in 1950 personal income was 227.6 billion, up 19 percent, and federal personal income tax collections were 18.1 billion, down 7.6 percent.

Early Cold War Budget Experiments

The Korean War reestablished expansionary economic spending policy, but not for fiscal policy reasons. The North Korean invasion that began on June 25, 1950, was strongly opposed by the United States. From 1950 to 1953 real federal purchases increased at 40.4 percent per year, driving real GNP up at 6.0 percent per year.

With the sudden jump in total demand, prices as measured by the all-item consumer price index (CPI) rose 8 percent from 1950 to 1951. Fortunately, the civil servants and institutional memory of the price control system from World War II were still available. An almost identical system was put in place and the inflation ended immediately and totally. The average annual rate of price increase for the rest of the 1950s was 1.4 percent, with the worst year of the peacetime Eisenhower administration, 1957, showing a 3.5 percent increase. It was followed by eight years of almost total price stability. From 1957 to 1965 the price index rose only 1.4 percent per year. Remarkably, the average annual increase in the CPI from 1950, before the Korean War buildup, to 1969, one year into the Vietnam War de-escalation, the average annual inflation rate was only 2.2 percent per year as measured by the all-item CPI with the 1967 base.[20]

The Eisenhower administration's economic advisers were not Keynesians. Arthur Burns, the first chairman of the Council of Economic Advisers (CEA) under Eisenhower, was sharply critical of Keynes in *The Frontiers of Economic Knowledge,* published while he was serving as chairman (although written before). Not surprisingly, there was no active expansionary fiscal policy while such men made policy. However, they managed to preside over three recessions during Ike's two terms. This forced considerable salvaging activity. The Eisenhower economic reports carried extensive recommendations of expansion and extension of the unemployment compensation system, improvement of job training, and public works expenditure.[21]

Indeed, the biggest federal public works program of the post–World War II period is the National Defense Highway Program begun by President Eisenhower. It set out to build a four-lane limited-access highway system connecting every city of 50,000 or more population and all the state capitals. It led to a relatively steady flow of funds from the federal government to the states and to highway construction companies for the best part of thirty years. Since the long-run growth rate of real investment in business structures has been very sluggish since about 1910,[22] this program increased employment in trades that the private sector had shifted away from. So it is salvaging expenditure. Without it there would have been less employment and investment in the construction industry— an industry already of great age but without government support, facing continual decline.

Eisenhower's second CEA chairman, Raymond J. Saulnier, was also unimpressed with the Keynesian revolution. Writing as a summary of Keynes's *General Theory:*

> From our point of view, then, Keynes has not been altogether successful in his reformulation of economic theory. His real contribution, I believe, is in his insistence that general economic theory, that is the theory of value and distribution, must be stated in terms which give full recognition to the operation of monetary forces, and in his attempt to construct a "monetary" theory of pro-

duction. Neither of these tasks seems to me to have been adequately accomplished, but Keynes has indicated some of the lines along which the development should proceed.[23]

Both Burns and Saulnier were unalterably opposed to any possibility of inflation. The fact that there was virtually no inflation in no way dampened their energy for searching out and decrying the potential for inflation. At the end of his second term, Eisenhower appointed a Cabinet Committee on Price Stability for Economic Growth, made up of Vice-President Richard M. Nixon as chairman and the obvious economic officers of the cabinet—Treasury, Agriculture, Commerce, Labor—and the chairman of the CEA. It also included the postmaster general and the special assistant to the president. Special Assistant W. Allen Wallis and CEA Chairman Saulnier could be called economists, although only Saulnier had advanced degrees in economics.

The Cabinet Committee report was released by President Eisenhower on June 29, 1959. It said, in part,

> It is the unanimous opinion of the Cabinet Committee on Price Stability for Economic Growth that our economy is now at a critical juncture urgently requiring action to forestall inflation and insure sound and sustained economic growth and progress. . . . We face a serious risk of price increases which not only would be directly harmful to American families but would seriously endanger the healthy prosperity now developing. . . . *Recommendations for immediate action* . . . not only is it imperative that the budget be balanced in the fiscal year starting next month (fiscal 1960), but it is important that the national debt be reduced. Any effort to increase expenditures beyond the levels recommended in your budget should be vigorously resisted. Holding the line on expenditures together with improved revenues from prosperous business conditions, would make possible some reduction of the debt. Not only must the line be held on the total of next years appropriations, but it is important that the greatest restraint and selectivity be exercised in authorizing programs for later years. Excessive authorizations, by making deficits or higher taxes likely in the future could create permanent inflationary forces.[24]

There is not the slightest hint of Keynesian or fiscal policy thinking in this statement. No recognition that government spending might increase output instead of prices. No recognition that all models in use at that time held increasing taxes to be deflationary, not inflationary, as stated.

Curiously, in 1960 there was a budget surplus on both an administrative and a cash basis as recommended by the Cabinet Committee. It was achieved by a large increase in receipts and a significant reduction in expenditure on an administrative budget basis or a large increase in cash receipts with no change in cash payments on a cash budget basis.[25] Fiscal policy, but not Eisenhower's advisers, predicted that such policies tend to depress the economy. A recession began in April 1960, which is widely credited with contributing to the defeat of Richard Nixon's presidential candidacy in the election that fall.

The recommended policies—restricted government spending and debt reduction—were totally ignored by the Kennedy administration, narrowly elected over Nixon in the fall of 1960. The next five years exactly achieved the good-growth, no-inflation goals of the Cabinet Committee, but with rising federal deficits on both a cash and an administrative budget basis. Federal administrative expenditures rose from 76.5 billion in 1960 to 96.5 billion (4.75 percent per year) in 1965 and on a cash basis from 94.3 billion to 122.4 billion (5.35 percent per year). Over that same period real GNP rose at a 4.72 percent annual rate and the inflation rate measured by the CPI was 1.28 percent per year. Gross public debt increased only 2.05 percent per year.[26]

The last five years of the Eisenhower administration (1955–60) were characterized by Paul Samuelson as the "Eisenhower stagnation." In that period annual rates of expansion were 2.17 for real GNP, 2.02 for consumer prices, and 0.67 for gross public debt. In technical economic terms, ending the Eisenhower years with a recession and beginning the Kennedy years with a recession biases the results against Eisenhower and in favor of Kennedy. However, historically that is what happened and how citizens and voters experienced it; and in the fiscal policy sense that bad policy under Eisenhower can be said to have caused the recession and better policy under Kennedy can be said to have eliminated it. Indeed, the eight robust years of Kennedy-Johnson are the only full eight-year presidential period without a recession in American history. They were the best years of the postwar era.

The modern language for dealing with recessions mostly emphasizes automatic stabilizers: programs like unemployment insurance, which automatically increases government expenditures whenever the economy slows down; and progressive income taxes, which automatically cut the average income tax rate whenever incomes go down. Hansen's notion of salvaging includes the idea that total government spending probably has to be increased to get people back to work whenever recessions are serious, since the automatic stabilizers at best only reduce the rate of fall. They do not cause output increases, although as the economy speeds up in a recovery they do reverse themselves and dampen the expansion.

Stein's observation that Republicans accepted tax cuts to ameliorate recessions is very weak. The tax cut of 1948 was wanted under any terms. Even Keynesian excuses to give their constituents more money would be accepted. However, the three Eisenhower recessions, a remarkable number in so short a time, did not lead the Republican administration to advocate tax cuts. Total federal receipts did fall in 1954 and 1958—both recession years when the economy lowered the receipts, not when lower receipts expanded the economy. As noted above, in the 1960 recession, even with built-in stabilizers, tax receipts went up.

Fiscal Policy Triumphant

The Kennedy advisers were unabashed Keynesians. That is made most clear in their first *Economic Report*, where they make a major change in the structure of the federal budget for purposes of economic stability, to be discussed below. They also proposed that the Congress adopt a range of rates of income taxation and delegate to the president the power to lower taxes within that range when the president and the CEA had strong evidence for the imminent onset of a recession. They further proposed that the Congress adopt a system for authorizing public works spending, but such spending would be triggered only by other strong signs of an onset of recession and the finding of need by the president and his economic advisers. The third part of the program was the usual extension of unemployment benefits and improved worker training programs.[27]

The Kennedy program, had it been adopted, would have solved a major dilemma in American fiscal policy—namely, the fact that all budget authority is given by the Constitution to the Congress. However, the Congress is designed to be a deliberative, slow-moving institution, which in a fiscal policy context means that by the time the solution to a recession is adopted the recession may be over and the delayed solution will make the succeeding expansion too strong. A slow-moving response to the economy is procyclical, not anticyclical.

A wonderful by-product of the Kennedy proposal would have been the necessity to list and prioritize public works. If a public work is necessary, it should be built now. If it is something the community would benefit from but it is not critical at the moment, then it could be added to the list of projects to be built in a future recession. This notion of nice but not immediately necessary public projects would greatly improve the discussion of public works. For example, the National Gallery of Art clearly is not necessary to the functioning of the country, since it did not exist for most of the history of the country. But it is widely accepted today as a good thing. It imitates in both name and collection the actions of most other countries. Building it in a depression means most construction workers and companies would otherwise be out of work, which means that a good thing is achieved at very little economic cost. To this day we do not debate what is the next unnecessary but nice thing we should build—say, a lodge at Zion National Park or an aquarium at Baltimore or a telescope in Hawaii. Which proposals are better than others? We decide with little consideration of their relative merits. A placement on Kennedy's proposed list would have encouraged such debates.

The historical evolution of the Kennedy budget reform proposals over the next two years clearly demonstrated the sluggishness of response in the political system. Reform of taxes to make them more responsive to changing cycles problems, written during 1961 and proposed to Congress in January 1962, became a proposal for a tax cut and reform in July 1962. With reform included, the usual flood of special pleaders hit the Congress like the *blitzkrieg* before the Polish cavalry.

Everyone wanted his or her special tax provisions expanded, his or her rates cut, and the budget balanced. Kennedy's proposal for a general rate cut and reform had been targeted to take effect in January of 1963.[28] By Kennedy's assassination in November 1963 the only certain directive to the administration from the Congress was that spending restraint was a necessary condition to achieve a tax cut. The ever anti-Keynesian Arthur Burns testified before the Joint Economic Committee of the Congress:

> Senator, let us make the assumption that the Government adopts a fiscal policy with a view to stimulating the economy and that this fiscal policy involves incurring deliberately a budget deficit of some size. Let us say that the planned budget deficit is $10 billion. Plan A, let us say involves increasing federal expenditures by $10 billion. Plan B involves, let us say, increasing expenditures by $5 billion, and also cutting taxes by $5 billion. Plan C involves, let us say, a cut in taxes of $10 billion. . . . The theory which is now fashionable among economists is that the first of these plans would be most stimulative. The reasoning is that if the government undertakes to increase the deficit by spending $10 billion, that much purchasing power will be promptly added to the economy. Those who take this viewpoint go on to argue that if, on the other hand, taxes are cut by $10 billion, a portion of that sum will be saved by individuals or by business firms. In other words the deficit of $10 billion created by a tax reduction will lead to an increase in the communities spending of something less than $10 billion.
>
> I disagree with this theory. . . . The reason why I think that plan C, to return to my example, is more stimulative than plan A is that under plan C individuals and businessmen will begin thinking very differently about the future. They will be in a position not merely to use the larger cash income which is at their disposal, but they may well be in a mood also to dip into their accumulated assets and to use their credit.[29]

To this very day (in the fall of 1996), *all* the better selling principles of economics textbooks teach the answer that Burns called the then fashionable (that is, Keynesian) plan A more stimulative.

President Johnson, who drove the Congress hard to pass the tax cut, conceded to the spending cutters and actually proposed an administrative budget expenditure for fiscal 1965 (July 1, 1964–June 30, 1965) below the figure the House Republicans were suggesting. In typical Johnson fashion, it was mixed up with many different budget figures. The budget, to most people at that time, meant the administrative budget. From fiscal 1964 to fiscal 1965, administrative budget expenditures fell from $97.7 billion to $96.5 billion. However, consolidated cash budget expenditures rose from 171.3 billion to 177.7 billion. On a calendar year basis the then in use federal budgets for 1965 produced a budget deficit of 4.7 billion for the administrative budget, $3.0 billion for the consolidated cash budget, and the National Income and Products Account (NIPA) accounts budget showed a surplus of 1.6 billion.[30]

In sum, the budget shift from calendar 1964, effectively unaffected by the tax cut, to fiscal 1965, with much of the tax cut in place, was probably slightly contractionary with spending restraints slightly overbalancing the effect of the tax cuts. Thereafter, the expansionary effect of further provisions of the tax cut taking place in the second year and the increase in federal government spending made the national government expansionary again.

In the 1962 *Economic Report,* the Kennedy administration announced a target unemployment rate of 4 percent. That rate was not achieved until January 1966. When achieved, the rate was then held at or below 4 percent for every single month through January 1970, with the exceptions of September and October 1967, when it averaged 4.2 percent. These were the best years for the unemployment rate since the end of the Korean War.

It was increasingly common to associate a tight labor market with inflation. The very popular Phillips curve, associating wage rates and unemployment rates, had been published in 1958, and by the mid-1960s was reproduced as a functional connection between inflation and unemployment rates in everything from textbooks to popular magazines. The CEA carefully tracked inflation and unemployment as the generally expansionary fiscal policy drove unemployment rates down.

Fiscal Policy as an Anti-Inflation Tool

Opponents of inflation like to assert that when inflation begins it continuously accelerates and makes things ever worse until it is successfully attacked and stamped out. There is no evidence for this notion. Most American inflations are short, clearly associated with an obvious cause, and not prone to lengthy acceleration. The exception is hyperinflation caused by excess money creation. But the United States has not had an hyperinflation since colonial times. Inflation has escalated in the sense that the inflation rate was higher each successive year for at least four years only five times since 1890. These escalating inflations are listed in Table 4.5.

There is considerable white noise in price data. Identification of the beginnings of an inflation from a series of annual price increases like those of 1963 to 1967 is impossible. Although the rate of price increase rises each year, the level remains below the probable error of three to four percentage points. Today we say the sequence in inflation rates for the years 1963–67 of 0.95, 1.32, 1.59, 2.43, 2.77 was the beginnings of an inflation. We do not say that the much more rapid increase from 1955 to 1957 of 0.88, 3.28, 3.60 was the beginnings of an inflation. In the next eight years the inflation rate averaged 1.34. In the five years after 1967 the inflation rate averaged 4.18, certainly above the threshold to measure inflation, but not by much and with no further escalation after 1970.

There was no surprise that inflation eventually appeared in the 1960s expansion. It had been predicted in every economic report of the president from 1962 onward. In a sense it was a goal. The clearly stated plan was to expand the economy and lower the unemployment rate until such time as serious inflation costs were encountered. Memoirs of the economic advisers from that time say

Table 4.5

Annual Rates of Inflation and Federal Government Outlays and Receipts as a Percentage of GNP in Years of Escalating Inflation at Least Three Years Long, 1890–1994 (in percent)

	World War I				World War II		
	Inflation rate	Federal outlays/ GNP	Federal receipts/ GNP		Inflation rate	Federal outlays/ GNP	Federal receipts/ GNP
1913	0.48	1.24	1.24	1939	−1.57	9.86	7.45
1914	1.43	1.39	1.39	1940	1.59	9.96	8.67
1915	3.13	1.39	1.25	1941	8.95	16.33	12.35
1916	12.16	1.14	1.22	1942	13.96	35.28	4.47
	Vietnam War				Energy crisis		
	Inflation rate	Federal outlays/ GNP	Federal receipts/ GNP		Inflation rate	Federal outlays/ GNP	Federal receipts/ GNP
1963	0.95	19.00	19.05	1976	5.75	22.08	19.08
1964	1.32	18.39	17.88	1977	6.62	21.61	19.29
1965	1.59	17.77	17.84	1978	7.32	20.92	19.62
1966	2.43	18.82	18.58	1979	9.09	20.77	20.13
1967	2.77	20.31	18.69	1980	10.80	22.51	20.27
1968	3.85	20.48	19.81				
1969	4.44	19.85	20.71				
1970	4.61	20.46	19.24				

	Gulf War-Energy Crisis		
	Inflation rate	Federal outlays/ GNP	Federal receipts/ GNP
1986	2.90	24.04	19.34
1987	3.85	23.45	20.11
1988	4.07	22.59	19.81
1989	4.86	22.43	20.11
1990	5.09	22.98	19.98

Sources: For 1939–80, *Economic Report of the President*, 1990, pp. 294 and 387; for 1980–90, *Economic Report of the President*, 1993, pp. 376, and 439; for 1913–39, *Historical Statistics of the United States Colonial Times to 1970*, Vol. 2, p. 1104. The receipts and expenditures are NIPA basis for 1939–90 and listed as budget for 1913–17.

that President Johnson ignored their advice to increase taxes to cover the increased costs of wars in Vietnam and poverty at the same time. Walter Heller said, "He [President Johnson] did not propose a tax increase until early 1967, and no tax action was completed until 1968, long after the inflation horse was out of the barn."[31]

Heller is too self-serving and implies precision of information that did not exist. In 1966 the inflation rate was 2.43 percent, not enough to say whether prices were rising or not. In the January 1967 *Economic Report of the President,* obviously written in late 1966, Johnson did call for a tax increase. But in 1967 the first-quarter real GNP fell for the first time since the 1960 recession. For the first half of 1967 the rate of real GNP expansion was only "a little over 1 percent."[32]

If the fathers of fiscal policy had learned anything, it was to not raise taxes in a falling economy. Consequently the delay from proposal to enactment of the tax increase was really rather short, not too long as Heller implies. Furthermore, the inflation rate for the whole of 1968 at 3.85 is at best marginally certain as inflation at all.

Even later CEAs thought of the late 1960s as a low-inflation era. "[We] compare the behavior of key macroeconomic indicators and policy variables during the relatively low inflation period from the second quarter of 1954 through 1970 with the relatively high inflation period from the fourth quarter of 1970 through 1982."[33]

In President Reagan's final *Economic Report,* the council, in part summing up the performance of the administration observed,

> The rate of inflation fell from 9.7 percent in 1981 to the 3.5 percent range, and unlike periods in the past, it has stayed in that range. Contrary to the fears of many, it will stay in that range and gradually drift down if the monetary authorities remain committed to reducing the rate of inflation to achieve price stability.[34]

So we see that inflation rising to a 3.5–4.5 level at the end of the sixties has been deemed a failure while a fall to the 3.5–4.0 level in the eighties has been deemed a success.

World Wars I and II and the Korean War produced very rapid consumer price increases. The great manager of the War Industries Board in World War I, Bernard Baruch, concluded that price controls were necessary in wartime.[35] Such controls were imposed during World War II and the Korean War, ending the inflations during those wars. Remarkably, when inflation resumed after the lifting of wartime controls, it never accelerated for more than two years. In the Korean case there was no postwar inflation at all.

During the Vietnam War, oil crisis, and Gulf War–oil crisis inflation accelerations there were no price controls. Peculiar wage and price controls were imposed by President Nixon in August 1971, but by then inflation rates had been falling for over a year. Those controls remained in effect nominally until April 1974, and they were at best marginally successful. For the eight months ending August 1971 the CPI rose at an annual rate of 3.8 percent, seasonally adjusted. In the next eight months the rate was 2.9, and the eight months after that, 3.5

percent.[36] When compared to World War II, when the rate fell from 10.8 percent in the partially controlled 1942 to 6.2 percent in 1943 and 1.62 percent in 1944, the Nixon controls must be deemed a failure.

The methods and publications of the price controllers of the 1940s were totally ignored during the Nixon controls. It seems reasonable to conclude that the people running the Nixon price-control scheme—politically active Republican business and economics experts—helped the price controls fail since they were ideologically committed to the proposition that they were a bad idea and probably would not work.

The Economic Stabilization Act amendments of 1971, which were the legal basis for the price-control scheme, required the *Economic Report of the President* to give an evaluation of how the system was working. The evaluations published in the 1973 and 1974 reports were most equivocal in answering this requirement:

> We believe it is probable that the controls did reduce the rate of inflation, but the magnitude of the reduction is uncertain. . . . But one cannot be certain that the controls had an effect on the rate of inflation. Still less can the size of the effect be gauged.[37]

> The effect of the controls program on the rate of inflation in 1973 cannot be known with certainty either today or ever.[38]

The difficulty of gauging the inflation decline is largely driven by the small possible decline. In the eight months before the price freeze, the inflation rate was only 3.8 percent. Why then was there a price freeze? The economic reports clearly indicated that the goal was more rapid economic expansion through expansionary fiscal policy.[39] The president and some of his advisers were afraid that inflation would force adoption of contractionary fiscal policy, thus defeating their economic expansion goals and possibly producing a recession like the 1960 recession that Nixon credited with causing his presidential campaign defeat that year.

The common theme of the inflation accelerations policies of the post–Korean War era is constant or falling federal expenditures as a share of GNP and rising or constant federal taxes as a share of GNP. That is, fiscal policy in the post–Korean War era was consistently anti-inflationary in every acceleration of inflation. The sole year 1968 can be identified as an exception to that case.[40] Fiscal policy does not seem to be a good tool for counteracting inflations. Neither fiscal nor monetary policy has been capable of counteracting the effects of international monopoly or war. Milton Friedman's contention that inflation is ever and always a monetary phenomenon is wrong for the postwar era.

Although President Nixon has been widely quoted as observing, "We are all Keynesians now," he was primarily an anti-inflationary Keynesian. The early years of the Nixon administration were an application of increased taxes through fiscal drag as an anti-inflation policy. Any increase in income causes a more than proportionate increase in tax rates and liabilities in a system with progressive income tax rates and no inflation adjustments in the income tax. In the early Nixon years most of the income increases were from inflation, not real expansion. However, the administration hoped the higher taxes combined with the spending restraints they were imposing, largely through winding down the Vietnam War, would end the inflation with rather minor increases in the unemployment rate. As always, a fiscal policy attack on inflation failed.[41]

The Deficit and National Debt Reemerge as Fiscal Policy Targets

From the election of Richard Nixon in 1968 to the present time, budgetary policy pronouncements from the leaders of the government, including their economic advisers, have been more and more a chorus of concern about the alleged adverse effects of large budget deficits and a rising national debt. Strangely, the more the government has railed against the national debt the faster it has grown. The source of increasing national debt is primarily budget deficits, but it includes the fiscal policy logic that budget surpluses are created to reduce private purchasing power, and so the debt should not be paid off if the budget is in surplus, since it increases private money holdings at exactly the wrong time. As mentioned above, this makes the national debt a ratchet. Of course, the national debt will never be liquidated.

The *Journal of Economic Perspectives* sponsored a symposium, "Fifty Years of the Council of Economic Advisers," in its Summer 1996 issue. On deficits, the conclusion of the authors were:

> Although the CEA always believed that the deficit was a serious problem, it did not, at least for the public record, make a calculation of the optimum path of the deficit. Its answer to the question of the proper size of the deficit was always "less," just as the Pentagon's estimate of the proper size of the defense budget was always "more."[42]

> During the first 25 years of the postwar era, both parties (Republicans and Democrats) came to accept the inevitability of large cyclically induced budget deficits. . . .
>   Even the terms of the dialogue about the effects of budget deficits and fiscal policy have altered sharply. Whenever the first forty or so *Economic Reports* discussed the subject of excessive budget deficits it was almost always in terms of a danger of inflation. . . . Currently, however, the economic effects of large deficits are almost universally discussed in terms of what they do to national savings rates and interest rates.[43]

Democratic politics applied to government spending, Buchanan and Wagner argue, functions well only as long as deficits are prohibited—regarded as a dire moral evil. Thus, arguments that deficit spending could be useful as a tool of stabilization policy might undermine the polity's immune system that prevents the emergence of borrow-and-spend as standard political operating procedure. . . .

It is hard to look back at the politics of America's federal deficit since 1980 and not conclude that there is a good deal of truth in Buchanan and Wagner's argument. The basic economic message is simple enough; "Cyclical deficit—good. Structural deficit—bad."

It is a heavy irony that made the American political party usually seen as most sympathetic to Buchanan's general philosophy—the Republicans—the carrier of the policies that he feared would emerge from the use of fiscal policy for macroeconomic stabilization.[44]

Later Cold War Budget Experiments

The years since 1970 have produced precious little discretionary fiscal policy, certainly none oriented toward economic growth (except for the Reagan administration). Stein thinks there were small expansionary programs proposed by Presidents Nixon in late 1971, Ford in 1975, and Carter in 1977. Schultze agrees and adds a proposal from President Clinton in 1993. All of these proposals fell in periods when both federal taxes and spending as a percentage of the economy were remarkably stable, as Table 4.6 illustrates.

Both Presidents Carter and Reagan, while campaigning for their first terms, promised to balance the budget by the end of the four years. Both promises were severely violated. Table 4.7 illustrates their budget results three ways: federal budget surplus or deficit, the same on an NIPA basis, and finally on a high-employment budget basis adjusted for inflation and interest effects.

The budget numbers are what most people call the budget. The NIPA numbers are the budget adjusted to make sense in a national income accounting (system of measuring GDP) sense. The two fiscal year columns vary, but not significantly. The NIPA should measure to some extent the effect on the economy or vice versa. Unfortunately it doesn't. The calendar year numbers for NIPA are not significantly different from the fiscal years, except for 1982. The last column, "Adjusted High Employment Budget," is startlingly different. All years are surpluses except 1982 and 1984.

A high-employment budget asks: What would the receipts and expenditures of the government be if the economy were operating at a high rate of employment? The surplus or deficit generated is then adjusted for inflation and changes in the market value of government securities. An increase in prices lowers the real value of the federal bonds held by market actors, since the bonds' face value, which is paid on maturity, is stated in nominal dollars. For an outstanding bond with a coupon of 5 percent, meaning it pays 5 percent of the par value, a rise in the market interest rate to 10 percent will almost halve the value of the bond. So when interest rates have risen, the government can pay off its bonds not by paying the par value, which never changes, but by buying the bonds on the market at the now lower market prices. These adjustments

Table 4.6

Federal Government Receipts, Expenditures, and the Composition of Expenditures as a Percentage of GDP, 1970–94, Selected Years (NIPA basis)

Year	Total Receipts	Total spending	Purchase of goods and services	Transfers to persons	Transfers to state and local governments	Interest paid
1970	18.8	20.2	9.7	5.9	2.4	1.4
1975	18.2	22.8	8.3	9.0	3.3	1.4
1980	20.2	22.4	7.7	8.9	3.2	1.9
1985	19.4	23.3	8.2	8.8	2.4	3.0
1990	19.7	22.4	7.4	8.7	2.3	3.1
1994	19.9	22.6	6.5	9.6	2.8	2.9

Source: Calculated from the *Economic Report of the President*, 1996, p. 373.

Table 4.7

Federal Surplus or Deficit in the Budget, on an NIPA Basis and in a High-Employment Budget Adjusted for Price and Interest Effects, During the Carter and Reagan Administrations (billions of dollars)

	Fiscal year budget	Fiscal year NIPA budget	Calendar year NIPA budget	Calendar year adjusted high-employment budget
Carter years				
1977	−44.9	−46.4	−46.4	24.9
1978	−48.8	−29.2	−29.2	46.4
1979	−27.7	−14.0	−14.8	46.2
1980	−59.6	−50.9	−62.3	51.8
Reagan years				
1981	−57.9	−58.9	−64.3	42.8
1982	−110.6	−113.6	−148.2	−61.7
1983	−195.4	−189.3	−178.6	17.7
1984	−175.4	−170.3	−176.4	−87.0

Sources: Economic Report of the President, 1981, pp. 316, 319 (for Carter) and 1985, pp. 318, 322 (for Reagan); and Robert Eisner, *How Real is the Federal Deficit?* (New York: The Free Press, 1986), p. 193.

were done and explained in great detail by Professor Robert Eisner of Northwestern University.[45]

Interpretation of the *budget* surplus has not been possible. Observers always confuse the effect of the government on the economy with the effect of the economy on the budget. A high-employment budget can describe independently the effect of the budget on the economy. If the high-employment budget is in surplus, it says that if the economy is at high employment, government receipts will exceed expenditures. Often it can also say what the surplus or deficit would be at other rates of employment, and thus how rapidly an expansion raises taxes and lowers spending. A rising deficit in a high-employment budget means that the budget is tending to expand the level of economic activity and income. An increasing surplus implies that the government is slowing the rate of economic expansion.

With Eisner's adjustments, the national debt in terms of how much the government would currently have to pay to get out of debt almost continuously fell from the end of World War II to the 1980s. When in 1996 Herbert Stein writes that the CEA *"always* believed that the deficit was a serious problem" (italics added),[46] he is saying that the CEA failed to apply elementary business arithmetic to the debt and to their analysis of problems. If they actually made decisions on the budget deficits they publish in their reports, then they often tended to contract the economy with full-employment surpluses even as they decried the imagined expansionary effects of the nominal budget deficits.

The Reagan Triumph, or Kennedy-Johnson Redux

Under Ronald Reagan there were tax cuts and federal purchase increases, which are illustrated in the 1980 and 1985 lines of Table 4.6. Most of the purchase increase was an extraordinary buildup in defense programs.

The tax decreases were argued by a group of economists and other policy experts, called "supply siders," as devices to increase government revenues and cut the deficits. The "technical" argument was apparently first made by Arthur Laffer, an economist, doodling on a cocktail napkin in a bar in Georgetown. He argued that as tax rates rose tax receipts also rose for a range of rates, but after some level, increases in rates should produce reductions in receipts. This far the argument is trivial to all economists. It is simply the total revenue curve from price theory applied to government. Graphically, the Laffer curve and total revenue curve are identical parabolas in most textbooks.

The next argument was that the income tax had become too high and was consequently raising less revenue than it could. The mechanism for raising more revenue from lower tax rates was an incentive to work. With lower tax rates, laborers and capitalists would significantly increase their work effort, which would produce significantly greater income. Hence, even paying lower tax rates would yield higher total taxes.

Neither the tax cut in 1948 nor the one in 1964 had produced such a result. But the tax changes of the 1960s and 1970s had significantly lowered income tax rates. Consequently it was unlikely that the reductions from even lower levels would produce Laffer's magical effect—and it didn't happen.

The Reagan budgets were expansionary in both Keynesian theoretical terms and practical experience. With spending up and taxes down, the rate of expansion of the economy significantly increased. But was it fiscal policy? If the criterion in the first sentence of this chapter is used, then the answer is yes. It is the only non–hot-war expansion of the economy in American postwar history. But the supply siders and many of their friends say not so. Fiscal policy means manipulation of demand, whereas the Reagan tax cuts induced work that produced income. A fiscal policy tax cut would produce spending of the tax cut by persons and businesses, which would expand the economy through demand. Did the private sector produce more because its customers were buying more, or did it produce more and earn more, enabling it to buy more? This is the chicken or the egg.

Since the 1930s, we have had economic theory arguing that increases in government spending and reductions in taxes will result in higher GDP. If Keynesian, it works through demand; if supply side, it works through supply. When such policies are applied, the rate of real economic expansion is significantly higher than it is the rest of the time.

There are in the 1990s professional economists who are willing to argue that increases in government spending simply reduce private spending and do not increase output at all. In his first economic report, President Reagan outlined a "long term program designed to increase economic growth and to reduce inflation. The key elements of the program were: 1, Cutting the rate of growth in federal spending. . . ."[47] But rapid real economic growth in the twentieth century occurs only when the rate of government spending is increasing rapidly. Table 4.8 illustrates both this point and the connection between government and investment.

Unfortunately, the government purchases in Table 4.8 are all-government purchases. Usually it is dominated by state and local purchases, it does not reflect fiscal policy or any other policy, and it is the sum of the spending decisions of many thousands of governmental units. However, it is clear that *all* high GDP growth rates occur with high government purchases rates. It further illustrates the statistical vacuity of the notion of crowding out. *Crowding out* is said to occur when the government takes resources away from the private sector. A common variant is that the government is a better credit risk than any private business. Consequently, when the government borrows more it makes less money available for business to borrow and the result is less investment.

There are two cases in Table 4.8 where the government growth increases and investment growth slows: the period 1929–49 in the long-run panel is one case. It is clearly an instance of investment collapse, not government aggrandizement. Had government purchases fell in that period along with investment, the Depression would have been worse and the war lost or unfought. In the short-run panel, the rate of government purchases increased in the period 1978–82 while the rate of investment rise dropped. Again in that case, the government is salvaging the system in dire economic distress, as the GDP expansion rate demonstrates.

When the government is not salvaging the system from collapse, investment

Table 4.8

Annual Growth Rates of Real GNP/GDP, Government Purchases, and Private Fixed Investment (in percent)

Period	GNP/GDP	Government purchases	Private business fixed investment
The long-run problem			
1900–1929	3.53	4.19	2.70
1929–1949	2.35	4.52	1.72
1949–1969	4.12	5.23	3.54
1969–1994	2.71	1.41	3.36
The short-run problem			
1969–1978	2.85	–0.15	3.75
1978–1982	0.38	1.68	1.25
1982–1988	3.86	3.45	3.42
1988–1994	2.00	0.97	2.39

Source: Updated from Harold G. Vatter and John F. Walker, "Stagnation and Government Purchases," *Challenge*, November-December 1992, p. 56.

grows fastest when government grows fastest. Business and government are not substitutes shifting along a social transformation function where if one gets more the other gets less. Rather, they are complements, such that when government grows rapidly so does investment, and when investment slows down either government maintains its expansion to salvage the system damaged by the slowing investment growth or compounds the damage by slowing itself. Surprisingly, in a well-run fiscal system, government purchases are a ratchet. They rise fastest when investment rises fastest, and they keep rising when investment falls.

If the nation had fiscal policy in the strict sense, government as a share of the economy should rise indefinitely. Mostly without fiscal policy, it did so rise from the early nineteenth century up to the 1970s or 1980s. As pointed out in Chapter 2, that government in some sense grows faster than the economy in capitalism has been known as Wagner's Law since the 1880s. As the rise in government spending has slowed down, so has the economy.

In summary, fiscal policy seems to have been used primarily for salvaging purposes in the United States. Purposeful manipulation of the federal budget to produce economic expansion is clearest in the 1960s and the 1980s. In both cases the expenditure side was substantially driven by military objectives. In the 1960s it was the Vietnam War and the War on Poverty. In the 1980s, it was the Cold War. Most citizens would probably agree that cold wars are better than hot wars, and wars to end domestic poverty are superior to wars to destroy foreigners either militarily or financially. Still, without the war appellation we find no expansionary fiscal policy for long-run growth in the United States.

The data seem more consistent with government spending as an expansionary tool than taxation as an expansionary tool. That is consistent with Keynesian theory. There seems little reason to believe that fiscal policy will restrain inflation or cause it in non–large-war situations. It is clearly theoretically possible, but it seems unlikely that the country would endorse a massive increase in resources shifted to the government in a short time for anything other than a hot war. So the possible expansions through fiscal policy are severely limited by the political system. Inflation is largely a phenomenon caused by forces like OPEC and large foreign wars that cannot be controlled by normal fiscal or monetary policy. If the spending expansion of World War II or the Korean War is called fiscal policy, it means fiscal policy can cause inflation, but such an inflation could not be controlled by either budget cuts or M_2 decreases without threatening the war itself.

The review of federal fiscal policy record since the Great Depression shows that fiscal activity played an important role in the rise of big government at the federal level. Of course, the great and growing magnitude of public revenues and expenditures was the expression of domestic societal and international forces, not fiscal goals. Those enormous fiscal flows and adjustments demanded that the federal establishment, whether competent or not, assume an even greater managerial responsibility for their effect on people and the economy. That administrative assignment was much augmented, formally at least, by the Employment Act's assertion of federal responsibility for maximum employment, and therefore the general performance of the economy.

The government bungled much of its managerial task over the years. But whether it at times pursued deliberate Keynesian fiscal policy or inadvertent Keynesianism or salvage objectives or Cold War actions or anti-Keynesian programs, or just plain fiscal reductionism, both macro and micro fiscal administration on a massive scale continued to grow. Hence the history of federal fiscal behavior is closely connected with the subject of growing administrative management, treated in Chapter 3 of this work. Like the evolution of governmental regulatory activity as usually defined, fiscal activity has made its substantial and irreversible contribution to the managerial component of big government.

Budgeting, Meaning, and Misinformation

The notion of connecting the revenue, expenditure, and borrowing of the government is usually credited to the British government, which produced the world's first national budget in 1820. Most modern industrial nations were experimenting with systems of budgeting during the late nineteenth and early twentieth centuries. It is useful to note that all of the great empires of the past, and most modern capitalist nations, were developed without the institution of the budget.

In most of the world, budgeting is the system developed in the United Kingdom in the nineteenth century. Most credit for this development is usually given to the liberal prime minister William Gladstone, although there were many participants in the development of budgeting.

In Britain, after an election, the majority party nominates a prime minister. The prime minister then names the members of the cabinet. This committee of the Parliament is the administration. The cabinet, under the direction of the prime minister and the chancellor of the exchequer, writes a budget. Typically it is a one-year plan covering most of the tax receipts, borrowing, and expenditures of the government. The plan is presented to the Parliament, which debates it but normally cannot amend it. At the end of the debate Parliament votes. If the vote is yes, the plan is executed. If the vote is no, the prime minister resigns, the sovereign dissolves the Parliament, and a new Parliament is elected.

The British budgeting system is widely imitated around the world. It is a quick, responsive system. The whole process from election through parliamentary adoption of the budget takes just a few months, far less than a year.

Budgeting to Restrain Spending

The first budget of the United States was for 1923. President Taft, a pro-budget man, had prepared one for every year of his term, 1909–12. However, the Constitution gives the powers to tax, borrow, and spend to the Congress, which ignored Taft's budgets. Neither his predecessor, Theodore Roosevelt, nor his successor, Woodrow Wilson, was interested in budgeting, although Wilson under great political pressure did propose a budget act shortly before leaving office, only to veto it when Congress passed it in 1920.

In the United States, budgeting began with city governments. It was a tool of the conservative "reform" movements in their attempt to restrain the spending of the famous big-city political machines. After cities, states began to adopt budgets, again as a device to restrain the growth of government. At the national level, budgeting was again a demand of the politically conservative, who believed with budgets the growth of government would be restrained. This is all nicely summarized by Jesse Burkhead:

> The pressures for a budget system in cities and in state governments came as these governments expanded their activities at the turn of the century, and again in the 1920s. The pressures for federal reform were strong only when federal outlays increased faster than the increase of economic activity, and only when this differential rate of expansion produced stringency in federal government finance.[48]

The federal government grew rapidly during World War I, causing all taxes to increase significantly, which fit Burkhead's point, and in 1920 a very conservative government was elected. The result was the Budget Act of 1921 requiring the president to present a budget to the Congress in January of each year. The

Table 4.9

Federal and State and Local Receipts as Percentage of GNP

	$millions			Percent		
Year	Federal receipts	State and local receipts	GNP	Federal	State and local	Total
1890	403		13,100	3.08		
1895	325		13,900	2.34		
1900	567		18,700	3.03		
1902	562	1,041	21,600	2.60	4.82	7.42
1905	544		25,100	2.17		
1910	676		35,300	1.91		
1913	714	2,018	39,600	1.80	5.10	6.90
1915	683		40,000	1.71		
1920	6,649		91,500	7.26		
1922	4,026	5,061	74,100	5.43	6.83	12.26
1923	3,854		85,100	4.52		
1925	3,641		93,100	3.91		
1927	4,013	7,722	94,900	4.23	8.14	12.37
1929	3,861		103,100	3.74		
1930	4,058		90,400	4.49		
1932	1,924	7,655	58,000	3.32	13.20	16.52
1935	3,706		72,200	5.13		
1936	3,997	8,412	82,500	4.84	10.20	15.04
1940	6,879	10,804	99,700	6.90	10.84	17.74
1950	40,940	23,153	284,800	14.37	8.13	22.50
1960	92,492	45,530	503,700	18.36	9.04	27.40
1970	193,743	108,898	977,100	19.83	11.15	30.98
1980	517,100	299,293	2,742,100	18.86	10.91	29.77
1990	1,031,300	712,700	5,567,800	18.52	12.80	31.32

Sources: Historical Statistics of the United States (Washington: U.S. Dept. of Commerce, 1975), Vol. 1, p. 224; Vol. 2, pp. 1105–1106 and 1125–1126; for 1980 and 1990, the data are for fiscal years from the *Economic Report of the President*, 1994, pp. 294, 359, and 367.

first budget director, in his first speech to the heads of federal departments, said to the president who was attending, "You ask us to do our part in helping to lift the burden of taxation from the backs of the people by a reduction in the cost of government."[49] The first goal of the budget promoters in the United States at all levels of government was to restrain public spending and taxation. However, the budget has been an unequivocal failure as a device to restrain the growth of government spending and taxing. Table 4.9 shows tax receipts as a percent of GNP for selected years of the last century.

For the period 1900–1915, federal taxes as a percent of GNP are monotonically declining. Yet this is the period when increasing elements of society demanded the adoption of a budget system to restrain the "out-of-control" growth of federal spending. The 1912 report of President Taft's Commission on Economy and Efficiency and numerous books described and advocated a "national budget system."

The unbudgeted World War I increased the size of the federal government substantially. That fact, plus the long pro-budget political campaign largely led by former president Taft and the conservative Republican political sweep in the 1920 election, led to the adoption of the Budget Act in 1921. It created two important new political institutions: the Bureau of the Budget to assist the president in writing the budget, and the General Accounting Office to assist the Congress in monitoring the president's performance in administering the budget.

The Bureau of the Budget prepared the first federal government budget from July to December of 1921. It was presented to the Congress by the president late in the year. It described the planned taxing and spending for the fiscal year 1923—that is, July 1, 1922, to June 30, 1923.

Table 4.9 shows federal tax receipts as a percentage of GNP falling from 7.26 in 1920 to 4.52 in 1923. That is the unbudgeted period. In the next period, 1923–29, the federal share of GNP averages about 4 percent, a fall from 1923 but not as big a fall as the unbudgeted period achieved. Clearly, in the first thirty years of the twentieth century, most declines in the federal government's share of the GNP occurred in the no-budget periods rather than in the budget periods.

The enormous relative growth of the federal government, which is such a striking part of this century, was driven by four overlapping events: the Great Depression, World War II, the Cold War, and the development of the welfare state. None of these was amenable to budgeting, particularly budgeting designed to restrain public spending.

The early budgets were largely detailed lists of the objects the federal government was planning to buy and estimates of revenues from various taxes. In nonwar periods the principal "objects" of expenditures were employees. Budgets were more organized in a manner to encourage the Congress to cut spending than in a manner to encourage debate about social costs and benefits. Burkhead observed:

> The object classification may also serve to strengthen the legislature in relation to the operating departments, although frequently with rather perverse effects. . . . The over attention to detail inherent in the object classification undoubtably encourages over attention to detail at all levels of budget review, *with a consequent inattention to the larger issues which ought to be presented in the budget but which remain buried in the object detail.*[50]

The presidents did faithfully budget and the Congress did usually follow the pattern of presidential recommendations, although jealously guarding its nominal constitutional control over all taxing and spending by imposing many small changes as the object format encouraged. There was, as Herbert Stein has noted, little tendency for the federal government to change. "During the 1920s the size of the federal budget had been fairly constant."[51]

The Great Depression, one of Burkhead's larger issues, imposed the first important test on the budget system. Stein observed:

> As a result of the automatic decline of revenues with falling incomes, and the payments on the veterans' certificates, the changes in the budget between 1929 and 1931 were very large relative to the size of the budget, and even of quite substantial size relative to the size of the economy in 1929. Receipts declined by almost 50 per cent and expenditures rose by almost 60 per cent. The swing from surplus to deficit was over 3 percent of the 1929 gross national product.[52]

President Hoover's budget for 1930 included estimates for revenues that were clearly based on the assumption that the economy was not declining. The more it declined, the greater the demands from Congress and other influential public groups that spending be increased. The veterans' bonus mentioned by Herbert Stein was passed over Hoover's opposition and forced large transfers from the government to veterans. Stein calls all this "fiscal stimulation by inadvertence."

Late in 1931, President Hoover decided to call for a very large tax increase to balance the budget. Stein says this was primarily a response to the British government's abandonment of the gold standard. The effects in the United States, according to Stein, were an increase in interest rates, an outflow of gold, and increased bank failures. The president, in his State of the Union message on December 8, 1931, observed:

> Our first step toward recovery is to reestablish confidence and thus restore the flow of credit which is the very basis of our economic life.
>
> The first requirement of confidence and economic recovery is financial stability of the United States Government.
>
> Even with increased taxation, the government will reach the utmost safe limit of its borrowing capacity by the expenditures for which we are all ready obligated and the recommendations here proposed. To go farther than these limits in either expenditures, taxes, or borrowing will destroy confidence, denude commerce and industry of their resources, jeopardize the financial system, and actually extend unemployment and demoralize agriculture rather than relieve it.[53]

In fact, the proposals of the president were to achieve a balanced budget in 1932.

As we now know, raising tax rates as an economy collapses will not increase revenues. It is more likely to accelerate economic decline, which is what happened. Hoover could not be blamed for not knowing the then-unknown Keynesian economics. But he can be blamed for the traditional, conservative, excessive reliance on a balanced budget. In the twenty-six calendar years 1894 through 1919 the federal government ran a deficit seventeen times—that is, from Hoover's twentieth to forty-sixth year of life. The national debt increased from $1 billion to $25.5 billion, while the nation won two wars and expanded from a significant regional power to the unquestioned dominant power of the earth. This massive increase in government debt and international power and responsibility did not cause a crisis of confidence in the bond market. Why would further debt increases do so?

Champions of the beliefs that bond traders' expectations will, if unfulfilled, cause serious declines in the economy were common in 1931, as they are today in conservative economic circles. The problem then was much as it is now, but the consequences were worse. To act to preserve the imagined expectations of bond traders in the face of economic collapse is to try to protect a few at the expense of the many.

The next year Hoover was defeated in a reelection bid. The economy continued to decline, and Hoover blamed much of that decline on the reaction of people in the "markets" to the notions of Franklin Roosevelt. There was a very long interregnum between the election of the president in the first week of November and his inauguration in the first week of March. During that interregnum the crisis got significantly worse, with Michigan closing all its banks and other states planning to follow Michigan's lead. Arthur M. Schlesinger Jr. reports that Hoover proposed to Roosevelt that

> a very early statement by you upon two or three policies of your Administration would serve greatly to restore confidence and cause resumption of the march of recovery.... It would steady the country greatly if there could be prompt assurance that there will be no tampering or inflation of the currency; that the budget will be unquestionably balanced, even if further taxation is necessary; that the government credit will be maintained by refusal to exhaust it in the issue of securities.[54]

Here we see budget balancing as a form of mental disease. In 1931, tax rates were increased. In 1932, collections and the economy declined further. Hoover's advice to Roosevelt was to do it again because the markets and the credit system expected it. This is a strange form of class war in which the rich and the securities-market–sophisticated have produced an overblown credit system leading to a bubble in the stock market and then a collapse. Because of their expectations, everyone's taxes must rise. There is no similar concern for the expectations of the formerly employed, the formerly profitable small businesses bankrupted by the financial collapse and the tax increase, or the former students driven out of schools by the decline in their parents' resources into an economy with no new jobs.

Budgeting had meant "Keep the cost and size of government down." The federal government did not grow under the Republican budgets of the 1920s. That meaning died with the removal of Herbert Hoover from office in March 1933. Depending on the measure of size used, the federal government grew relative to the economy until 1960 on an employment and purchases basis, until 1970 on a receipts basis, and until 1990 on an expenditures basis. See Table 4.10. It is clearly in the era of budgeting that most of the federal government's

Table 4.10

Measures of the Size of the Federal Government (in percent)

Year	Receipts/ GDP	Purchases/ GDP	Expenditures/ GDP	Employees/ labor force
1940	6.5	6.0	9.5	2.7
1950	13.8	6.5	15.0	4.9
1960	18.0	10.8	18.0	5.8
1970	19.1	9.9	19.4	5.7
1980	19.1	7.7	21.8	4.1
1990	18.6	7.7	22.6	3.8
1993	18.1	6.4	22.1	3.4

Sources: Calculated from *Economic Report of the President*, 1994, pp. 268–269, 359, 306–307, 318–319; and *Economic Report of the President*, 1975, p. 249; for employment in 1940, *Historical Statistics of the United States, Colonial Times to 1970*, Vol. 2, pp. 1102, 1141. All employment, expenditures, and purchases include the armed forces.

relative growth has occurred. The broadly understood goal of budgets—to restrain government growth—clearly failed.

Budgeting as a Fiscal Policy Tool

Although Franklin Roosevelt had included a balanced budget in his goals during the presidential campaign of 1932, and he did dutifully submit a budget to the Congress every year as the law required, he could not be said to have budgeted in the usual sense. His management system is described in detail by Janeway.[55] He would listen to advice on how to deal with the problems the country faced. Whenever Roosevelt heard an idea he thought possibly useful, he would have a proposal drawn up and sent to the Congress to try the project. He never considered himself limited by the budget he had submitted, nor did the Congress.

When the performance of an agency assigned to some problem was found wanting, Roosevelt would propose assigning the problem to some other, often newly created agency. He would strip authority from the old agency but would not propose its abolition. Consequently, the number of new federal agencies grew faster than the number of new tasks, which were growing rapidly. Such a system does not seem to conform to any of the standard notions of budgeting or fiscal policy.

As the welfare state developed, its principal programs, old-age pensions, dependent and survivors income, unemployment compensation, and Medicare were financed by special "trusts" consisting of a dedicated tax and an expenditure formula. These constitute the biggest part of the continuing growth of the federal component of big government. Defense is bigger whenever war, cold or hot, expands considerably. But the continual, year-after-year, unrelenting growth of government is the welfare state. There is no possibility of an end to the welfare state, as there was an end to the Cold War.

The national government chose to treat the trusts as programs separate from the rest of government and typically did not include them in the budget. This noninclusive budget came to be called the *administrative budget*. Later, all the trusts were added together and called the *trust budget*. The trust budget included the highway trust financed by a gasoline tax, which is really a public works rather than a welfare state program.

Particularly with the expansion of the government in World War II, it became obvious that the effect of the government on the economy was not measured by the traditional budget. This led to the development of the *consolidated-cash budget*. This budget measured total government expenditures and receipts by combining administrative and trust accounts. Presumably, if the government was spending more into the private economy than it was taxing away from the private economy it was contributing to the private economy.

The consolidated-cash or cash budget evolved out of estimates of the income-increasing–expenditures of government done by Lauchlin Currie in 1935. The detailed construction of the budget was done by Budget Director Grover Ensley during the war and it was accepted as a budget rather than as a supporting document because of the extensive use and promotion of the idea by the CED in 1947.[56]

One major problem this method solved was the peculiar treatment of Social Security in the budget soon to be known as the administrative budget. In the late 1930s the Social Security trust had very large receipts and very small expenditures. *The surplus was invested in Treasury securities.* The Social Security trust account treated the purchase of the securities as an expenditure, so the trust was always exactly in balance. This trust surplus was thus turned into a budget deficit![57]

By the time of the Eisenhower administration there were three standard budgets: administrative, trust, and cash. None of the budgets was on an accrual basis. It had been recognized in the 1920s that government accrual accounting was necessary to accurately depict the effects of various policies. During the 1960s various methods of connecting government receipts and expenditures with the national income accounts were developed. As noted above, Gayer had attempted some primitive accrual accounting in his 1938 estimates of government income-generating expenditure.

The income account, or *national income accounts budgets,* included rudimentary accrual of some tax receipts. For example, the corporate profits tax was recorded when earned by the corporation rather than when paid, which was typically several quarters later. As more finely developed in the late 1960s and the 1970s, these budgets represented receipts, expenditures, and deficits, not on an actual experience basis but on a normative rate of economic performance basis. The early national income accounts budgets developed in the Kennedy-

Johnson years reported on a normative 4 percent unemployment rate. Later under Nixon this was split into two budgets, one called *high employment,* reporting receipts and expenditures that would occur at 5 percent unemployment, and another called *full employment,* reporting on the rates of spending and taxing at 4 percent unemployment. In more recent years the normative rates of employment in the income accounts budget have been raised to 5 and 6 percent. There is a detailed description of this budget in the 1971 *Economic Report of the President.*[58]

When the accounts of the government are measured several different ways it is possible to get several different deficit figures for any significant total like receipts, expenditures, or deficit. That has been the case with the federal government for almost fifty years.

> The use of these three concepts of the federal budget (Administrative, Consolidated-Cash, and National Income) frequently led to confusion, especially after all three were highlighted together in one large lead-off table beginning with fiscal 1963, the first Kennedy budget. The three provided alternative formulations of receipts and expenditures and consequently different figures regarding the government surplus or deficit. To illustrate the kind of confusion that existed, for the fiscal 1968 budget the Associated Press reported budget expenditures of $135 billion, United Press International reported $172.4 billion, *The New York Times* $169.2 billion. All of the totals referred to "the" budget.[59]

For the fiscal 1969 budget, President Johnson, on the advice of the President's Commission on Budget Concepts, adopted a *unified budget,* which technically combined all the budget systems. The unified budget provides a single total for the budget with special reports that effectively cover the old administrative budget, trust budget, cash budget, and income accounts budgets. There are also complex reconciliations of the various budget concepts published in the Unified Budget and sometimes in the *Economic Report of the President.*

Budgeting as Political Fad

Curiously, the Congress, which according to the Constitution has all budgeting authority, had never budgeted. Budgeting in the traditional sense as taught in economics, home economics, and accounting has very simple themes. First, collect all the resources available. Second, list all of the demands for goods and services. Third, if resources exceed demands, supply the demands and save the extra or cut taxes in the government case. If demands exceed what the available resources can supply, then (1) cut demands, or (2) increase resources through (a) increased income or taxes or (b) increased debt.

For most of the history of federal budgeting, the Congress has received the budget as a single unit from the president, broken it into parts consistent with the committee structure of the Congress (which is not quite the same as the department structure of the administration), and proceeded to decide on the parts without ever discussing the effects of the parts on the whole. For example, the Foreign Relations Committees passed bills authorizing spending on projects involving foreign relations and the Postal Committees passed bills on postal spending. The Ways and Means Committee of the House of Representatives was the principal authority and author of tax bills. Ways and Means could and did ignore the spending decisions. The other committees could and did ignore the revenue decisions.

The actual laws authorizing the operation of the government in a typical year are eleven to thirteen appropriations bills that typically but not universally authorize spending for one year. These bills, with modifications, are passed every year. Most taxes are in effect indefinitely but their provisions are modified annually. The set of laws controlling spending and taxing for a year have no name. They are commonly confused with "the budget." Legally, the budget is the proposal of the president for some year. There are no cases where the Congress accepts the president's proposals unmodified.

In the Congressional Budget Act of 1974, the anti-budget behavior of the Congress was directly addressed. The fiscal year was shifted from July 1 to June 30, as it had been since 1842, to October 1 to September 30. The Congress authorized two new budget committees to specifically address budget problems. The budget process was broken into two logical steps. From the presentation of the budget by the president in January to May, the Congress was to study and debate the macroeconomic issues. By the end of May it was to have adopted total spending, taxing, and borrowing amounts to optimize aggregate economic behavior in the coming year. Then from June to September it was to make the micro decisions: how much defense, postal service, welfare, and tax subsidies.

The role of the budget committees was to enforce the aggregate budget decisions made in May and guide the reconciliation done in September. The reconciliation was to be a great debate accommodating the micro decisions with the macro decisions. If the nation truly needed more public services than the macro decision would allow, then a debate on increasing taxes or debt would be appropriate. If the micro totals were too big and the necessity arguments too weak, then the decisions of the spending committees would have to be cut back. This was all to begin in 1976 with the enactment of the fiscal 1977 budget. None of the discussion regarding the act addressed the long-run growth of the economy.

This is being written in fiscal 1997, twenty years after the Congressional Budget Act took effect. In that period there has been one reconciliation debate. Congress did not like it and does not do it. Instead, it passes appropriations and taxes much as it did in the past. Often they can be said to exceed the guidelines the budget committees are to enforce. But as yet the budget committees have not been able to veto the behavior of the other committees. It seems Congress will not budget in the traditional sense.

Presidents have often championed schemes to improve the budgeting process.

Lyndon Johnson, greatly impressed with the work of Robert McNamara and his "whiz kids," imposed the system they were using at the Pentagon on the entire federal establishment. It was called planning programming budgeting systems (PPBS). Essentially it required every federal program to provide a cost-benefit analysis of itself for the forthcoming year and show how that was most likely to evolve over time.

In a perfect PPBS world, the high-level managers would receive a detailed outline of the evolution of the costs of government over the next several years and the benefits associated with those costs. Unfortunately, most of the civil service had not a clue as to how to do a "correct" cost-benefit analysis. They were faced with questions like what the current dollar value was of increasing the life expectancy of alligators in southern Alabama. There are no market data. Of course they made up the answers; no one could meaningfully evaluate or aggregate them.

While the civil service attempted to learn the PPBS system, it was used as part of the management of the Vietnam War, where it failed totally. President Nixon formally abandoned PPBS early in his term. But some local governments were adopting it as much as a decade later.

President Johnson's unified budget put together the administrative and trust budgets that President Eisenhower had separated in the 1950s. Both presidents described their changes in budget systems as improvements. As noted earlier, surpluses in the Social Security Trust Funds were reported in the budgets of the late 1930s as deficits in "the budget," since the Treasury had to issue bonds to the trusts in the amount of their surpluses. Those funds were then spent to finance the government generally. If the Treasury or the Social Security Trusts just save the money (not spend it), the economy definitely declines.

In 1983 a commission directed by Alan Greenspan recommended a large increase in payroll taxes for the Social Security Old Age Trust. These taxes, like those in the 1930s, were to exceed trust expenditures. They are now carried in the public accounts as off budget receipts and expenditures. Again, the Treasury receives and spends the trust receipts. If it didn't, the government would continually take out of the economy more than it spent into the economy, which would contract the economy.

If the Social Security Trust surpluses are reported as part of the total federal government they also reduce the deficit. If reported separately they seem to say we are saving for the old age of the baby boom population, which is an act separate from usual government acts and so reasonably treated as separate. Eisenhower's trust budget is back but now it is called *off budget receipts and outlays*.

For fiscal policy purposes, a payroll tax slows the economy down about the same as an income tax. So budgets aimed at fiscal policy questions should include the trust accounts. For other goals, they may be better excluded. The current pattern is to include for two or three presidential terms, then exclude for a while.

Multiple budgets for multiple goals make more sense but are harder to explain.

President Carter championed "zero-based budgeting." In its simplest form it assumes that all government programs have a beginning budget of zero. As the president and Congress are convinced of their value, the acceptable budget rises. This was never formally adopted, possibly because it requires an annual debate on questions such as whether the Department of Defense should exist, a silly question that takes time away from the meaningful question of how we should modify defense spending.

A number of states have adopted sunset laws. They assume all spending on a project must be reviewed every ten or fifteen years. The biggest saving under the Oregon sunset law was the abolition of the Board of Watchmakers, a quality control program with three part-time employees. In Colorado, the program that most completely failed the first round of sunset law reviews was the sunset law.

More than any other slogan, the "annually balanced budget" has been championed as the way to get government spending down. Thirty-five states have called for a constitutional convention to create a balanced budget amendment to the Constitution. It was introduced into the Oregon Legislature and passed in less than a week with no public hearings. Meanwhile, Oregon has seven publicly owned colleges and universities, all of which teach introductory economics using textbooks that explain how fiscal policy means using the deficit as part of macroeconomic control.

In 1995, the House of Representatives passed a Balanced Budget Amendment and in 1996 the U.S. Senate defeated it by one vote (most think it was Mark Hatfield of Oregon). Past and current presidents, cabinet members, congressmen, and senators often champion this simple rule. They have all worked with the budget; they know that there is not one budget, but several. Typically they don't say which one should be balanced. Is it the administrative budget, the unified budget, one of several income accounts budgets, or the congressional budget?

Statements of the sort, "When little Alanis is born she is $XXX thousand in debt," where XXX is national debt divided by population, are continually shouted and published by people who should know better. In such statements they ignore that by the same logic little Alanis will inherit $XXX worth of federal bonds so that her net wealth inheritance from the process is zero.

Economists behave little better. The Nobel Prize winner James Buchanan years ago argued that the burden of debt was passed to future generations, the opposite of economic thinking since David Ricardo. Buchanan's model clearly assumed full employment. His contribution was a new notion of burden. Since people bought federal bonds voluntarily on a market, they could not be burdened. The burden was to pay taxes to pay off bonds. Since taxes are coercion, they are burden.

In a short-period fiscal policy model, there normally is no full employment. Debt caused by cutting taxes would expand the economy through expanded consumption and investment. That is, the government borrows so that consumers and businesses can spend. Income is created that funds the debt, and there is no burden anywhere.

More modern conservative economists like Robert Barro have argued that people expect a Buchanan-like burden whenever national debt is increased. Consequently, their "rational expectations" lead them to save sufficiently to pay the taxes when they come due. Consequently, increases in government spending and cuts in taxes for fiscal policy reasons fail, since rational expectations drive spending down while fiscal policy models expect it to rise.

Both Buchanan, who accepts the short-run effects of fiscal policy if there is unemployment, and Barro, who says there are no positive effects either long run or short run, require people to expect debt increases to imply tax increases. But the logic of the national debt in a fiscal policy world is a ratchet. *Debt never goes down, so taxes to pay it off need never be imposed.*

Some of the debt is regularly paid off. The bonds are paid by issuing new bonds, not by imposing taxes to pay the debt off. The general trend of national debt throughout American history is up. It was paid off once under Andrew Jackson, but a recession promptly recreated it, as fiscal theory predicts. Why would Americans think high national debt means higher taxes, when neither historical statistics, Treasury practice, nor empirically oriented economic theory requires it?

Meaningful budget discussions require the discussants to know which budget they are talking about. For a year like 1973, that would be either the unified budget or the income accounts budget in either the high- or the full-employment versions. For a year like 1958, it would be the administrative budget, the trust budget, or the cash budget.

The U.S. government budget cycle takes four years. The president prepares a budget from January to January. Congress then enacts the budget from January to October 30. The budget is then enforced for a fiscal year. After the fiscal year it is audited, which can take more than a year in some cases. When we say Fiscal 1996, we mean the budget year October 1, 1995, to September 30, 1996. In any calendar year the government is working on four fiscal years. This produces the pattern in Table 4.11.

All phases of the budget cycle are public. Technically, preparation occurs in the executive office of the president; practically, a large staff spread over a large number of offices does the work. When final-cut or inclusion decisions are being made, the part of the community affected gets word of the decisions from friends in the cabinet, civil service, or Congress who want particular programs. Then the lobbyists go to work intensely. If there is a cut there is usually an appeal, sometimes in the press. Journalists figured out during the Cold War that the United States had an annual missile crisis every fall when some of the many proposed missile programs were cut from the Pentagon budget.

Enactment by the Congress is the most public part of the process. Both houses of Congress hold detailed hearings on virtually every spending and tax program. Again, the lobbyists thrive. Most are then published.

Table 4.11

Stages of Fiscal-Year Budgets in a Calendar Year

Calendar year 1997	Fiscal year 1999	Fiscal year 1998	Fiscal year 1997	Fiscal year 1996
January	Preparation		Enforcement	
February	by OMB	Enactment	by president	Audit
March	and	by	and cabinet	by
April	president	Congress		GAO
May				
June				
July				
August				
September				
October			Audit	
November		Enforcement	by	
December		by president and cabinet	GAO	

Source: Robert D. Lee Jr. and Ronald W. Johnson, *Public Budgeting Systems* (Baltimore: University Park Press, 1973), pp. 94–99.

Enforcement—the actual spending of the money and collecting the taxes—is probably the least public. In part, that is because a fiscal year budget has been intensely debated by the government and the public for twenty-one months before it takes effect. Still, there are continual comments about how the current programs are working and should be modified. When the General Accounting Office was created, it was hoped it would be the source of fine new public accounting systems to enable the government to better measure what it was doing and how to do it cheaper. Mostly it has become a simple watchdog for the Congress to keep the president spending as directed. Every year it finds some theft, misspent funds, and silly programs. It is useful but not fundamental work.

Since the federal government has more than one budget and is continually working on at least four fiscal years, meaningful statements about budgets should include which type of budget is being discussed and for what fiscal year. Public discussions of budgets in the press, speeches of congressmen and economists, and petitions for referenda on the balanced budget virtually never pass this test. *The minimum rule for scientific work is to state your information in a way that enables others to check it.* American commentary about the federal budget virtually never reports both the fiscal year and budget type discussed. Consequently in a scientific sense these discussions have no meaning.

Many good economists have tried to make budgets meaningful for fiscal policy. Currie, Gayer, Brown, the CED, Eisner, and the CEA under Presidents Kennedy, Johnson, and Nixon are among the contributors mentioned in this chapter. But progress in this area is being reversed. There is much discussion of the budget, macroeconomic policy, the debt, and the deficit in the *Economic*

Report of the President, for 1996 from Clinton and for 1993 from Bush. But there is no mention of income accounts or full- or high-employment budgets or any other adjustment necessary to make meaningful connections between the unified budget and the career of the economy. There are no adjustments for the inflation or interest-rate effects of the debt. Fiscal policy as developed from 1936 to the Nixon era is not part of modern American government. The debts and deficits and their connections to macroeconomic events are clearly mismeasured in the public pronouncements of the president and his economic advisers, as well as most other political leaders.

Notes

1. John Maynard Keynes, *The General Theory of Employment, Interest and Money* (New York: Harcourt, Brace and Company, 1936), pp. 94–95.

2. Alvin Hansen, "Mr. Keynes on Underemployment Equilibrium," *Journal of Political Economy* 44, no. 5 (October 1936), pp. 667–686.

3. Alvin Hansen, *Full Recovery or Stagnation* (New York: W.W. Norton, 1938).

4. Arthur D. Gayer, "Fiscal Policies," *Papers and Proceedings of the American Economic Association,* March 1938, pp. 90–112.

5. Ibid., p. 107.

6. Ibid., p. 111.

7. Alvin Hansen, *Fiscal Policy and Business Cycles* (New York: W.W. Norton, 1941).

8. Ibid., pp. 346–347.

9. Hansen, *Full Recovery or Stagnation,* pp. 267–289.

10. Hansen, *Fiscal Policy and Business Cycles,* p. 84.

11. Ibid., p. 85.

12. E. Cary Brown, "Fiscal Policy in the 'Thirties: A Reappraisal," *American Economic Review* 46, no. 5 (December 1956), pp. 857–879.

13. Ibid., p. 869.

14. Committee for Economic Development, *Taxes and the Budget: A Program for Prosperity in a Free Economy* (New York: Committee for Economic Development, 1947).

15. Herbert Stein, *Fiscal Revolution in America* (Chicago: University of Chicago Press, 1969), p. 204.

16. Ibid., pp. 200–202.

17. Harold G. Vatter, *The U.S. Economy in World War II* (New York: Columbia University Press, 1985), pp. 104–110.

18. Alvin Hansen, *Business Cycles and National Income* (New York: W.W. Norton, 1951), p. 532.

19. Stein, *Fiscal Revolution,* pp. 206–220.

20. *Economic Report of the President,* January 1978, p. 313.

21. Reuben E. Schlesinger, *National Economic Policy: The Presidential Reports* (Princeton: D. Van Nostrand, 1968), pp. 35–51.

22. Harold G. Vatter, John F. Walker, and Gar Alperovitz, "The Onset and Persistence of Secular Stagnation: 1910–1990," *Journal of Economic Issues* 27, no. 2 (June 1995), pp. 591–600.

23. Raymond J. Saulnier, *Contemporary Monetary Theory* (New York: Columbia University Press, 1938), p. 375.

24. Cabinet Committee on Price Stability for Economic Growth, "Interim Report to the President," reprinted in *The Annals of the American Academy,* 1960, pp. 133–138.

25. *Economic Report of the President,* January 1967, pp. 284–285.

26. Ibid., pp. 214, 263, 279.

27. *Economic Report of the President,* January 1962, pp. 72–77.

28. Stein, *Fiscal Revolution,* pp. 422.

29. Cited in ibid., pp. 449–450.

30. *Economic Report of the President,* January 1967, pp. 284–286.

31. Walter Heller, "Activist Government: Key to Growth," *Challenge* 29, no. 2 (March/April 1986), p. 7.

32. *Economic Report of the President,* January 1968, p. 4.

33. *Economic Report of the President,* February 1986, p. 26.

34. *Economic Report of the President,* 1989, p. 58.

35. Bernard Baruch, *American Industry in the War* (New York: Prentice-Hall, 1941), pp. 380–385.

36. Calculated from *Economic Report of the President,* January 1973, p. 252.

37. *Economic Report of the President,* January 1973, pp. 61–62.

38. *Economic Report of the President,* January 1974, p. 108.

39. *Economic Report of the President,* January 1973, pp. 51–56.

40. John F. Walker and Harold G. Vatter, "The Princess and the Pea; or the Alleged Vietnam War Origins of the Current Inflation," *Journal of Economic Issues* 16, no. 3 (June 1982), pp. 597–607; Charles B. Garrison and Anne Mayhew, "The Alleged Vietnam War Origins of the Current Inflation," *Journal of Economic Issues,* March 1983, pp. 175–186; and John F. Walker and Harold G. Vatter, "Demonstrating the Undemonstrable," ibid., pp. 186–195.

41. Herbert Stein, "A Successful Accident: Recollections and Speculations about the CEA," *Journal of Economic Perspectives* 10, no. 3 (Summer 1996), pp. 15–20.

42. Charles L. Schultze, "The CEA: An Inside Voice for Mainstream Economics," *Journal of Economic Perspectives* 10, no. 3 (Summer 1996), pp. 33–36; and Stein, "A Successful Accident," p. 18.

43. Schultze, "The CEA," pp. 34, 36.

44. J. Bradford DeLong, "Keynesianism, Pennsylvania Avenue Style: Some Economic Consequences of the Employment Act of 1946," *Journal of Economic Perspectives* 10, no. 3 (Summer 1996), p. 48.

45. Robert Eisner, *How Real is the Federal Deficit?* (New York: The Free Press, 1986), pp. 78–94.

46. Stein, "A Successful Accident," p. 18.

47. *Economic Report of the President,* January 1988, p. 23.

48. Jesse Burkhead, *Government Budgeting* (New York: John Wiley, 1966), p. 28.

49. Quoted in ibid., p. 28.

50. Ibid., p. 130, emphasis added.

51. Stein, *Fiscal Revolution,* p. 14.

52. Ibid., p. 26.

53. Cited in ibid., pp. 33–34.

54. Arthur M. Schlesinger Jr., *The Crisis of the Old Order* (Boston: Houghton Mifflin, 1957), p. 476.

55. Eliot Janeway, *The Struggle for Survival: A Chronicle of Economic Mobilization in World War II* (New Haven: Yale University Press, 1951).

56. Stein, *Fiscal Revolution,* pp. 230–231.

57. Ibid., p. 124.

58. *Economic Report of the President,* January 1971, pp. 70–74.

59. Robert D. Lee Jr. and Ronald W. Johnson, *Public Budgeting Systems* (Baltimore: University Park Press, 1973), p. 233.

CHAPTER FIVE

The Rise of the American Welfare State

The long-run expansion of the welfare state as conceived here, after World War II, was a major contributor to the growth of government in general. Its expansion, using the criterion of expenditures in particular, was dominated by the federal government's share of total all-government welfare outlays. That dominant role was due primarily, at least up to the 1970s, to the social insurance component at the federal level. Veterans' benefits and education are excluded here from the definition of the welfare state because such aid long antedated the mixed economy era.

Table 5.1 below shows that the total of real social welfare expenditures under the selected public programs increased at an annual rate of about 7 percent between 1950 and 1991. This was approximately twice as fast as real GNP or GDP. They might have risen relatively even faster had it not been for the politico-economic competition they chronically faced with the not-so-Cold-War military budget at the federal level. With real national defense outlays slowly, slightly, and reluctantly drifting downward after the end of the Cold War, Americans began to confront more starkly and with highly emotional controversy the extent of their commitment to their welfare state. That commitment came under unrelenting attack by right-wing elements in the mid-nineties.

It is because of the persistence of this adversary Cold War–welfare state relationship, along with the absence of universal health care entitlement, that the U.S. welfare state may be termed peculiar. (This health care gap was briefly treated in Chapter 3.) Implicit in that adjective is comparison with the typical European welfare state—that is, one in which the social consensus demanding welfare as an entitlement has been less sullied by competing Cold War military expenditures. Also implicit in making the comparison is the hypothesis that in these other mature social market systems the community has developed a pro–economic-growth consensus—a consensus that could be realized only if the real government outlay growth rate approximates the real socially demanded GNP rate, whatever that might be.

Table 5.1

Social Welfare Expenditures Under Public Programs ($millions)

Years	Social insurance	Public aid	Health and medical	Housing	Other social welfare	Grand total
1950	4,947	2,496	2,064	15	448	9,970
1960	19,307	4,101	4,464	177	1,139	29,188
1970	54,691	16,488	9,753	701	4,406	86,039
1980	230,000	73,000	27,000	7,000	14,000	351,000
1992	617,000	208,000	70,000	21,000	22,000	938,000
Average annual real percentage changes						
1950–92	7.56	6.53	2.39	13.95	5.20	6.58
1950–70	9.81	7.02	3.78	18.06	9.17	8.08
1970–92	5.55	6.09	1.14	10.34	1.72	5.24

Source: Economic Report of the President, 1995, pp. 278, 341. Deflators for 1950 calculated. All deflators are for gross domestic product except "health and medical," which is CPI for medical care. Current dollar data in top panel are from *Statistical Abstracts*, 1975, p. 280 and 1995, p. 374. The listed categories include administrative expenditures and capital outlay.

Delineation of what constitutes the civilian welfare state embracing all levels of government requires treatment of the distinction between welfare entitlements and means-tested "poor law" programs. Because so much of the "poor law" type programs are deeply rooted in past laissez-faire history, there is an interpretive risk in identifying such programs with the welfare state in the era of big government. Nevertheless, the rise of the affluent society, and the public's accompanying humanistic insistence on a war on poverty and a social safety net, have produced augmented spillover effects on means-tested programs from its newer entitlement institutions. This interrelationship between the two warrants a common treatment for both programmatic types under the welfare state rubric, so long as the distinction is retained for certain interpretive purposes.

Delineating the Welfare State

The welfare state as conceived herein is not an explicitly programmed economic income-distribution institution. Nor is it in the strict sense designed to relieve acute distress. That is exclusively a "poor law" function that, however, has been blanketed under the broader definition indicated. Nor does the welfare state embrace all varieties of government social policy. For example, government encouragement of collective bargaining, or environmental policy, or public infrastructure services such as sanitation, sewerage, and education, are not hallmarks of the welfare state.

The strictly conceived welfare state (i.e., entitlements) employs the insurance principle (self-help), embracing premium-linked social security. Unlike private insurance, both high-risk and low-risk individuals are obligatorily covered. The strictly conceived welfare state emphasizes entitlement rather than means tests. Benefits are received as a right. Welfare state "insurance" applies universally for all persons within the covered group. It is committed to a safety net that is designed to provide a material minimum promising escape from want and poverty for those covered. It vastly expands the transfer payment. It is consistent with regressive taxes. It is committed to high employment (e.g., the Employment Act of 1946) and therefore, assuming more or less stable work hours for a growing labor force, economic growth.

And finally, the welfare state evolves. A prime example of its evolutionary character is the extension of coverage under its social insurance programs. In the U.S. case the number of civilian employees covered by the Social Security Act's Old-Age, Survivors, Disability, and Health Insurance (OASDHI) was about 66 percent of total paid civilian employment in 1950; but by 1970 the percentage had jumped to 88, and in 1991 covered persons accounted for 95 percent. The self-employed were not covered at the beginning of the 1950s, but by 1955 about 7 million had already been blanketed in.[1]

The expenditure programs included here in the welfare state category are shown in Table 5.1. As noted earlier, there are two major exclusions from the table: veterans' programs and education. The veterans exclusion is due partly to the fact that those programs were discussed earlier in Chapter 3, but also because (1) they represent no historical discontinuity in the social consensus toward their entitlements as between laissez-faire and the welfare state era, and (2) in real expenditure terms they grew at only a moderate rate from 1950 to 1994 and not at all after the mid-1970s. Their career reflects primarily that of foreign wars together with health and aging changes within the veteran population itself.

The exclusion of educational expenditures is a different matter. It will be recalled that the explosion in such outlays was mainly connected with the community's presumption that the baby boomers had a right to a public school education. That is why the state- and local-dominated real total of educational expenditures jumped up to a yearly rate of 8 percent between 1950 and 1970 and then collapsed to only 2.4 percent annually during the next two decades. This is not the long-run welfare state in action, and should not be confused with the general slowdown in the welfare state's growth after the mid-seventies. It is due rather to a demographic hump differing distinctly from the long-run growth in the elderly population, which provided the entering wedge for establishment of an abiding institution embracing public retirement benefits and Medicare.

The much smaller stream of real federal expenditures for education also exploded between 1950 and 1970. This is partly because the federal government showed some response to the baby boom at the elementary and secondary levels of schooling, instituting federal aid to such education for the first time.[2] The

Table 5.2

Real "Poor Law" Means-Tested Spending (1987 dollars)

Year	Spending	Span	Annual percentage rate of increase
1950	27,959	1950–92	5.30
1960	40,853	1950–70	6.02
1970	90,035	1970–92	4.64
1980	167,150		
1991	244,433		

Source: See Table 5.1.

federal government spent increasing amounts in those two decades to subsidize both public and private higher education. This latter development has been explained previously as due to the immediate postwar's G.I. Bill plus the subsequent upsurge in women's higher education enrollment, a groundswell in demand that continued through the 1980s. Women's enrollment soared and bachelor's degrees conferred on females rose between 1960 and 1970, by far the greatest decadal increase, by 9.5 percent a year!

But the special and historically limited character of the federal role in those developments is shown by the fact that its real expenditures for *all* levels of education, public and private, were only 29 percent higher in 1991 than they had been in 1970.[3] This is an annual percentage increase of only 1.22 per year. Its expenditures made a definite contribution to government growth up to about 1970, but for the whole era after World War II they failed to match the growth rate pattern of the real welfare state outlays (except for "Other Social Welfare") depicted in Table 5.1.

Growth of Social Welfare Expenditures

If we examine the columns in Table 5.1 showing the deflated annual expenditure rates for the selected series, we have a bird's-eye view of the welfare state's career and the size of its contribution to all-government growth. The grand total in the last column of deflated average annual expenditure rates shows a very high average yearly growth rate of almost 7 percent over the whole postwar era, 1950 to 1991. By far the fastest growth in the total was in the first twenty years, after which it slowed down distinctly. But even so, its growth rate from 1970 to 1991 was still much higher than that of real GDP.

If we calculate a total for all means-tested real "poor law" series in Table 5.1, we get a similar difference between the two subperiods as shown in Table 5.2. *This difference in the two periods is the basic pattern for the postwar era.* It is seen in almost every component series.

By way of partial explanation, reference to John Kenneth Galbraith's interpretation may well be pertinent. Galbraith has suggested that, at some historic point, increased economic well-being of the community became a major cause of spreading interest in "economic security"—that the public's urge to attack the material hazards of modern economic life increased "in the sense that people have more to lose."[4] This partial interpretation derives support from the empirical fact that the yearly average compound growth rate of real per capita disposable personal income soared 2.24 percent from 1950 to 1970, and in the sixties was a phenomenal 3 percent. But from 1970 to 1991 the annual rate dropped to 1.68 percent.

The eminent historian of economic growth, Moses Abramovitz, rounds out Galbraith's interpretation about the effect of affluence with the assertion that the attack on poverty in recent times derives in part from a "sense of deprivation which stems from inability to consume or possess the goods that people somewhat better off can have. This sense of deprivation is intensified as communication and advertising develop."[5] Here we have a combination of social impulses from Galbraith's relatively well-off and Abramovitz's relatively deprived that generates a current of political activism leading to correction of the imbalance by the state. And the correlation with the rate of per capita income growth is striking. Here the market system scores, for it is the evolving mixed market system that has been primarily responsible for the secular rise in per capita income. Indeed, it is income growth that eases both the spread of the welfare safety net and efforts to redistribute that income.

Scanning the substantial real growth rates of the component series in Table 5.1 demonstrates that those welfare state expenditures were an intrinsic part of the growth of big government. And overall they were a big part. As late as 1991, after a slowdown, the welfare state grand total in the table, at $855 billion in current dollars, was equal to 44 percent of the $1,945 billion of all-government expenditures (the percentage was the same in 1992).

But there is more to be gleaned from public program data. The strictly welfare component of the welfare state—that is, the overwhelmingly dominant social insurance series, grows faster in every long-run subperiod than does the grand total. It also grows faster in the shorter decadal periods, except for the 1960s. The most explosive decade for social insurance is the 1950s, when almost 7 million self-employed were covered under the Social Security Act's OASDHI for the first time, and 14 million more civilian wage and salary workers were blanketed in.

For "poor law" expenditures the most explosive growth decade is the Kennedy-Johnson War on Poverty period of the 1960s. The Galbraith interpretation scores here. It is worth noting that after the 1960s the separate "poor law" grand total holds its relative ground compared to social insurance, with annual real expenditures averaging about 34 percent of the grand total of all welfare state expenditures.

For each of the two decades after the 1960s the growth rates decline for all series except housing. The worst decade for the welfare state's growth is clearly and not surprisingly the Reagan presidency decade of the 1980s, when the real grand total rose only 3.66 percent annually (1980–91). This is the first decade in the postwar era in which the welfare state growth rate fell to only about one percentage point above the level of the real GDP rate of 2.45 percent a year.[6] The welfare state was already under attack, especially the "poor law" component. Even social insurance suffered, but it still managed to exceed the poor GDP growth by a whole percentage point. That attack accelerated in the mid-1990s as the conservative Republican sweep mounted its Contract with America, forcing political liberalism to conduct a rearguard action. While that attack would no doubt fail to dismantle the welfare state, it threatened to arrest its growth for an indeterminate period, and therefore its continuing contribution to the expansion of government. Whether the Contract with America can slow down the pace of welfare state growth to the extent that it will no longer outpace even the pitiful 2.5 percent GDP rate desired by the Federal Reserve conservatives is doubtful as retirement for the baby boomers arrives.

Careers of the Welfare Components

A brief survey of some of the major components of the series listed in Table 5.1 will more informatively reveal the character of the welfare state as an institution, and at the same time suggest what kinds of market system inadequacies and social pressures are reflected in the table's expenditure categories.

With respect to market inadequacies, a certain duality of effects needs to be noted. On the one hand, the changing market system fostered a long-run rise in per capita income that provided, as previously noted, a material basis for pro-welfare attitudinal changes even in the more well-off community. On the other hand, the market's development process condemned a large stratum to lives of deprivation, chronically or episodically at risk, people who found such conditions unacceptable, and who gradually acquired spokespersons and organizations to represent their interests politically. This was pointed out with respect to housing, for example, in Chapter 3.

The fact that to be effective the pressures had to focus on the political sphere was accentuated by the inadequacy of the private insurance market:

> Everybody at some time runs the risk of getting sick or injured, becoming disabled, widowed, or unemployed, or requiring financial support during old-age for longer than anticipated. These are not risks fully serviced by the private insurance market, which either rejects the opportunity to provide insurance or supplies insurance which is judged inadequate. The failure of the private market is predictable. A private insurer is not going to provide insurance against sickness or unemployment when he is incapable of judging its cause (the moral hazard problem); he will provide health, injury and permanent health insur-

ance, but only at a price determined by the distribution of bad risks and for a predetermined indemnity (the adverse selection problem); he will finance unanticipated longevity, but since he cannot usually secure a guaranteed real return on his investments he is not in a position to specify the real income he will pay to be retired (capital market failure).[7]

The universality of these privately uninsured threats in the context of an historically high-income society, numerous market failures including private insurance insufficiencies, and the breakdown of the family's provision for retirement needs is obvious. Furthermore, the growing democratic demand for distributive justice has made social insurance and extended "poor law" solutions inescapable.

The four major components of the predominant, social insurance core of the welfare state are the Social Security Act's OASDI (which became OASDHI after the institution of Medicare in 1965–66) public employee retirement, unemployment insurance, and workers' compensation. The first of these programs now covers about 58 percent of the civilian noninstitutional population. The smallest in expenditure terms is unemployment and job services, and now covers 97 percent of wage and salary workers.

Enough has already been said previously about the Social Security Act's characteristics viewed as a response to the Great Depression shock and to the subsequently evolving public pro-welfare consensus.[8] The vital place of the act in the growth of government has also been treated. Expenditures for the four components in 1992 were as follows (billions of current dollars):[9]

OASDHI including Medicare	416.6
Unemployment and employment services	41.2
Workers' compensation	44.1
Public employee retirement (civilian)	79.8
Total	581.7

Under the workers' compensation system all states now provide some employer-financed, state-administered income payments and medical services, possibly together with rehabilitation services. Almost all workers today are to some degree protected against work-connected injuries or death. Dependents are likely to be partly supported with allowances and/or inflation adjustment.

Workers' compensation made gradual progress, with considerable business support and despite some labor union hostility, in the laissez-faire era. By 1920, thirty-eight states had established at least some weak sort of program, and archaic legal barriers to employee protection had been largely overwhelmed. Total expenditures for compensation drifted up gradually in real terms during the Great Depression decade, even as work-injury frequency rates declined a lot. But that economic crisis period produced no noteworthy surge in compensation expenditures to rival the larger social insurance revolution.

The drop in work-injury frequency rates in the 1930s inaugurated a plateau in the rates lasting into the 1990s. In that stable context, real total benefits by publicly regulated private insurance carriers, the states, and self-insurers began to soar to very high annual rates after World War II—that is, throughout the whole era of the growing welfare state. Indeed, their pace was very close to that for total social insurance expenditures.

Therefore the coverage of workers' compensation—a state-administered, compulsory, non–means-tested social entitlement program that had moderate beginnings during laissez-faire but exploded with respect to both expenditures and types of services provided after World War II—demonstrated a close functional linkage with the strictly conceived welfare state. It will thus be viewed herein as a legitimate component of social insurance. With its total expenditure flows of $44 billion in 1992, workers' compensation equaled 7 percent of all social insurance outlays.

Public Employee Retirement

Public employee retirement (PER) programs are officially viewed as a part of social insurance. From a welfare state perspective this seems reasonable, and their widespread neglect in much of the welfare state literature seems quite odd. But some minor qualifications are probably appropriate for the purposes at hand. In the first place, the federal expenditure totals are unfortunately heavily laden with outlays for retired military personnel and their survivors.[10] The welfare state referred to herein is viewed as a civilian phenomenon in partial competition with the military establishment.

It is possible, however, to segregate federal civil service retirement from the totals. One way to do so is to trace the record of civil service pension coverage, beneficiaries, and benefit payments under the federal contributory system. That record shows how the federal government, assuming the role of ideal employer, pioneered with a significant response to the growing pension movement in the last laissez-faire decade by instituting a contributory pension, disability, and survivor program for civil service employees in 1920. That system stretched far beyond the petty, mincing, selective arrangements of the state and local governments in that decade.

The initial federal coverage applied to about 300,000 workers out of a total of some 613,000 FTE employees and half a million civil service workers.[11] By the next year there were only 6,500 annuitants (retired plus disabled), as might be expected.[12] The growth in the system in the twenties was steady but modest, although the number of annuitants increased much faster than employees. Expenditures for benefits to civil service workers for retirement had reached only $18 million by 1929.[13] Thereafter they exploded to $72 million in 1940, so that with falling prices they jumped to a real annual growth rate of 15 percent. They were making enormous relative gains over transfers for the much larger veterans' benefits.

Meanwhile, the number of civil service employees was growing by over 60 percent, 1929 to 1940, and retirement coverage was more than keeping pace. Thus, the federal level of the retirement component of social insurance was expanding very fast over the Depression decade. After the war—by 1952 for example—with 2 million[14] employees covered out of a civil service FTE total of about 2.3 million, the program had become a very active participant in the new welfare state. At that date there were already 375,000 annuitants (beneficiaries), or 16 percent of the number of civil service workers. In 1940 they had been 13 percent, in 1929 only about 4 percent. Benefits paid out in 1952 amounted to $600 million.

Then the great acceleration began in earnest. From 1950 to 1991, in the context of a sluggishly growing federal civilian employment, the number of annuitants rose at a vigorous annual rate of 6.4 percent, and the total of real benefits paid out at an even more robust 8.9 percent. In 1993, federal civil service contributory retirement benefits totaled about $35 billion in current dollars.[15] Real annual benefits per civil service beneficiary had also risen steadily throughout the postwar era until the 1980s, when the rise stopped dead in its tracks.

State and Local Social Insurance Systems

In the case of PER systems at the state and local level, we find them to stem distinctly from the welfare state era. Unlike workers' compensation, there are practically no PER roots in the laissez-faire era prior to 1929. Only six states had set up retirement programs for their civil service workers before that year.[16] Most large cities had established some modest, selective pension arrangements for the police, firemen, and some teachers.[17] In a quaint reference to those selected pensioners in the late 1920s, the Fraternal Order of Eagles in a pamphlet declared itself strongly in favor of a general social retirement system by remarking, "those who through years of humble toil have helped to create the wealth by which taxation is borne, are just as much entitled to honor and independence in their old age through pensions as the teacher, the judge, and the fireman."[18]

State and local government expenditures for PER in 1929 were only $61 million for an FTE total of 2.4 million employees.[19] As a rough indicator, it may be noted that the ratio of PER outlays to (civilian) employees in 1929 was about .07 for the federal government and .03 for the state and local governments. Writing in the early 1930s, the President's Research Committee on Social Trends touched upon the underdeveloped state of affairs at that time, regarding pensions at the state and local level, with scattered passages:

> The first old age (state) pension law was passed in 1923 and only four additional acts were adopted before 1929. . . . Up to the end of 1928 only 6 states had passed such laws and all of them involved county option. In three years,

> 1929 through 1931, eleven states passed old age pension laws; of these 6 were mandatory. There are, then, 17 states in 1932 with some provision for old age pensions. . . . Paralleling this movement have been . . . the inauguration in about half the states of plans for pensioning public school teachers and the adoption in most of the cities of retirement systems for some employees.[20]

In New York City in 1934, out of a total of 35,000 teachers (excluding substitutes), there were only 3,648 on the pension list.[21] Significant PER programs clearly had to await the impetus of the powerful social forces that crystallized in the Great Depression, forces very similar to those that generated the New Deal and its Social Security Act.

As the Depression decade unfolded, real state and local government expenditures for PER rose strongly at 8.5 percent a year in the context of an FTE employee total annual rate rise of only 2 percent.[22] Similarly, real state and local payments to persons for pensions gave a very strong annual leap: 9.2 percent.[23] Pension payments had clearly experienced their takeoff decade. The accompanying sluggish growth in employees failed to anticipate what lay ahead in the future for the commitment to PER. The public's commitment probably did not dream of what it was getting in for.

Anticipated or not, state and local PER was caressed by the magic wand of the welfare state social insurance wand. State and local employment exploded between 1950 and 1970 at more than a 4 percent annual growth rate, much faster than the sluggish federal. At the same time, PER was inspired to expand expenditures for retirement at more than twice the employment pace: 9.5 percent a year! An even greater gap between the two rates developed over the next twenty years: 2.2 percent for state and local employees and a whopping 6.6 percent for real PER expenditures.

The phenomenal rise in PER expenditures to 46 billion current dollars in 1992[24] reflected not only the public's fiscal and coverage commitment but also the rapidly mounting, unheralded number of beneficiaries necessarily accompanying the fast growth of state and local employment—the heart of big government's expansion. The ratio of beneficiaries to FTE employees stood at a minuscule 5.25 percent in 1940. In 1950 it was almost 8 percent. Thereafter it rose steadily, along with real benefits per beneficiary, until it had reached about 35 percent in 1991.[25] This compared with 82 percent for federal annuitants relative to FTE civilian employment.[26]

This all added up to over 6 million annuitants and beneficiaries, including the federal civilian, in the context of over 15 million all-government civilian FTE employees in 1991, along with $73 billion in civilian PER payments. If the welfare state contributed to the rise of big government, the rise of big government as measured by public employment in turn contributed to the burgeoning employee retirement department of the welfare state's social insurance division.

Social Insurance for Health Care

The great gaping hole in the U.S. social insurance safety net was the continuing absence of universal health insurance coverage, such as has existed for a long time in most other high-income, mixed market systems. This lacuna persisted into the mid-1990s. The chief American substitutes were Medicare, a concession to the elderly made in 1965 in the form of an addition to the Social Security system, and a "poor law" companion piece of legislation for the needy of all ages, Medicaid. The common birth of the two programs attests to the joint character of insurance and means-tested institutions in the postwar welfare state.

The matter of the social roots giving rise to special attention by government on behalf of the elderly has been looked at earlier in this chapter in connection with pensions. The same special attention was given to aging veterans, as previously noted. Now again, the elderly were singled out, in this case for health care. One student of the political and social origins of Medicare has emphasized that the aging cohort was particularly acceptable to the general public as a deserving group that had "through no fault of their own . . . lower earning capacity and higher medical expenses than any other adult age group," adding that they bene-fited from a "considerable legitimacy" enjoyed by the now well-established Social Security system.[27] Medicaid, on the other hand, expressed, in addition to other factors, the augmented consciousness of the gaping hole in American health care for the poor during a decade that was eminent for its great social concerns.

These two institutions, plus a handful of other piecemeal programs, became the vehicle for enormous increases in public health outlays in the decade after 1965. Private expenditures exhibited a parallel rise. Private market price admin-istration by suppliers was the chief single culprit responsible for the cost in-creases. One analyst has well spelled out the strategic determining factors:

> More than half of the increase in total expenditures over the period 1960–89 can be attributed to medical price inflation, more than a third to changes in use or kinds of services and supplies, and almost twenty to an increase in the size of the population. More fundamentally, the rapid growth in national expendi-tures on health care seems to be related to the following factors: the aging of the population, the secular growth of the institution of third-party payment, the technology-augmenting sophistication of medical treatment, and the increase in the number and relative earnings of health care providers.[28]

It seems highly probable also that the federal government's pro-health tax expenditure policies (e.g., exclusion of contributions for medical insurance pre-miums and medical care, exclusion of untaxed Medicare benefits, the deductibil-ity of medical expenses) stimulated, as well as reflected, the rapid growth of private health insurance, an overconsumption of certain kinds of specialty medi-cal care, and a consequent partial reason for medical care price inflation.[29]

The total of public outlays for health in all levels of government rose in price-deflated magnitudes (deflating with the CPI medical care index) at a yearly compound rate of about 6.5 percent from 1960 to 1991, which in both periods was far in excess of the real GNP rate. After the institution of Medicare and Medicaid, the real annual growth rate for the total outlays for both programs, with Medicare persistently the larger, approximated 5.6 percent in 1970–90. In other words, both programs in combination rose well over a percentage point faster than the rapidly growing total of all real public health expenditures after 1970. The sum of the two had reached 59 percent of total public health outlays in 1992 (current dollars). Since public health care belongs to any functioning welfare state, it is clear that in the United States, government expenditures for it were a big participant, even as they likewise spurred the long-run growth of big government. Small wonder that the conservative Republican anti-welfare forces in the 1990s leveled their big guns at these two programs. Of course, their attack, reflecting the enormous support for Medicare in particular, was couched in terms of "saving" it by arresting it. Indeed, in all welfare areas targeted for retrenchment, their claim was that they were "reforming" the programs.

Yet with all these public health outlays, somewhere between 30 and 40 million Americans lacked either public or private health *insurance* coverage in the early nineties. Those millions had to rely on public assistance, such as Medicaid, or private charity, or their own resources. That condition has been aptly described as "financially and morally staggering for the supposed wealthiest and wisest country in the world."[30]

The itemized programs in the social insurance component of the welfare state were tabulated in Table 5.1. Medicare outlays were about 31 percent of the $382.3 billion OASDHI total contained in the social insurance total therein for 1991 (32 percent in 1992).[31] They had risen strongly from their 1970 proportion of 19 percent. Not surprisingly, health costs were outrunning pensions. The total of OASDHI expenditures (pensions plus Medicare) were outrunning GNP. They were about 3.6 percent of current dollar GNP in 1970, but 6.2 percent in 1990 and 6.9 percent of GDP in 1994. Even without the Medicare component, OASDHI was growing much faster than GNP, partly because its pension coverage of the civilian population was expanding.

But the health care factor bore the chief responsibility for the high growth rates, which were a function of more services rendered and zooming prices. Deflating nominal outlays with the consumer price index for medical care instead of the PCE deflator would slow down the growth rates by almost two percentage points; but Medicare expenditures, for example, would still rise yearly by a vigorous 5.7 percent. The cost explosion made it increasingly difficult for the working poor and for smaller enterprises in particular to meet the burgeoning premium payments required. More important, the explosion greatly complicated the task of cost containment that would have to accompany any universal health care system such as initially proposed by the Clinton administration in the early nineties.

The same general pattern of rapid growth, however less rapid than health, occurred with respect to the total social insurance component of the welfare state. For example, if the expenditures for that component, as presented in Table 5.1, are expressed in ratio to current dollar GNP, they were relatively as follows:

1950	1.72%
1970	5.41%
1991	9.82%

The social insurance component was bigger than the "poor law" component by the end of the 1950s, and it grew much faster. And as usual, it grew relatively faster from 1950 to 1970 than in the following two decades.

Welfare State Means-Tested Programs

The private market system has always spun off, for many in the population, destitution and socially threatening, uncared-for, ill health—hence, a long series of public welfare programs and reforms going back to before the reign of Queen Elizabeth. But the economically developed United States, in the agony of its Great Depression and under the impetus of the New Deal, gave birth to new and greatly expanded "poor law" type institutions that joined with the freshly established social insurance system to inaugurate a common welfare state.

Expenditures for those major welfare state programs outside the dominant social insurance component are listed in Table 5.1. The total for those means-tested items in that table, in millions of dollars, has also been tabulated above. Comparison of the real means-tested expenditure totals with the real social insurance outlays in Table 5.1 shows that the former were considerably larger in 1950 than social insurance. But thereafter the social insurance heart of the welfare state took off, and already in 1960 they were much larger than all of the real income-tested programs. In the next decade of the War on Poverty and the Great Society, the latter ever so slightly outpaced insurance entitlements; but over the following two decades, insurance expenditures came to reach over twice the size of total indigent aid programs.

In the decades after the exploding welfarism of the Kennedy-Johnson sixties, both types of welfarism experienced growth rate slowdowns. The sixties was the growth heyday of the welfare state, just as they were for the growth of the economy in general. A bit of calculation from the tally of the real income-tested totals will reveal that, like social insurance, those expenditures suffered a particularly drastic slowdown in the Reagan decade of the eighties, growing annually at only 2.7 percent. Such retrenchment was in accord with the president's welfare goals under his New Federalism. The Reagan-Bush years were the worst for the expanding welfare state, with the general assistance expenditures components growing but little faster than the sluggish 2.45 annual percentage for real

GNP. Social insurance managed to squeeze through with an expansion rate only about one percentage point higher than that for GDP. As one leading welfare analyst of the record has noted:

> New AFDC rules rendered some recipients with low earnings ineligible for further aid. Food stamp benefits were lowered.... New subsidized housing starts were drastically curtailed. States were encouraged to apply for authority to administer experimental workfare programs.... Categorical distinctions were strengthened.... Benefit reduction rates were increased ... and ... the traditional attitude that the welfare system is a seedbed of sloth and dependency reclaimed dominance from the upstart view that welfare is a right of the poor.[32]

Even Social Security came under attack, as it did again later under the Contract with America, particularly on the grounds that the trust fund and the taxed working population would not be sufficient early in the next century to provide for the growing population of elderly retirees. Ignoring the favorable effects of future productivity increases, the employed (i.e., future retirees) were incited to mount a confrontation with the upcoming body of retirees. There was even a rebirth of the deceptive allegation that the trust fund could "go bankrupt" and thus destroy the capacity of the de facto pay-as-you-go system to meet its benefit obligations. The long slowdown in economic growth and the persistent stagnation in real income per wage earner and per family provided a festering backdrop for a resurgence of such illusory retrenchment attitudes.

But it was nonetheless clear in the early nineties, before the next attack by the Contract with America, that the gigantic income-support institution had only suffered some loss in momentum. A pickup in the expansion rate of real expenditures was already apparent after 1988. For example, a couple of real "public aid" total payments (Supplementary Security Income, or SSI, and Aid to Families with Dependent Children, or AFDC) jumped back up to a yearly increase from 1988 to 1992 of 8 percent and 2.6 percent, respectively; and the annual real cost of federal food stamp disbursements zoomed at a 10.2 yearly percentage increase between 1988 and 1993.[33] Total current dollar outlays for the three programs totaled $65 billion in 1992.

The forces in society and the economy responsible for the whole postwar era's growth in expenditures and beneficiaries for the public means-tested programs were also partially responsible for the parallel growth of social insurance. They included:

- The emergence, initially with the Great Depression and the New Deal, of a widespread conviction that indigence, like unemployment, is in general not a product of individual, innate incompetence but is created exogenously by the economy.
- The continuing replacement of the agrarian with the urban family, a historical process prompting offspring to wish to relinquish material family support for a growing body of unemployable elderly forebears.

- The multiplication of ever more vast inner-city blight in the great metropolitan centers, with attendant human destitution, disease, and threatening sociopolitical turbulence.
- The attitudinal effects of a socially humiliating contrast between spreading poverty and affluence resulting from the secular rise in per capita income: welfare measures as an expression of guilt feelings.
- An abiding general compassion, heightened by a communications revolution that spread the public's awareness of indigent needs.
- An increased militancy on the part of certain disadvantaged groups like the Black Panthers and Gray Panthers.
- A shocking increase in single parenthood among poverty-stricken, poorly trained women with small children, led by blacks and increasingly common in all groups; it is noteworthy that compassion for *children* is central to the very origin of the AFDC program.
- A deep-rooted public conviction that minimally decent shelter constitutes a human right, conjoined with certain segments within a politically influential construction industry.
- Widespread support for governmental provision of medical care. In a series of personal interview surveys of representative cross sections of U.S. adults during the 1970s, the majority felt that the federal government should see to it that every person receives adequate medical care.[34]
- An abiding public conviction that hunger is unacceptable, conjoined with a politically powerful farm interest group dedicated to securing government direct and indirect supports for food marketing and farm income.
- The repercussions of the civil rights movement.
- The activities of the Lyndon Johnson regime in the sixties: assumption of greater federal responsibility for both social insurance and public assistance, e.g., the War on Poverty, Medicare, Medicaid, and the resurging affirmation that welfare is a matter of right for the disadvantaged.
- The very growth of the many ingredients of the welfare state itself augmented the strength, cohesion, and political clout of their constituencies, even the mentally ill and their families[35] and thus contributed to the assured institutionalization of entitlements and other income-support programs.[36]

The momentum that the sixties imparted to the institutionalization of welfarism carried over still quite strongly into the seventies, even though the process suffered some particular setbacks from such influences as the growing cost burden of an ever-rising needful population, excessive inflation, a very serious slowdown in economic growth, and a constant real median family money income, as well as real wages after 1973.

The leading components of the means-tested system, involving all levels of government, using the current dollar expenditures criterion, are presented in Table 5.3. The programs are arranged in two panels: noncash and cash. As usual,

Table 5.3

Major Public Means-Tested, Income-Support Expenditures, Selected Years, 1950–91 (billions of current dollars)

	1950	1960	1970	1980	1990	1993
Noncash benefits						
Medicaid and prior vendor						
medical payments	(X)	.5	5.3	23.3	64.9	76.0
Food stamps	(X)	(X)	.6	8.7	14.2	22.0
Housing benefits	.1	.2	.7	9.2	17.5	(X)
Cash aid						
AFDC and prior ADC	.6	1.1	4.9	13.9	21.2	23.0
SSI and predecessors	1.6	2.0	3.0	7.9	16.6	21.0
Earned income credit	(X)	(X)	(X)	2.0	5.9	9.0
General assistance	.4	.4	.7	1.4	3.2	(X)

Sources: U.S., Department of Health, Education and Welfare, "Social Welfare Expenditures, 1950–75," *Social Security Bulletin*, January 1976, *passim*; Tax Foundation, *Facts and Figures on Government Finance* (Baltimore: Johns Hopkins University Press, 1990), p. 210, No. D43; U.S. Congress, Congressional Budget Office (CBO), *The Economic and Budget Outlook: Fiscal Years 1995–1999*, January 1994, p. 42, Table 2–6; and numerous editions of the *Statistical Abstract*. This last-named source for 1994 gives total refunds for 1992 of $9.2 billion.

(X) Not available, inapplicable, or inconsequential.

the omissions include education and veterans' assistance; there are also many other programs of modest size that are passed over.

It will be seen at once that only five programs make up by far the major ingredients of the means-tested elements in the U.S. welfare state. It will also be apparent that noncash benefits as a group are much larger than cash aid, owing to the dominant Medicaid outlays. A number of writers have called attention to and commented upon this programmatic allocation. For example, economist Henry Aaron states that "the American public has declared unmistakably that it is willing to provide to those in need of aid such commodities as basic housing, food, and health care, but it is unwilling to give poor people the cash to buy these items themselves."[37]

It seems proper to explain the noncash emphasis, despite the American worship of free choice generally, as an expression of political pressure on government by interest groups that are more influential than the pertinent beneficiary constituencies. It will also be observed from Table 5.3 that all of the programs experienced explosive growth in the 1970s, even if the numbers were to be discounted for inflation. And the growth in the three noncash programs was much faster than the two big cash aid systems. They moderately bested the high inflation of that decade.

The career of Medicaid on the expenditure measure has already been scanned. It clearly became the heart of the means-tested element in the welfare state. The number of households receiving Medicaid assistance, another measure of size and growth, jumped from 5.4 million in 1970 to over 10 million twenty years later. Over 31 million persons received some kind of Medicaid assistance at some time during 1992.

The Food Stamp Program

Food stamps actually got a pilot program start late in the New Deal period, but the program was local and temporary, ending during World War II. The Kennedy-Johnson sixties saw more temporary pilot food stamp structures reestablished intermittently through a balky Congress. But it was not until 1973 that the institution was made into a permanent, nationwide (with enormous benefit differences between the states), minimum food program for the needy.[38] However, food stamps were also paralleled by the New Deal's school lunch program instituted in 1935 under Public Law 320. That program of combined support for children's nutrition and farm income, unlike the food stamps' growth pattern, was a continuous one, bolstered by subsequent legislation in 1946 and 1949. As early as 1940, about 2.5 million children were participating, and the number continued to increase to 10 million in 1950, reaching its surprising historic maximum, however, of about 25 million as early as 1973.

The development of a growing constituency to supplement the farm bloc's influence apparently helped finally to make the food stamp program a lasting one that was able to expand greatly over the years:

> In the early years of the food stamp program, representatives of the so-called hunger lobby helped to stimulate congressional hearings designed to bring public attention to the severity of hunger and malnutrition in the United States. The hearings received substantial press coverage, and testimony by doctors and nutritionists helped to create public sympathy for expanding the food stamp program.[39]

The food stamp benefits were also price indexed to the cost of living in 1973, the second program following SSI to be indexed.[40]

The number of participants in the food stamp program, who were typically presumed to be candidates for available jobs, rose dramatically from an already large 11.6 million persons in the pre-permanent year of 1972 to 21.1 million in 1980 and, following a decade of no increase, to 27 million in 1993. The food stamp system, partly state and local administered, thus ultimately became a very large ingredient of the welfare state, with estimated expenditures, all federally financed, of $22 billion in 1993 and almost 11 million participating households (11 percent of all households). The food stamp program was much costlier than the school lunch program, with its $22 billion compared to $4 billion for school lunches in 1993.

Housing Benefits

The contemporary housing program for the poor consists chiefly of low-rent public housing and rent supplements paid under an amendment (Section 8) in 1974 to the New Deal's Wagner-Steagall Housing Act of 1937. That original act was designed to serve three goals: stimulate construction, alleviate unemployment, and offer housing help for some of the poorest families. It did not include a formal rent supplement system. Local housing authorities were encouraged to decide, under presumed state enabling legislation and with federal subsidies, whether or not—and no matter where—a public housing project would be constructed. This legally autonomous authority under the 1937 act continues to develop, own, and operate the public housing under its jurisdiction and is exempt from property taxes.[41]

The New Deal program barely got off the ground before the war converted it into a minuscule measure for housing in-migrant defense workers. Thereafter it continued to languish until it experienced a modest boost in the sixties. However, new construction was being largely negated by demolitions and other losses, which totaled 290,000 a year in the fifties and 360,000 annually in the next decade.[42] Meanwhile, the baby boom and family household formation was skyrocketing. These and related developments in the inner cities prompted the addition of the rent supplement program to the low-rent public housing program in the mid-sixties.

The rent supplement measure for existing facilities squeezed through a reluctant Congress in 1965. "The chief innovation of the rent supplement program was to vary assistance systematically with tenant income in order to focus federal outlays on the neediest."[43] A contract between the Department of Housing and Urban Development (HUD) and a developer provides for supplementary payments when newly constructed units are occupied.[44]

To win support for the programs from segments of an often reluctant construction industry, the federal HUD department, in cooperation with the local housing authority, inaugurated in 1965 the so-called turnkey arrangement, whereby private developers are invited to propose a construction plan and site acquisition. Then the local housing authority, after selecting and approving a proposal, promises to purchase the completed facility. The housing arrangement function can be turned over to private corporations.[45] New construction under turnkey projects did quite well until the overall slowdown in total low-rent unit growth in the period after 1975.

Expenditures under the two types of housing assistance were absurdly low as late as 1970: about $241 million for rent supplements and $460 million for public housing costs. But after the 1974 amendment to the 1937 act, rent supplements took off. By 1975, expenditures for the two were about equal at some $1.5 billion each. As the program evolved after that year, the real public housing expenditures for rent supplements rose very rapidly over the long run, but for low-rent housing construction and operation the long-run increase was less than 1 percent a year. Indeed, the number of such housing units, after vigorous growth from 1950 to 1975 slowed down, came to a halt in 1988, and dropped absolutely thereafter. There were 1,323,300 low-income public housing units of all sizes in 1992, whereas there had been 1,378,000 in 1985.

However, the *households* receiving benefits continued to fill up those units: 2.6 million of them in 1979, and 4.5 million in 1992. A varying 50 to 60 percent of these households were below the poverty level. Hence, the big increase in real public housing expenditures of 7.5 percent annually after 1975, and over 11 percent a year in the eighties was overwhelmingly for Section 8 rent supplements for the burgeoning recipient population. It is therefore the explosion in real rent supplements for low-income assistance after 1975 that brought up housing expenditures to a level that warrants their inclusion here in the welfare state tables.

Aid to Families with Dependent Children

If ever a welfare policy had a checkered career, the split federal–state and local financed and administered AFDC was it. Here was a program whose benefit levels and eligibility criteria reflected, like Medicaid, a high degree of state and local autonomy and variability under detailed guidelines laid down by the Federal Family Support Administration of the Department of Health and Human Services. Throughout its entire controversial history, up to and including President Clinton's determination to "end welfare as we know it," the program was under constant attack even as it expanded into a big welfare system affecting the lives of millions of Americans. No matter how frequently investigations reiterated that the incidence of fraud was minimal, AFDC youth and adult recipients were always kept under a cloud for their alleged laziness, work avoidance, propensity to have more babies, efforts to become permanently dependent (despite the fact that at least 50 percent leave the program within two years, 85 percent within eight),[46] maneuvers to acquire maximum benefit combinations of the all too numerous hodgepodge of welfare programs, and greed for too generous allowances. The program was under continual attack and modification designed to infuse it with adjustments that would (1) eliminate its built-in work disincentives and encourage employment (somewhere) as an alternative; (2) ferret out those among the beneficiaries who were "able to work" as distinguished from those "unable to work"; (3) link up a formal work training and work availability program with AFDC; (4) engineer appropriate work incentive devices; (5) prevent those potentially AFDC-eligible among the working poor from becoming actually eligible; (6) develop and strengthen an emphasis on children among the beneficiary cohort; and (7) correct inequalities among the states in the state and local governments' costs and real benefit levels. The majority of modification measures were always focused on stimulation of the employment alternative: self-reliance vs. dependency. Alternatively put, "workfare" was chronically juxtaposed with AFDC "welfare." The provision of alternative employment, however, was typically left in a penumbra.

The program originated, like so much of the contemporary welfare state, under the New Deal. It was part of the 1935 Social Security Act and its Social Security Administration (SSA), setting up Aid to Dependent Children (ADC). As one scholar has insightfully noted, however, at the time "no one envisioned the growth in divorce and dissension that was to convert the Aid to Dependent Children's program from a minor, relatively uncontroversial, program into the focal point of the welfare reform debate in the 1960s and 1970s."[47]

The ADC welfare system was of course necessarily expanded—for example, by additional amendments to the SSA in 1950 that allowed benefits to the mother of the children as well as the children. After all, motherhood was historically complementary with child care. Further amendment in 1961 extended coverage to the dependent (under eighteen years of age) children of unemployed parents. This policy was developed later to blanket in, by state initiative, families' health by long-term unemployed fathers, the so-called AFDC-UF provision of the law. Hence, about a fifth of all AFDC families came to be male-headed.[48]

A program that was originally viewed as of minor magnitude became frighteningly large. Attacks on it mounted, pushing for the jobs alternative. Amendments to SSA in 1962, in addition to the significant name change from ADC to AFDC, attempted to allow continued coverage combined with earned income. The states were required to deduct work-connected expenses from earnings before they could reduce benefits.[49] But then and always afterward there was still a tax of some sort that ate into job remuneration. Sometimes the tax involved the loss of part or all of other welfare benefits that the AFDC beneficiary was also receiving, such as food stamps or Medicaid. Thus, work disincentives in program modifications persisted, sabotaging the very self-reliance objectives of the changes made. However, time was incrementally on the side of self-reliance. The work-stimulus philosophy did succeed by the end of the 1980s in making more earned income retention possible without loss of beneficiary status.[50]

As the sixties unfolded, it became increasingly apparent that the "working poor" very frequently earned less than many AFDC beneficiaries, heightening criticism of the program's "generosity." To add to the controversy, the number of the female-headed families was skyrocketing, creating millions more eligibles, to say nothing of the fact that the program participation rate of those increasing eligibles was also rising. That rate reached 94 percent as early as 1971.[51]

Enter the heyday of AFDC—as usual, the sixties. The number of recipients, which had increased by a strong 3.25 percent a year during the fifties, jumped to over 12 percent annually in that decade. So did the number of families covered, and children embraced by the program rose 11.5 percent a year. Real total AFDC expenditures topped both at almost 14 percent! Such growth in the "welfare burden" was even too much for the liberal administrations of the period. The

Congress in 1967 jumped on to the workfare bandwagon, instituting a freeze on total recipients. But the freeze never materialized. How could it? However, Congress did enact another modified and liberalized work incentive (WIN) amendment. WIN, like the other standard self-reliance alterations, made little difference in practice.

The terrifying caseload and outlay Frankenstein, as it was viewed by opponents of the AFDC program, set the stage for the next two decades' mounting workfare constraints. The opposition was remarkably successful in its efforts at constraint. In the seventies, for example, the rise in the rate of family recipients' growth dropped to 4.2 percent annually; and in the eighties the rate fell again, to less than 2 percent. "The attack on entitlement was legitimated through research embedded in new, more restrictive eligibility requirements, culminating in the 1988 passage of the Family Security Act."[52]

Real total AFDC payments growth was permitted to be devastated by inflation, collapsing to a mere 2.5 percent a year. In the next decade there was no growth at all. Indeed, real total payments were lower in 1991 than they had been in the past year 1975. That meant less real benefits per family, per recipient, and per child, for their numbers were slowly edging up.

So again, growth in the AFDC expenditures component of the welfare state, like the number of low-rent housing units in that component, was arrested after the mid-seventies under the hammer blows of the retrenchment crusade. The slowdown was aggravated by President Reagan's New Federalism drive to counter President Carter's more liberal efforts, by shifting the administration of the welfare system, and ultimately the tax sources to pay for it, back to the state and local governments.[53] But AFDC was still a big welfare program, and its long-run slowdown nonetheless found it with over 14 million recipients and $22 billion of benefit payments in 1992. This was far too much for the Contract with America Republicans.

Supplemental Security Income

The federal Supplemental Security Income (SSI) program, administered by the Social Security Administration, is a much less controversial public aid institution than AFDC. That is primarily because, being addressed to needy elderly over sixty-five, the blind, and the disabled, the work objective cannot be insinuated into a beneficiary's claim. Furthermore, the average monthly payment levels at, for example, $358 in 1992, have been too low to elicit much righteous indignation ($381 per family for AFDC!). Indeed, most states supplement the basic SSI payment.

Since the roots of such public assistance, particularly for the indigent aged, go far back into the laissez-faire era, it is reasonable to ask why the categorical program for that group can be identified with the welfare state. The positive answer to that question calls for a brief historical review.

Before the SSI, there were state and locally administered categorical programs for the aged and the blind who passed a means test. The disabled were widely neglected until they were blanketed in by the SSA in 1950.[54] Some of the funds for such programs, which included both money payments and social services, came from the federal government. But the federal share, indicative of its pre-welfare state nature, like the neglect of the disabled, was very niggardly. For example, one study records *total* public assistance expenditures in 1929 at $60 million, and reports that the source of those funds was entirely state and local governments.[55] However, after the New Deal the federal share of old-age assistance payments jumped up; for example, in 1940 it was about 50 percent.[56]

Thus, important developments, as usual, came with the Great Depression, and the Social Security Act. The federal government entered the picture, via the SSA, with its "noncontributory old-age program" of grants-in-aid public assistance for the elderly over sixty-five. That innovation was expected to be largely transitory until the OASDI system of the SSA got under way and took over. Its presumed temporary importance was made more plausible by the fact that most state old-age assistance programs were going bankrupt from the "temporary" economic crisis.[57] Only about 10 percent of the eligible elderly were getting old-age assistance.[58]

It did not prove temporary as a program, however. The federal government had for years helped finance to some degree the state and local governments with their public assistance programs, and the number of eligibles was secularly growing. Hence, for almost forty years after passage of the SSA, public money payments and social services to the needy aged, blind, and disabled were still administered by the state and local governments, but the dispensation of that assistance was increasingly out of funds (grants-in-aid) provided in ever larger proportions by the federal government under SSA stipulations. But the level of federal payments was still quite low, and the state and local governments in many cases supplemented the federally provided benefits. The federal portion of the total payments probably amounted to about 45 percent by 1950, over 50 percent in 1955 and 1960, and about 57 percent in 1973, on the eve of SSI. This was the characteristic drift toward a greater federal share of the funding that characterized the welfare state.

Other important changes of a welfare state nature came in 1972, when the Congress established the SSI program, combining the three categorical programs, to take effect in 1974. The new program made four major innovations in the categorical "poor law" type institutions: (1) the three categorical measures were integrated administratively into a single program; (2) administration of federal grants was transferred from the states to the federal SSA; (3) a *nationwide minimum income* was provided for all beneficiaries of the program; and (4) benefits were indexed, like food stamp benefits, to the cost of living, beginning in 1974. Uniform *national* eligibility requirements and payment standards were instituted. These changes solidified the welfare state character of assistance to the needy elderly, blind, and disabled.

States could choose to supplement the basic federal payment, both fiscally and administratively. In the inaugural year of SSI in 1974, the federal minimum monthly cash payment, at $91 for the aged individual and $142 for a disabled person, was higher than that paid by about three-quarters of the states.[59] Federal SSI outlays in 1975 were $5,716 million, and state-administered payments only $162 million.[60]

Increases in SSI and its predecessors' real expenditures for, and beneficiaries among, the affected groups have made but modest contributions to the growth of the welfare state since World War II. For the whole period 1960–90, real expenditures rose annually at only 2.25 percent. The total number of recipients, with the aged recipients falling absolutely and the larger number of disabled rising substantially, increased by only 1.85 percent a year. The absolute fall in the number of aged SSI beneficiaries—for example, from 2,286,000 in 1974 to 1,475,000 in 1993—appears to support the belief in the first days of the SSA that public assistance, as distinguished from social insurance, for the elderly would prove to be transitory; almost all of the elderly would eventually be blanketed into social insurance via rising years of compulsory contributions and extension in coverage of the system. The record for OASDHI retired worker beneficiaries supports that early expectation: 1,771,000 in 1950, and from 15,958,000 in 1974 to 26,104,000 in 1993, when about 95 percent of the jobs in the country were covered, as noted previously.

The biggest growth decade for both elderly and disabled was not the famed sixties but the seventies, when real outlays rose 2.8 percent and beneficiaries 2.95 percent annually. The surge was primarily due to a jump upward in both outlays and beneficiaries in the first year of SSI. Despite the sluggish growth for the postwar era as a whole, the program was large in the 1990s, as indicated in Table 5.3. Federal spending for SSI totaled $21 billion in fiscal 1993, a real annual rate of increase over 1990 of 3.23 percent.[61]

The Earned Income Tax Credit

After years of awareness and viewing with alarm, the neglected working poor were finally targeted for welfare through a federal tax expenditure measure, the earned income tax credit (EITC). Unlike some of the other welfare programs, the EITC had no incipiently institutionalized roots in either the laissez-faire era or even the Great Depression. Its roots were rather in the great welfare decade of the sixties.

The EITC is not means tested by an ordinary social welfare agency. But it is nonetheless income-tested because it is addressed to the disadvantaged category of taxpayers with incomes surrounding the poverty-income line. It is a cash aid, public, antipoverty device. On these two criteria it is clearly a welfare program.

EITC's official birth was, as might be expected, in 1969, when the President's Commission on Income Maintenance emphasized in its report that millions of full-time workers earned incomes so low that they belonged in the poverty class.

Indeed, they and their families at that time accounted for almost one-half of the official poor.[62] Work for them was not doing the hallowed job that employment was supposed to accomplish, through workfare, for the army of other welfare beneficiaries. This shocking situation not only sullied the workfare, self-reliance model but also undermined the ethical foundations of the welfare state.

But it took five more years from the time of the President's Commission report to get legislation addressed to the awkward problem. The EITC was finally instituted in 1974, the memorable year of the SSI, as part of the Tax Reduction Act of that year, and went into effect a year later. Tax expenditures are, as pointed out in Chapter 3, revenue losses, an officially accepted concept that sounds less threatening to political conservatives than more welfare or more government spending. But more welfare spending is exactly what EITC involves. However, the tax "concession" approach of EITC, plus the support it seemed to extend to the worshipped work ethic, made the program sufficiently palatable to the conservatives to get it through Congress.

The EITC pays out cash refunds to "working poor" families with children (childless taxpayers with low incomes became eligible beginning in 1994) on the basis of their individual federal income tax return. Note that targeting children again helped give the initial impetus. Only persons legally required to file such a tax return can be eligible. Of course, there have been over the years millions of low-income eligibles who filed returns but failed to claim a credit (the IRS caught many of these; we don't know the numbers). This unfortunate feature precluded the receipt of refunds for a noteworthy percentage of low-income earners for many years. The Internal Revenue Service (IRS) in 1990, and probably somewhat earlier, attempted to correct this massive omission by calculating and paying the EITC to taxpayers who appeared eligible even though they did not claim a refund.[63] Throughout most of the 1980s the average number of monthly EITC recipients hovered around 19 million.

Refunds under the EITC rise at a given percentage up to a certain income point. This is the subsidy range of income; it yields the maximum refund amount. That income point in 1975 was $4,000, and the maximum refund was $400.[64] Above such income point in 1975 there applied a "phase-out" percentage, which in that year was the same as the rate in the subsidy phase. This rate applied to income up to $8,000, which at that time was the "refund cutoff income" where the refund process was exhausted.

In the ensuing years the credit rates, maximum refunds, income points, and cutoff incomes were raised substantially. In 1993 the credit rate had risen to 18.5 percent, the maximum refund to $1,434 ($1,511 for two or more qualifying children), and the refund cutoff income to $23,050. Benefit credits were not affected by the receipt of other welfare benefits from AFDC, Medicaid, SSI, food stamps, and low-income housing.[65] As percentage increases, the changes between 1975 and 1993, other than the credit rates, compare favorably with the increase in the CPI over that period.

Clearly, there has been a work stimulus from EITC up to some point in earned income. But after that point the stimulus encountered mounting disincentives until it was no longer operative. As one writer has commented, "we must recognize that reducing benefits as income increases is perfectly equivalent to taxing income."[66] Hence, EITC was the subject of much controversy over the years regarding its antipoverty thrust versus its work incentive and disincentive effects.

Data on the total refunds paid out and the number of recipients for the early years of the program are sparse. The tax expenditure data for those years provide only the totals for the nonrefundable portions of the claims![67] Average monthly recipients totaled about 21 million in 1980, and rose to 28 million in 1988. This number jumped to 40 million by 1992! Total refunds rose throughout the eighties, and the Congressional Budget Office reported $9 billion for fiscal year 1993 (Table 5.3) with an estimate of $22 billion for 1999.[68] While the total refunds were therefore growing rapidly, even in price-deflated terms, they were but a modest percentage of all federal outlays and accounted for some 17 percent only of the cash aid listed in Table 5.3 for 1993.

Conclusion

The measure of the rise of the civilian welfare state and its contribution to all-government growth has emphasized here the vast expenditure increases. But it is the people affected that perhaps show best the enormous extension of government influence in this realm of big government. The term "universal program" applied to the social insurance segment of the welfare state, and accounting for almost three-fourths of all income supports, is indicative of that segment's comprehensive influence over people's lives. After all, the social insurance sphere is basically addressed to the human problems that the poor share with the nonpoor.

There were 166 million workers who were fully insured for retirement and/or survivor benefits under Social Security in 1992. Women accounted for 47 percent of the total. There were over 4 million retired persons and dependents, survivors, and disabled workers actually receiving Social Security payments. In addition, there were about 26 million beneficiaries of civilian public employee retirement systems in 1991. Also, there were over 9 million first-payment beneficiaries of state unemployment insurance in 1992. And finally, there were 94 million workers covered by workers' compensation protection in 1991 (in a civilian labor force of 125 million).

In the income-tested category, where the numbers were generally smaller, there were over 18 million households receiving at least one noncash benefit in 1992. AFDC recipients numbered over 13 million and SSI over 5 million in that year. The vast totals for the two programs do not include the myriad smaller welfare programs, aside from those for educational purposes and for veterans. They are vast totals even when the large overlap among recipients is acknowledged.

Income security and antipoverty objectives were paramount in the developing welfare state. It was the social antipoverty impulse, "poverty amid affluence," that made the sixties the biggest decade for the expansion of that institution in the post–World War II era. It is true that on the official, strict, money-income criterion of the poverty line, the percentage of the total population below that line, after a dramatic drop in the sixties, paralleled the stagnation of real wages and rose again substantially between 1978 and 1992. But without the welfare state, millions more would have joined the impoverished stratum. For example, in 1993 some 31 percent of the highly impoverished black population were officially below the poverty line. But in the absence of government money transfer payments, 40 percent would have been below it.[69] When full allowance for all welfare benefits is made, the percentage of blacks below the poverty level was brought down to about 25 percent in 1992.[70]

It is widely known that for the elderly of all races, social insurance alone prevented many millions from falling below the poverty threshold. Equally well known is the fact that in the lowest personal income quintile of the population, over 90 percent of their total income came from the income-support system.[71]

It is revealing to recognize that, aside from income from work, *earned benefits* from the welfare state system (e.g., Social Security, veterans' pensions, unemployment compensation, workers' compensation, government employee pensions) account for a very high proportion of the total income of the poor. It is estimated that about three-tenths of that income comes from the means-tested programs.[72] These two facts about their income sources dispel some typical, popular conservative misconceptions about laziness, alleged partiality toward dependency, and lack of work incentives on the part of welfare state beneficiaries.

The explanatory structure used herein has again revealed its cogency in this review of the welfare state's rise. The operation of the market system produced a long-run growth in per capita income. This rise released the abiding social culture currents pressing for the provision of material minima to the lower rung of the social ladder. Concurrently, that very market system income achievement revealed to an ever more glaring degree its own incapacity to alter sufficiently the income inequalities and associated sociopolitical disparities always characterizing the system's functioning.

The Great Depression triggered the new social response. The disillusionment with the exercise of economic responsibilities by the private business stratum amounted to a profound pervasive, public shock, coming as it did following the 1920s "New Era" of laissez-faire, or "intact capitalism," as Joseph Schumpeter described it. The old slogan of private "property rights versus human rights" resurfaced explosively. The substitution of a broad militant consensus favoring humanistic, collective, political approaches for the brute individualism and voluntarism endogenous to the private market system billowed across the social spectrum. Governmental solutions were inaugurated.

The state and local governments had quickly proved inadequate to cope with the economic breakdown of the 1930s. The conservative argument that the breakdown was a temporary emergency was soon seen as an illusion. The time-honored partiality toward state and local government measures was replaced with a fresh focus on the need for intervention by the traditionally viewed, more threatening federal power.

While the new welfare solutions thus invoked possessed American character-istics, their historic significance was and is greatly enhanced by the fact that the process was matched by developments in many other countries having advanced market economies. The welfare state component of the social market economy in the United States soon became thoroughly institutionalized, just as it did in those other nations. Thus the tripartite analytical framework employed in the present work—the market's own evolution, the societal currents of the larger culture, and the changing government role with respect to those two—is extremely clari-fying for the interpretation of the welfare state's appearance and subsequent growth.

Notes

1. Percentage calculated from data in *Statistical Abstract,* 1979, p. 331, No. 529; 1993, p. 372, No. 586; and the *Economic Report of the President,* January 1993, p. 385, Table B-32.

2. Under the Elementary and Secondary Education Act of 1965. See Irwin Gar-finkel, "Income Support Policy," *Discussion Paper,* Institute for Research on Poverty, University of Wisconsin-Madison, April 1978, p. 39. Photocopied.

3. Calculated from data in *Statistical Abstract,* 1994, p. 154, No. 227.

4. John Kenneth Galbraith, *The Affluent Society* (Boston: Houghton Mifflin, 1958), pp. 109, 111.

5. Moses Abramovitz, *Thinking about Growth* (New York: Cambridge University Press, 1989), p. 305.

6. All short-period GDP and other rates for economy are calculated on the basis of three-year averages for the initial and terminal years.

7. Organization for Economic Cooperation and Development, *Social Expenditure, 1960–1980* (Paris: Author, 1985), p. 56.

8. A survey by the National Opinion Research Center in 1986 found that on average the public supported assistance to very low-income families at a level 16 percent higher than the official poverty threshold. See Fred Groskind, "Ideological Influences on Public Support for Assistance to Poor Families," *Social Work,* 39, no. 1 (January 1994), p. 83.

9. *Statistical Abstract,* 1995, p. 357, No. 552; p. 375, No. 585; and p. 376, No. 587. Includes administrative expenditures and capital outlay. Retired military pay has been subtracted from the federal total on p. 357, No. 552.

10. *Historical Statistics to 1970,* Part 1, p. 332.

11. Coverage is from Domenico Gagliardo, *American Social Insurance,* rev. ed. (New York: Harper Bros., 1955), p. 186; the FTE employees estimate is from Solomon Fabri-cant, *The Trend of Government Activity in the United States Since 1900* (New York: National Bureau of Economic Research, 1952), p. 182–183, Table B6; the number of civil service workers is estimated by W. Andrew Achenbaum, *Old Age in the New Land* (Baltimore: Johns Hopkins University Press, 1978), p. 121, and *Historical Statistics,* Part 2, p. 1102, Series Y-311.

12. Gagliardo, *American Social Insurance,* p. 187, Table 24.

13. U.S. Department of Commerce, *The National Income and Product Accounts of the United States, 1929–74* (Washington: GPO, 1977), p. 343, Table 3.12.

14. Coverage from Gagliardo, *American Social Insurance,* p. 186; civil service total from *Statistical Abstract,* 1953, p. 380, No. 407.

15. *Statistical Abstract,* 1995, p. 382, No. 597.

16. Achenbaum, *Old Age,* p. 121.

17. Ibid.

18. Cited in Clarke Chambers, *Seedtime of Reform* (Minneapolis: University of Minnesota Press, 1963), p. 162.

19. Expenditures from U.S., Department of Health, Education, and Welfare, *Social Security Bulletin,* January 1976, p. 8, Table 1; employees from Tax Foundation, *Facts and Figures on Government Finance,* 1990 ed. (Baltimore: Johns Hopkins University Press, 1990) p. 22, Table A20.

20. *Report, Recent Social Trends in the United States* (New York: Whittlesey House, 1934), pp. 848, 1199–1200, 1444–1445.

21. *World Almanac,* 1936, p. 497.

22. Expenditures calculated from *Social Security Bulletin,* January 1976, p. 8; and *Historical Statistics,* p. 346, using personal consumption GNP deflator in 1982 dollars. Employee estimates calculated from *Facts and Figures,* p. 22 and *Statistical Abstract,* 1953, p. 393, No. 424.

23. Calculated from *National Income and Product Accounts,* p. 343.

24. *Statistical Abstract,* 1995, p. 304, No. 481.

25. Estimated from *Statistical Abstract,* 1994, pp. 319 and 379, Nos. 493 and 586, respectively.

26. Ibid., pp. 348 and 378, Nos. 533 and 585, respectively.

27. Theodore R. Marrmor, *The Politics of Medicare* (Chicago: Aldine, 1973), pp. 15, 97.

28. Mark J. Warshawsky, "Factors Contributing to Rapid Growth in National Expenditures on Health Care," in U.S. Department of Labor, Pension and Welfare Benefits Administration, *Trends in Health Benefits* (Washington: GPO, 1993), p. 65.

29. These points are advanced by Stuart Dorsey, "Employee Health Benefits and the Federal Income Tax," in U.S. Department of Labor, *Trends in Health Benefits,* ibid., pp. 91, 94–95.

30. Peter J. Ratican, chairman, president, and CEO of Medicare Health Plans, "A Blueprint for U.S. Health Care," *Business Forum,* Winter Special 1991, p. 14.

31. Calculated from *Statistical Abstract,* 1995, p. 375, No. 585.

32. Henry J. Aaron, "Six Welfare Questions Still Searching for Answers," *The Brookings Review* 3, no. 1 (Fall 1984), p. 16.

33. Calculated from data in *Statistical Abstract,* 1994, pp. 383, No. 598 and p. 386, No. 602. The personal consumption expenditures deflator is applied to deflate the nominal totals. Food stamp program participants increased by 8.4 million, or 45 percent, over the same period.

34. Richard T. Curtin, *Income Equity Amoung U.S. Workers* (New York: Praeger Publishers, 1977), pp. 1, 105.

35. *New York Times,* October 14, 1995, pp. 1, 8.

36. See Jeffrey M. Berry, *The Interest Group Society* (Boston: Little Brown, 1984), p. 91.

37. Aaron, "Six Welfare Questions," p. 16.

38. Garfinkel, "Income Support Policy," p. 38.

39. Berry, *Interest Group Society,* p. 185.

40. Garfinkel, "Income Support Policy, p. 48.

41. Henry J. Aaron, *Shelter and Subsidies* (Washington: The Brookings Institution, 1972), p. 111.

42. *Economic Report of the President,* 1968, p. 150.

43. Aaron, *Shelter and Subsidies,* p. 134.

44. Ibid., p. 135.

45. *Economic Report of the President,* 1968, p. 152.

46. David T. Ellwood and Lawrence H. Summers, "Poverty in America: Is Welfare the Answer or the Problem?" *Working Paper Series,* National Bureau of Economic Research, Paper No. 1711, October 1985, p. 20. Photocopied.

47. Garfinkel, "Income Support Policy," p. 32.

48. Robert H. Haveman, "Work-Conditioned Subsidies as an Income-Maintenance Strategy," Subcommittee on Fiscal Policy, Joint Economic Committee, U.S. Congress, *Concepts in Welfare Program Design,* Paper No. 9 (Part 1), 93d Cong., 1st Session, (Washington: GPO, August 20, 1973), p. 37.

49. Garfinkel, "Income Support Policy," p. 36.

50. See "Social Security Programs in the United States," *Social Security Bulletin,* 52, No. 7 (July 1989), p. 67.

51. Garfinkel, "Income Support Policy," p. 100.

52. Teresa L. Amott, "Black Women and AFDC: Making Entitlement out of Necessity," in Linda Gordon (ed.), *Women, the State, and Welfare* (Madison: University of Wisconsin Press, 1990), p. 290.

53. U.S. General Accounting Office, Comptroller General, "Perspective on Income Security and Social Services and an Agenda for Analysis," *Report to the Congress,* August 13, 1981, p. 28.

54. Walter A. Friedlander, *Introduction to Social Welfare,* 2nd ed. (Englewood Cliffs, N.J.: Prentice-Hall, 1963), p. 274.

55. *Social Security Bulletin,* January 1976, pp. 6, 8.

56. Gagliardo, *American Social Insurance,* p. 61.

57. Daniel Levine, *Poverty and Society* (New Brunswick, N.J.: Rutgers University Press, 1988), p. 255.

58. Gagliardo, *American Social Insurance,* p. 51.

59. Garfinkel, "Income Support Policy," p. 72. The monthly payment figures are from the *Statistical Abstract,* 1980, p. 354, No. 570.

60. *Statistical Abstract,* 1980, p. 357, No. 574 and 358, No. 576.

61. The 1993 current dollar estimate is from U.S. Congress, CBO, *The Economic Budget Outlook: Fiscal Years 1995–1999* (Washington: GPO, January 1994), p. 42.

62. Garfinkel, "Income Support Policy," p. 40.

63. John Karl Scholz, "Tax Policy and the Working Poor: The Earned Income Tax Credit," University of Wisconsin-Madison-Institute for Research on Poverty, *Focus,* 15, no. 3 (Winter 1993–1994), p. 3.

64. These data on credit rates, etc., in this and the following paragraph are taken from ibid., pp. 2–3.

65. U.S. Department of the Treasury, IRS, *Your Federal Income Tax,* No. 17, 1993, p. 269.

66. Irwin Garfinkel, *Welfare Reform: A New and Old View,* University of Wisconsin-Madison, IRP, Reprint Series, No. 373, p. 66. Reprinted from *The Journal of Institute for Socioeconomic Studies,* 4, no. 4 (Winter 1979).

67. See, e.g., the *Statistical Abstract,* 1980, p. 267, No. 445. Refundable totals for 1983 and 1984 were $1,213 million and $1,123 million respectively; *Statistical Abstract,* 1985, p. 310, No. 494, footnote.

68. CBO, *The Economic Budget Outlook: Fiscal Years 1995–1999,* January 1994, p. 42.

69. *Statistical Abstract,* 1995, p. 485, No. 754.

70. Ibid.

71. Garfinkel, "Income Support Policy," p. 55.

72. Winifred Bell, *Contemporary Social Welfare* (New York: Macmillan, 1983), p. 105.

CHAPTER SIX

International Influences and the Expanding American Role

The vast extension of global economic and political relations after World War II induced a depth of involvement by the United States that was unmatched in any period of its previous history. However, the readily available record of that growing involvement is not a matter for full review here. Rather, the concern will be primarily with those parts of the record that have implications for U.S. government participation in the expanding international economy.

The character of the federal government's necessarily growing response to the continuing enlargement of global interdependence will undoubtedly, as in the past, take the form primarily of administrative management. Budgetary requirements should be moderate, and the associated public employment rise also modest. This means that to sketch the future interventionist pattern, lacking *numeraires,* only a qualitative survey of the likely policy areas and strategies is, with some exceptions, feasible. Restriction to qualitative analysis of the objective factors underlying and prompting policy measures is also necessary. For example, the domestic economic policies of the big trading nations and their foreign balances are interconnected. But exploration of the large intergovernmental management responsibilities that those interconnections will require in the future is an overwhelmingly nonquantitative undertaking.

Trade and Related Policies

Some of the major foreign balance developments that have shaped, and will continue to determine, the global policy setting of the United States, may be noted at the outset. Two of the basic influences on the United States emanating from its global connections are (1) the foreign balance in relation to the domestic economy, and (2) the U.S. share of the world's exploding international transactions (real world merchandise exports grew over three times as fast as global output, 1965–90). The long-run careers of these two proportions represent two of the conditions shaping policy responses because the government has historically been dedicated to supporting domestic economic interest organizations in their relations with international markets.

As to the first objective measure of foreign balance influence, it is clear that the linkage has quantitatively increased over the long run. In the more distant past, for example, U.S. exports of goods and services amounted to only 5 or 6 percent of its GNP; and imports were about a percentage point less. Those ratios continued to obtain after World War II up to the early 1970s. But thereafter exports accounted for an economically much more significant 12 percent of GNP on average, and imports a bit more (emergence of the notorious negative trade balance). The import rise was spurred by U.S. growth, foreign competitiveness, and a historic decrease in overall tariff rates. Hence, the stake of the domestic economy in the international market, and the consequent concern of a dedicated government, approximately doubled. There is little evidence that this historic rise will be reversed in the foreseeable future.

As for the U.S. share of world total exports, the pressure for government support rises to resist a falling proportion, and also rises to reinforce an increasing fraction. The share was very large in the years immediately after World War II as America poured out aid to war-devastated economies and U.S. superior productivity outsold the world. For manufactured commodities in world export trade in manufactures, it was a whopping 29 percent in 1953; but by the 1970s it had plummeted to an average of 13 percent.[1] The high export share also obtained for all merchandise in the early years of the postwar era; then it also fell until it stabilized at somewhat over 11 percent beginning about 1980.

U.S. export competitiveness, and therefore a supportive government with a sophisticated "national export strategy,"[2] has increasingly had to confront the rising technological challenges and spreading industrial policies pursued by other advanced countries, as well as the emerging strong competition from the newly industrializing nations and the developing world. The connection between competitiveness and the disparities in labor's working conditions in these tiers of differentially advanced countries has made those disparities a matter of growing international concern and consequent policy involvement.

The U.S. share of world merchandise imports has risen over the long run, as has its proportion of world commercial services exports. Services constitute by far the most rapidly growing export category. The surge of imports over the last quarter-century is dominated by imported capital goods. U.S. imports of capital goods, except automobiles, as a proportion of total imports rose from 10 percent in 1970 to 27.5 percent in 1994. The imported capital goods, less automobiles, as a percentage of nonresidential fixed investment rose from 3.7 percent to 27.6 percent over the same period. Obviously, a return to higher tariffs would lower the quality and quantity of available investment.

This brief quantitative review of the historically large export dependency of the U.S. domestic economy in recent times is designed to show that certain developments in the economic setting for government policy have made, and will continue to make, policy ever more imperative. Similarly, the growth in U.S. import dependency demands ever greater attention by government's foreign and domestic strategies. Furthermore, the growing import volumes provide the setting for augmented responsibilities on the part of the United States that are prompted by the demands of other countries for their own economic health. *All these enlarged responsibilities are two-way streets.*

Closely connected with such trade responsibilities and strategies is foreign exchange policy that deeply involves every federal administration and the Federal Reserve. The exchange value of the dollar relative to foreign money units impacts the volume of U.S. exports and imports. Since that impact affects foreign countries' buyers and sellers, their economies are stimulated or dampened. For example, the Clinton administration in late July 1994 strove to bolster the exchange value of the dollar because it believed that "a renewed decline would be counterproductive to the global economy."[3] This action was supported to the tune of several billion dollars by the Bank of Japan.

Such interrelationships lead to continual international cooperative efforts designed to adjust foreign exchange ratios so as to be as optimal as possible to often rival participants. Efforts of this kind command center stage and have become institutionalized in contemporary times, especially since the collapse of the predecessor International Monetary Fund's fixed exchange rate system. That arrangement had been established by the 1945–46 Bretton Woods agreement, but was scuttled largely by U.S. dollar devaluations in 1971 and 1973.

The ramifications of the government's trade management burden are revealed in considerable part by the years of often strained negotiations entailed in the evolving implementation of the free trade objectives of the 1947–48 General Agreement on Tariffs and Trade (GATT). That vicissitudinous saga reached a historic zenith with the conclusion in December 1993 of the so-called Uruguay Round of multilateral trade barrier reductions. The 117 participating countries, accounting for about 85 percent of world trade, endured an ebb and flow of negotiations for almost eight years before concluding the round.

GATT entangled the U.S. participants with the foreign trade problems of the tier of developing and newly industrializing countries and their many-sided relations with the economically advanced nations (e.g., the Group of Seven). The entanglement also included trade and exchange rate strategies generated by the new postwar regionally integrated collectives, such as the 1957 European Economic Community, the 1960 European Free Trade Association, the Gulf Cooperation Council, and the 1992 North American Free Trade Association (NAFTA). As the 1971 *Economic Report of the President* noted, "the relationship between the United States and the European Economic Community is a major consideration in the formation of both our trade and our balance-of-payments policies."[4]

GATT also ensnared U.S. representatives in negotiation tasks emanating from various countries' special discriminatory strategies, such as nontariff barriers, subsidies, and dumping. Indeed, U.S. antidumping measures, twisted in order to sabotage GATT's free trade thrust, are widely advocated by protectionists in and out of the U.S. Congress. Finally, there was and remains the growing managerial obligations to establish and pursue international dispute settlement procedures.

The Uruguay Round also affected future U.S. domestic economic performance and its consequent government management responsibilities. The round's average reductions of 40 percent in world import tariffs promised larger U.S. exports and therefore higher output, employment, and probably productivity. Of course, they also promised more imports and consequently less domestic output and employment—thus illustrating the typically contradictory nature of international economic changes, a systemic characteristic that can only increase government management reactions.

The domestic advantages of the tariff reductions diffuse through various sectors of the economy, that is, they more or less penetrate areas of government interest. For example, important favored sectors include textiles and apparel; electronic and other high-technology products; intellectual property rights such as patents, copyrights, and trademarks; the expanding category of services in which the United States excels, such as telecommunications, professional and financial intangibles; agriculture; and trade-related investment. As two authorities have perceptively commented, "nothing is more domestic than international trade policy."[5]

More on the domestic front, the Uruguay Round GATT milestone demands that the U.S. federal government will have to accord to foreign service suppliers treatment equal to that given to domestic suppliers of services. It must also ensure that foreign affiliates of U.S. multinational corporations have the right to export as much of their output as they wish. It must actively participate in GATT's new World Trade Organization's (WTO) dispute settlement panels and enforce the panels' decisions representing the consensus of the WTO's 123 member governments.[6] It must use GATT dispute resolution procedures before taking unilateral action. It must avoid using U.S. food safety standards, or other technical product regulations and business practice laws, as disguised trade barriers against foreigners. Further on domestic public management tasks, the Uruguay Round will require a reduction in federal tariff revenues of between $2 and $3 billion a year.

Enter the Budget Enforcement Act of 1990, requiring either an equivalent spending cut or tax increase. Thomas L. Friedman, writing in the *New York Times,* reviewed some of the possible fiscal solutions proposed by the White House to deal with those estimated GATT tariff revenue losses.[7] The possible spending cuts ranged widely through the grand sweep of the federal government's policies: farm subsidies and price supports, certain tax filing schedules required of some foreign-controlled firms, assignment of Social Security numbers to all newborn babies, reforms at the Pension Guaranty Corporation, and so on. Some compensating tax increases were also suggested—for example, on casino revenues from Indian reservations and how retailers account for inventory!

Connections, such as indicated in this list of possible adjustments, between the government's growing international responsibilities and its domestic policies, reveal a future filled with ever greater managerial activities by government. In its contemporary setting, as the era of increasing global intimacy unfolds, the United States can coordinate its international and domestic economic policies only if it negotiates continually in concert with other countries. This compelling insight has been perspicaciously expressed by one analyst: "The cooperation of other key nations [is] a necessary condition for the success of any American domestic economic strategy."[8]

But there are of course additional sources of involvement. For example, there is the well-known proliferation of U.S. and foreign multinational firms since World War II, a development that contributed much to the vastly expanded internationalization of finance, with its attendant interest rate policy involvement. The increase in American owned and managed multinationals was also principally responsible for the large expansion in the American stock of private foreign direct capital placements abroad from $12 billion in 1950 to $549 billion in 1993. As pointed out in the 1992 *Economic Report of the President,* "foreign direct investment flows, which are manifest in the operations of multinational corporations, have grown since 1983 at an unprecedented rate of 29 percent a year, roughly four times that of the growth of output (in current prices)."[9] U.S. firms owned one-fourth (and the United States hosted 22 percent) of the world's foreign direct investment stock in 1992. But at this point the concern is primarily with trade rather than capital flows or stock, even though the multinationals apparently augment their trade by expanding foreign direct investment. Much of their "trade" is intrafirm transactions. They accounted for over 75 percent of total U.S. merchandise trade by 1990, and around 40 percent of that was intrafirm. Protection and support, in the broadest sense, of these private investments and this private stake in their trade, will undoubtedly require continuous government surveillance, as it has historically ever since the early splurge of U.S. capital export in the very late nineteenth century.

The hosting of foreign direct investment in the United States in recent times far outdid in relative magnitude the nineteenth-century hosting of the primarily portfolio (securities) investment in the United States by England and France. The direct investment inflow was particularly large in the 1980s into the manufacturing sector, chiefly through acquisition of existing U.S. enterprises. It has been estimated that the impact on the domestic manufacturing sector will be to improve productivity and international competitiveness, raising exports and reducing imports in the affected industries.

Government enters this sphere of incoming foreign direct investment by multinationals through rules such as stipulations regarding the use of locally produced goods, requirements that foreign multinationals export part of their output, limitations on input purchases out of the foreign exchange revenues the multinationals receive, and specifications in the case of national security exceptions. These governmental rules are of course similarly relevant for the foreign affiliates of U.S. multinationals. Government administrative management in the future will have to include efforts to establish common multilateral rules for transnational investment throughout the world because it will be necessary to get "benefits that stem from the global production networks of multinational corporations."[10]

An additional area of governmental involvement that has been, and will of course continue to involve some of the work of the U.S. treasury under secretary for international affairs, is the taxation of multinationals, both foreign and U.S. owned. The U.S. Treasury Department's "external revenue service," in tandem with the Departments of Commerce, State, Defense, and so on, must continually deal with tax exemptions, deferrals, "first-crack" credits, and deductions in the context of a "rivalrous relationship between Home's and Foreign's tax collectors."[11] Optimal strategies of each and every government "for taxing corporate net incomes constitute the dominant factor in the division of spoils between source and host countries."[12] The U.S. Revenue Service will long have its hands full dealing with the fact that, among other avoidance tricks, multinationals manipulate their prices on intracorporate transactions in order to make their profit appear in tax-minimizing places. Internationally, the abiding adversary relationships characterizing multinational taxation will necessitate continuous negotiation to settle differences in the years ahead.

Japanese multinational corporations strongly lobbied against U.S. state government unitary taxes. These are taxes that allocate the total profits of a multiregional or multinational corporation by formulas that ignore the company-generated interregional profit shifts and instead say that profits in a state are the percent of total sales, and/or employees, and/or assets that the company earns in the state times total company profit. The Japanese, unaware of American institutions and traditions, did not realize that the unitary tax formulas were developed to protect businesses from predatory governments that could devise formulas that say, for example, 80 percent of U.S. Steel is in Pennsylvania and 75 percent in Ohio, thus taxing more than 100 percent of profit.

We must expect increasing lobbying of domestic governments by foreign governments and businesses. There will be cases when, say, the German government lobbies Congress for a policy while Mercedes-Benz lobbies a state legislature for its opposite. U.S. governments at all levels and businesses will lobby foreign country governments in similar ways.

Waxing World Environmental Cooperation

"More and more, national and international environmental problems are being seen not as two separate arenas of activity, but as a continuum," reported the *EPA Journal* in 1990.[13] The writer of this prophetic statement calls our attention to the fact that international environmental issues were first brought into focus by the Stockholm Conference on the Human Environment in 1972, one outcome from which was the creation of the consequential United Nations Environmental Programme (UNEP). The London *Economist* declared in 1989 that "if any issue cries out for international co-operation, it is environmental regulation. Pollution respects no borders. . . . It will be one of the most intractable political issues of the 1990s"[14]

Powerful, objective facts impelling international action on this front are very potent: population growth, the vast flow of toxic and nontoxic wastes produced particularly by the more affluent societies, and environmentally damaging decisions by one country that ignores national borders. When "pollution or other environmental problems spill across borders, international rules and cooperation will be necessary."[15] However, environmental issues are also indirectly increasing international competitiveness and trade. The worldwide explosion in environmental regulatory activity has spawned the development of pollution control technology, for example, and this is an area in which the United States happens to excel. Indeed, it has become the world's leading exporter of environmental equipment.[16]

The makeup of U.S. official foreign economic aid programs, which rose more than threefold in the 1980s compared to the seventies, has to an increasing extent addressed environmental goals. This change has paralleled a drop in the ratio of official military to economic foreign aid with the end of the Cold War. In 1993, for example, the ratio was 17 percent, compared to 52 percent for 1946–93. The compositional shifts within economic aid have furthered natural resource management (e.g., forests) and the development of environmentally healthy infrastructure projects.[17] These shifts require substantial, technical, and administrative guidance.

The same trends are developing in the loans made by the International Monetary Fund (IMF) and the International Bank for Reconstruction and Development (IBRD, or World Bank), institutions, and policies involving active U.S. participation. The American president of the World Bank, Barber B. Conable, declared in 1989 that "the Bank and others in the development community have learned that protection of the environment warrants specific and discrete emphasis. . . . Environmental issues cut across all development sectors and are affected as much by domestic politics as by international trade practices."[18] Of the total World Bank loans in fiscal year 1989, 38 percent contained environmental elements.

Conable appropriately noted the close connection between the environment and unchecked population growth in the developing regions of the world. Since the environment is borderless, so is the population threat. Conable adds, "the challenge is too great for us to await the impact of general social improvement on population growth rates."[19] The high priority of the issue is underscored by the fact that the notable United Nations Conference on Population and Development in Cairo in September 1994 was the third such meeting in only twenty years.

The council of the internationally influential Organization for Economic Co-operation and Development (OECD), in which the United States is a major participant, in 1985 called for assessment from an in-depth environmental stand-point of all development assistance projects and programs.[20] The great breadth of policy concerns at the meeting of environment ministers that year was revealed by Lee M. Thomas, U.S. Environmental Protection Agency administrator: conventional and toxic air pollutants, water pollution, hazardous wastes (especially their transborder transportation), and global atmospheric issues. Natural resources management in general was added as an area of participation for all members by the Australian minister for employment and industrial relations. The meeting emphasized that the scale of environmental deterioration in some parts of the Third and Developing World was approaching the crisis stage. Specifically, the savage deforestation in Latin America and elsewhere will become an ever larger negotiable issue for the United States and other industrialized countries in the years ahead, because it threatens (1) wood imports potential, (2) the ability of those regions' rain forests to continue to provide global carbon absorption services, and (3) a diverse world of endangered wild fauna and flora.

International institutions to secure negotiation and response in the area of nuclear safety were established by a forty-nation agreement at the International Convention on Nuclear Safety, which took effect in 1994.

> Signers of the agreement are required to submit an immediate report on atomic installations and, if necessary, urgently carry out improvements to upgrade the safety of sites. The agreement sets out a framework for a review of a nation's atomic sites by other countries. Neighboring countries, in particular, may call for an urgent study if they are concerned about a reactor's safety and a possible radioactive fallout accident affecting their own populations and crops.[21]

This would seem at minimum to subject U.S. nuclear facilities around the Great Lakes, Puget Sound, and the Columbia River to Canadian regulation, and nuclear plants in the Rio Grande basin as well as the southern California coast to Mexican regulation. These areas include the giant federal installations at Hanford, Washington, and Alamagordo, New Mexico, which are the heart of the U.S. atomic weapons program.

It is quite plausible that differing environmental policies in countries at varying levels of development and per capita income, on top of different capacities to assimilate pollution by natural processes, can dictate foreign policy attention. This follows from the impact of these two factors on comparative advantage and therefore relative prices in international export competition. For example, the higher the per capita income, the greater the popular demand is likely to be for a good-quality environment with its associated costs. Hence the widespread conviction in high-income countries that their environmental regulations unfairly discriminate against domestic export firms when they compete with firms in countries that have lower environmental standards and costs.[22]

However, it appears that only the future will reveal the scope of the required international negotiation efforts on this pervasive issue. So far, experience suggests that the matter is largely of potential significance. One careful survey has concluded that pollution control measures have not as yet "exerted a systematic effect on international trade and investment."[23] In general, "the differentials in the costs of complying with environmental regulations and in the levels of environmental concern in industrialized and industrializing countries have not been strong enough to offset larger political and economic forces in shaping aggregate international comparative advantage."[24] The point is not that the environmental regulation costs are irrelevant; it is only that they are at this point in history overshadowed by such things as production cost differences and exchange rates.

Foreign Aid, Support, Intercession

It is perhaps trite to say that U.S. foreign policy implements its long-run self-interest. But in the case of foreign aid and intercession in the affairs of other countries, it could be ingenuous to interpret even ostensibly humanitarian policies as unrelated to the nation's presumed maximization goals. Even the State Department's minuscule, humanitarian Peace Corps cannot but build good-will for the United States.

For a half-century the United States has been a world leader in providing grants and credits, first to the war-ravaged, noncommunist industrial countries, and then to poor developing countries. Its subsidized food exports have often allayed starvation and the threat of famine in recipient lands. It will no doubt continue to do so, at least in crisis situations under International Disaster Assistance.

The strategy of directing assistance to developing countries stems in part from an influential but weakly supported empirical presumption that its contribution to recipients' economic betterment promises reciprocation in the form of expanding markets for American products and capital exports. That widespread presumption, of course, actually "does not reflect the national interest, but rather, sectional and industrial interests promoted at the expense of the taxpayer."[25] History suggests that this fact is not likely, however, to seriously undermine either the influence of that extensively believed presumption or the associated targets of assistance strategy. Furthermore, the chronic existence of global violence, rebellions within nations and tribes, authoritarian government slaughters, ethnic genocide, and terrorism coexisting with the humanitarian, pro-democracy, economically maximizing, and national security objectives of U.S. foreign policy, obviously generates an overlap. *This overlap only strengthens the now historic, well-established policy of foreign aid and intercession.* It is true that national security dominated the foreign support policies during the Cold War— "The USA invented aid as a device to win over, or at least keep neutral, the uncommitted countries."[26] Indeed, by the mid-1960s it could be said that "aid would never have attained anything like its present level if it had not been for the Cold War."[27] Although as late as the 1980s, official "military" aid averaged about one-third of total foreign aid (the rest being economic), it was still undoubtedly accurate to say, in the spirit of the Mutual Security Act of 1951, that "two-thirds of U.S. aid is security-related assistance."[28]

As of the present, the anticommunist element of the 1948 Marshall Plan and the rebuilding of Europe's noncommunist economies, President Truman's 1949 Point Four program of technical assistance "for making the benefits of our scientific advances and industrial progress available for the improvement and growth of underdeveloped areas";[29] Nelson Rockefeller's Partners in Progress; and President Kennedy's 1961 Alliance for Progress, "designed to forestall revolution by raising the living standards of ordinary people throughout the southern two-thirds of the Western Hemisphere,"[30] are only highlights of the past, for the Cold War is over. The United States currently proposes to prepare to fight "only" two regional wars simultaneously. U.N. peacekeeping operations, such as that in Bosnia, will be cautiously and selectively supported jointly by the Departments of State and Defense, even as the Congress delays on overdue appropriations for the United Nations and the administration busies itself with combating waste and alleged fraud in that organization.

At least equally stimulative of economic intercession is the fact that the international competition facing the U.S. business community has been heating up. That development, alongside the national security overlap, must continue to invigorate the overall global strategy that employs the foreign aid instrumentality. Thus, it is not accidental that the long-run fall after 1953–61 in real official military aid, administered by the Department of Defense, was accompanied by long-run constancy in real official economic aid, administered by the State Department, after 1946–52 (translated into real magnitudes by appropriate deflators).[31] The annual volume of real economic aid during 1989–92, dispensed primarily by the State Department's Agency for International Development (AID), modest as it was in amount, was almost equal to the annual average for the 1980s as a whole.

One long-established assistance program has been connected with the dispensing of food, implementing the 1954 Agricultural Trade and Development Act (PL 480), or U.S. "Food for Peace" plan. The strength of the program in the past stemmed from a combination of humanitarianism, security strategy, and the fact that it "was based in considerable measure on a desire to get rid of U.S. agricultural surpluses generated by domestic agricultural policies."[32] PL 480 provided grants for emergency relief or community development, sales of farm commodities for local currencies, loans from those receipts to U.S. firms operating in the recipient countries, and grants or loans to the governments in the receivers. During one period, PL 480 was a quite large program. For example, in fiscal 1965, sales for local currencies, commodity grants, and dollar credit sales were about 30 percent of all economic assistance.

However, it would appear that PL 480 is one assistance program that has but a modest future. It funded less than 2 percent of total food exports in 1993, a magnitude that represented only some 10 percent of all government help to farmers; and government stocks of the particular commodities shipped under PL 480 became inconsequential.[33] The one residue of the program that could amount to much in the future is erratic shipments, under Title II of the act, to meet acute crises, such as in Bosnia or Rwanda. Probably much more important for the future is the impending multilateral work that will be required to coordinate national farm policies.

Annual funding for all foreign aid by 1994 was running at some $18 billion, which was about 1.2 percent of total federal expenditures. Given the overlap of the economic with national security, there are a multitude of pressures that are likely to expand these magnitudes and their administrative accompaniments. The Clinton administration's proposal for a new Foreign Assistance Act, for example, emphasized six weighty international inducements for continuing aid: building democracy; promoting peace (presumably this covers U.S. interventionist peacekeeping); promoting sustainable development (programs for health, education, family planning, water and sanitation, roads, ports, agriculture, and environmental preservation in developing countries, and including no doubt the 1961 Peace Corps of the Christian missionary tradition);[34] providing humanitarian assistance (e.g., funds for refugees and disaster assistance); advancing prosperity through trade and investment (e.g., through the work of the Export-Import Bank and the Overseas Private Investment Corporation, and through agricultural credit programs); and "advancing diplomacy" through the work of the State Department.[35] Verily, this is an almost unlimited agenda—administratively, if not financially.

Multilateral Influences

Comprehensive as this agenda is, its orientation around a legislative act necessarily gives it a primarily unilateral American focus. Hence there must be added a host of activities resulting from the increasing demands made upon the United States to participate in the assistance work of overlapping multinational institutions, both established and ad hoc. That addition is diverse and far-reaching in its budgetary and administrative scope. A few examples will indicate that reach. There is under multilateral aegis with U.S. involvement and with assistance aspects:

1. Support for the World Bank's International Development Association (the United States is a "Part I" major financial contributor) and International Finance Corporation
2. The implementation of several international commodity agreements to support prices (e.g., coffee, sugar, wheat)
3. Cooperative stabilization of foreign exchange ratios through the IMF

4. Loans for development under the IMF
5. Assistance dispensed through the United Nation's Food and Agriculture Organization
6. Assistance by the Inter-American Development Bank and the Asian Development Bank
7. GATT
8. Participation in the global negotiation work of the U.S. International Trade Administration
9. Cooperation with the UN Conference on Trade and Development (UN-CTAD)
10. Participation in some of the previously discussed multinational environmental assistance organizations, such as the Convention on International Trade in Endangered Species of 1973 (CITES), the 1987 Montreal Protocol on Substances that Deplete the Ozone Layer, and the International Seabed Authority set up under the 1958 Law of the Sea Conference
11. The United Nations' population fund
12. The Development Assistance Committee of the OECD

Many of these activities and organizations are not exclusively concerned with assistance. But all are either directly or indirectly so concerned, and there are interconnections among their functions that require administrative input.

Multilateral intercession is another matter. Much of that activity falls under the immense national security dominion, such as containment of nuclear proliferation (one task of the United Nations Security Council). But there are many activities less directly connected, such as multilateral cooperation on petroleum imports, the international paramilitary work of the Drug Enforcement Administration, the repression of international terrorism, the nonproliferation duties of the International Atomic Energy Agency, the Migration and Refugee Assistance Program, and the international war crimes tribunal.

The Trade in Weaponry

It is remarkable that the devotion of administrative management to the prominent American role in the international export trade in arms to governments and subnational groups is widely ignored. GATT's Uruguay Round, for example, had nothing to say about arms trade. U.S. weapons sales (totaling $12.4 billion in 1994 and equal to more than half the world's weapon supplies) are of course assistance in the sense that they help recipients defend themselves against presumed foreign threats or help recipient governments stay in power when threatened by internal dissent. In a certain sense they are also good business, for it may be presumed that recipients become linked to their U.S. suppliers through a resulting dependence on a continued flow of spare parts and related commodities or services along with technical know-how. However, from the U.S. economic standpoint alone, that outflow is not very significant.[36] Of course as might be expected, the State Department and the Defense Department typically attempt to justify substantial federal financing of arms sales on the grounds that they are economically important to U.S. business and labor. A national security argument might be more cogent and effective from an agency standpoint; after all, the Pentagon, through the U.S. Arms Control and Disarmament Agency, may be the seller of the weapons or, if not, it and/or the State Department must approve the transactions.

The United States unilaterally and multilaterally has permanently committed itself to restricting the export of arms. One of the chief multilateral instrumentalities for exercising controls has been the Coordinating Committee for Multilateral Export Controls (CoCom), created as far back as 1949 as an informal organization connected with the North Atlantic Treaty Organization (NATO). CoCom subsequently added Australia and Japan to its associates. The future role of this institution is of course uncertain, although its link with an uncertain NATO need not be iron-clad. In any case, there are a number of other international instrumentalities that have been set up to control the weapons trade, such as those implementing the Nuclear Non-Proliferation Treaty; the twenty-nation "Australia Group," formed in 1984 to impede the spread of chemical weapons; and the fourteen-nation 1987 Missile Technology Control Regime. Undoubtedly for a considerable future period, additional multilateral controls will be instituted and implemented to mitigate "threats related to weapons of mass destruction from the former Soviet Union."[37] After all, these policies and organizations represent the federal goal of "promoting peace," albeit on the multinational level—the only level that has much meaning for that goal.

In defense the United States promotes foreign consumption of fighter aircraft to achieve "scale economies." This has led international consortia to produce the fighter planes designed in America. The United States sees this as good. Other nations have created a consortium to produce Airbus airliners to compete with Boeing. The United States deems this bad. Yet the former tends to monopoly and the latter produces *some* competition.

Other Areas Requiring Coordination

There are at least two additional, linked national policy categories that in the upcoming years are likely to necessitate substantial, continuing international negotiation: fiscal (plus monetary) management and growth management. These policies influence the complex network of prices, the balance of payments, interest rates, private investment flows, and exchange rates. Therefore, all countries have a stake in dealing cooperatively with the impacts of their fiscal, monetary, and growth measures on that network. For example, the January 1989 *Economic Report of the President,* after noting that wide exchange-rate swings in the late eighties prompted officials from many countries to seek greater exchange rate stability through increased "coordination of sovereign policies," declared further

that "to achieve a stable value of the dollar requires not only predictable and restrained monetary policy along with sustainable real growth in the United States, but
also similar economic conditions abroad."[38] The report emphasized that

> a promising approach for increasing the stability of exchange rates focuses on
> the coordination of domestic policies toward inflation and economic growth.
> Under this approach, the leading industrial countries adopt mutually compati-
> ble economic policies to achieve sustained growth with low inflation.... No
> country acting alone can achieve both price and exchange-rate stability....
> Productive policy cooperation among countries includes ... consistent mone-
> tary and fiscal policies.[39]

Vito Tanzi, of the IMF economic staff, incisively theorizes that operation of
factors in the above-described network strongly shaped the deterioration in the
U.S. balance of payments on current account in the 1980s.[40] The road to international macropolicy coordination has barely been opened, but some traffic already
on that road is suggested by the Plaza Agreement of 1985, the Tokyo Summit of
1986, and the Louvre Accord of 1987. Commitment to economic policy coordination through these organizational steps was largely implicit, but the Statement
of the Group of Seven in December 1987 was more specific in listing the policy
intentions and undertakings agreed upon.[41]

As noted earlier in the discussion of GATT's Uruguay Round, the major
industrial countries are importantly involved in the necessary coordination despite their relative insulation owing to their large size. Both demand management
and tax reform are pertinent cooperation candidates, particularly through their
possible effects on cycles and growth. Tanzi calls attention to the links between
expansionary fiscal measures and the balance of payments:

> Acting independently, countries may be reluctant to pursue expansionary fiscal
> policies, because of the balance of payments effects of these policies. But, in
> theory at least, they could all benefit, and neutralize the effects on the balance
> of payments, if they all pursued fiscal expansion at the same time.[42]

If the United States presumes it can unilaterally pressure Japan to deficit finance
increase in its public infrastructure (to open up U.S. business opportunities
there), surely it must acknowledge its administrative commitments to its own
declamations—that is, "coordination of macroeconomic policies across countries
can help governments increase sustainable growth worldwide.... International
macroeconomic policy coordination continues to be essential."[43] One might say,
to reverse and modify the earlier quoted generalization by Shultz and Dam,
nothing is more international than domestic macropolicy.

Conclusion

In the context of a world of historically sovereign states, the U.S. market
system's network of evolving vested interests is interwoven with another net-

work of often conflicting, but on some issues nationwide, organized pressure groups. These pressure organizations have generated in turn a large third network of governmental administrative engineering whose function is to reconcile or otherwise resolve the continuing flood of demands by the organization network. The totality of this developing pattern, with the first network as prime mover, describes the theoretical framework for explaining the third network's activities in the global arena.

As in other connections throughout this work, the character and magnitude of the governmental superstructure and its policies may be traced back to the evolving and continually modified market system via the societal response to that evolution. The public policies in turn reshape the market system, changing its structure and modus operandi.

The third network being examined at the moment is the federal government's global interventionism. Here the general goal of the pressure network is ostensibly the national interest. But this is hardly clarifying in view of the disparate makeup of the pressure labyrinth. More specifically, we can detect three main classes of pressures constituting the second network. In order of strength, general national security vies with specific vested interests for the position of prime importance, with humanitarian and global welfare impulses at the bottom.

It is tempting to think that national security, being presumably backed by nationwide patriotism coupled with fear, is by far the leading class of pressure types within the second network. And when one looks at the relative share of governmental resources ostensibly devoted to national security, such a belief seems to be correct. For example, the Defense Department still has almost 900,000 "civilian" employees, and the national defense budget still approaches $300 billion. No other officially allotted, internationally oriented resources, taken in toto, even approach those magnitudes. For example, the State Department's employees number about 25,000, and the whole budget for all "international affairs" runs about $19 billion (1995). Even if one were to add several other internationally oriented "peace" programs, we would still be far below the total "national security" magnitudes.

However, despite those contrasting totals, it may nevertheless still be reasonable to say, as above, that national security vies with, rather than overwhelms, the special vested economic interests for top position in the hierarchy of pressure classes. The chief reason for saying so is evident at once if the term "military-industrial complex" is called up. The term reminds us that interlaced with general patriotism and fear is the very potent and strategically focused cosmos of millions of people with a material stake in the military establishment, together with billions of dollars of sales flowing to the myriad of businesses getting the military contracts. An article in *The Brookings Review* in 1996 reported that the Pentagon was prepared to allow defense companies to bill it for the costs, in many billions of dollars, of their surging mergers and acquisitions![44] Still others have indirect stakes in national security outlays and employment—for example, the state and local governments and those who enjoy the related public goods supply provided by those governments. People plus firms plus state and local governments—a truly gigantic "lobby" representing special vested interests that thrive on the pecuniary translation of patriotism and nationwide fear.

Members of Congress, asserting an expertise reflecting military-industrial constituency pressures, call for additional weaponry that the Pentagon says it doesn't need. During the 1996 election campaign, Doug Bandow of the conservative Cato Institute severely criticized conservative Republican groups for advocating significant increases in defense spending when "the United States . . . faces no serious security threat. And current spending is already greater than necessary to defend the country."[45] According to Bandow the Heritage Foundation advocated a $20 billion per year increase in defense spending. William Kristof advocated a $60–80 billion increase. Hally Barbour, chairman of the Republican Party, advocated an increase totaling $140 billion annually. Francis Fukuyama and Edward Luttwak have advocated significant but uncosted defense expansions.[46]

Humanitarianism, environmentalism, and development assistance pale in comparison to national security and economic vested interests. This can be indicated in a crude, quantitative way. Official economic aid totaled about $24 billion in 1993. Total funding for development assistance in 1994 was about $7 billion. Among a long list of donor countries, the United States has been in the bottom group so far. Barring a big swing in the American organizational consensus, it would appear that future international activity by the U.S. government will depend overwhelmingly on the overlapping national security–special-vested-interest classes of pressure.

The highly qualitative character of federal international interventionism is, like other types of administrative engineering, inadequately grasped by looking at budgetary and employee data alone. This judgment is supported by the fact that the interventionism is conducted by departments and committees within government branches and agencies that are but loosely identified with the usual aggregative data for those instrumentalities. Hence, unlike the earlier analysis of administrative management in this work, wherein a single public instrumentality could usually be identified for analysis, in the foreign policy sphere the interventionism is widely dispersed administratively.

Numerous groups within ostensibly domestic policy or presumably joint domestic and foreign branches of the government are involved in international tasks to varying extents. Whatever judgment is made about the Defense Department on this matter of tasks, it is clear that the State Department is devoted to international work. However, its outlays of about $6 billion in 1995 were not very well connected functionally with the much larger "international affairs" outlays of almost $19 billion. Who filled this enormous gap? All we know is that "conduct of foreign affairs," the basic function of the State Department, was allocated $4 billion of the $19 billion. We also know that the CIA, the FBI, the

Drug Enforcement Agency, the Nuclear Regulatory Commission, the Energy Department, the Labor Department, the Commerce Department, the Agriculture Department, the Postal Service, the executive office of the president (including the National Security Council), certain congressional committees, the U.S. Information Agency, the U.S. International Development Cooperation Agency, NASA, the Export-Import Bank, the Peace Corps, the U.S. Arms Control and Disarmament Agency, and the U.S. International Trade Commission, among others, are all participants in the global "third network." Clearly, the pressures for international involvement have established a vast though loose-knit institution whose future is assured by the expanding configuration of global problems.

Notes

1. William H. Branson, "Trends in U.S. International Trade and Investment Since World War II," in Martin Feldstein (ed.), *The American Economy in Transition* (Chicago: University of Chicago Press, 1980), p. 196.

2. *Economic Report of the President,* 1994, pp. 214–215.

3. *New York Times,* July 22, 1994, p. C1.

4. *Economic Report of the President,* 1971, p. 164.

5. George P. Shultz and Kenneth W. Dam, *Economic Policy Beyond the Headlines* (New York: W.W. Norton, 1977), p. 133.

6. *GATT Newsletter,* Focus No. 109 (July 1994), pp. 4–5.

7. Thomas Friedman, *New York Times,* July 15, 1994, p. C2.

8. Edward K. Hamilton, "Introduction and Overview," in Edward K. Hamilton (ed.), *America's Global Interests* (New York: W.W. Norton, 1989), p. 22.

9. *Economic Report of the President,* 1992, pp. 201–202.

10. Ibid., p. 215.

11. Richard E. Caves, *Multinational Enterprise and Economic Analysis* (London: Cambridge University Press, 1982), p. 233.

12. Ibid., p. 226.

13. Susan R. Fletcher, "The Environment: Moving Up on the International Agenda," *EPA Journal* 16, no. 4 (July/August 1990), p. 7.

14. *The Economist,* May 6, 1989, p. 67.

15. *Economic Report of the President,* 1994, p. 238.

16. Ibid., p. 180.

17. Fletcher, "The Environment," p. 10.

18. *Finance and Development* 26, no. 4 (December 1989), p. 2.

19. Ibid. p. 6.

20. *OECD Observer,* 135 (July 1985), p. 7.

21. *New York Times,* "40 Nations Agree to Shut Down Nuclear Plants Deemed Unsafe," September 22, 1994, p. A11.

22. Alison Butler, "Environmental Protection and Free Trade: Are They Mutually Exclusive?" *Federal Reserve Bank of St. Louis Review* 74, no. 3 (May/June 1992), pp. 8–9.

23. H. Jeffrey Leonard, *Pollution and the Struggle for World Product* (Cambridge: Cambridge University Press, 1988), as cited in Maureen L. Cropper and Wallace E. Oates, "Environmental Economics: A Survey," *Journal of Economic Literature* 30, no. 2 (June 1992), p. 698.

24. Ibid.

25. Raymond F. Mikesell, *The Economics of Foreign Aid* (Chicago: Aldine, 1968), p. 11.

26. I.M.D. Little and J.M. Clifford, *International Aid* (Chicago: Aldine, 1966), p. 88.

27. Ibid., p. 90.

28. John Marttila, "American Public Opinion: Evolving Definitions of National Security," in Edward K. Hamilton (ed.) *America's Global Interests*, p. 305.

29. H. William Brands, *The United States in the World: A History of American Foreign Policy* (Boston: Houghton Mifflin, 1994), p. 283.

30. Ibid.

31. *Statistical Abstract*, 1995, p. 812, No. 1331.

32. Mikesell, *The Economics of Foreign Aid*, p. 192.

33. Congressional Budget Office, *Enhancing U.S. Security Through Foreign Aid*, (Washington, GPO, April 1994), pp. 68–69.

34. William Woodruff, *America's Impact on the World* (New York: John Wiley and Sons, 1975), pp. 60–61.

35. Congressional Budget Office, *Enhancing U.S. Security*, p. 4.

36. Norman S. Fieleke, "A Primer on the Arms Trade," *New England Economic Review* (November/December 1991), p. 60.

37. Congressional Budget Office, *Enhancing U.S. Security*, p. 19.

38. *Economic Report of the President*, January 1989, p. 123.

39. Ibid., pp. 122–123.

40. Vito Tanzi, "Issues in Coordination of Fiscal Policies," *Finance and Development* 25, no. 4 (December 1988), p. 16.

41. Ibid., p. 17.

42. Ibid.

43. *Economic Report of the President*, February 1991, pp. 34–35.

44. Lawrence J. Korb, "Merger Mania," *The Brookings Review* 14, no. 3 (Summer 1996), pp. 22–25.

45. Doug Bandow, "Dole's Military Card," *New York Times*, July 6, 1976, p. 15.

46. All of the above cited persons and institutions are current or past advisers to Republican governments.

CHAPTER SEVEN

Why Government Must Continue to Grow

There is no possibility that the great relative growth of total government in the United States can continue indefinitely. It could not get so large that it became the total economy. Hence the question regarding the future is whether its rise will or will not keep pace with the expansion of the economy. To formulate the issue in this way is to imply, of course, that dreamers hoping or expecting absolute contraction in the size of total government are making an erroneous forecast. In advancing and empirically supporting the argument that the government's size will increase about as fast as the total economy, there is a concomitant contention that contraction of the present size is impossible.

The measurement of size in the case of government unfortunately requires a *numeraire* that encompasses more than the conventional criteria, such as revenues, expenditures, and number of public employees, although these certainly have a claim on measurement. But as emphasized in Chapter 3, the *numeraire* must include the enormous volume of managerial governmental activities that influence human economic activity and economic performance. The expanding career of such government influences has been traced in earlier chapters, and it remains here necessary only to develop the point that the managerial functions grow of necessity out of the very *modus operandi* of (1) the market system's evolution; (2) what Schumpeter called the "capitalist order"; and (3) the human culture currents, including public attitudes and government itself, accompanying the evolution of (1) and (2).

Certain assumptions must be made at the outset. One is that it is an essential law of motion in a capitalistic market system, insofar as it persists in even modified form, that it must expand or it will die. This is a general characteristic stemming from the aggregation of a core of business enterprise individually dedicated to the expansion of assets—that is, accumulation and technological advance in the sphere of production. While this fact does not pinpoint a *rate,* it does assert a positive long-run expansion at some rate. Asset expansion for the core enterprises requires sales expansion—that is, long-run growth in aggregate demand. But that demand need not emanate entirely from the domestic private economy itself.

A second assumption is that the human community is also dedicated to long-run rising total output. This assumption is appropriate certainly for an economy and society that are already technologically advanced—that is, "industrialized" and in possession of a historically high per capita income. Even if the country's population, unlike the United States, is no longer growing, it is proper to presume a social consensus that insists if at all possible on a long-run increase in real per capita income. Alternatively put, the historical achievement of a high per capita income apparently has a social ratchet effect. The emergence of any long-run decline in per capita income is unacceptable to the community, and it will take steps to correct such a development. This is the assumption of a social economic growth consensus.

A third assumption is that the innate drive for expansion in the market economy and the community's insistence on economic growth reinforce each other. Hence, it is reasonable to presume continued long-run economic growth and development.

The relative growth of big government in historically recent, and only recent, times is not unique to the United States. This fact strengthens the presumption that the phenomenon is generated by powerful forces innate to most advanced, high income, industrial societies. There is nothing aberrant about the U.S. experience. Furthermore, acknowledgment of the enormous, endogenous power of those forces is reinforced in the American case by the recognition that they had to overcome an exceptionally strong socioideological opposition to augmentation of the governmental establishment in general.

Six decades ago it was plausible to most Americans to believe that the Great Depression's upsurge of public clamor, and consequent public intervention into the economy and the nexus of traditional property relationships, was only temporary. It would all presumably disappear when the inevitable cyclical recovery, with its decisive assistance from private investment, had occurred and brought the return to full employment. But the intervention established several big new institutions, like Social Security, that were destined to become abiding components of an upcoming "social" market economy, or mixed economy. It was furthermore ideologically devastating to both the conventional wiseacres and the social interventionists that, after a whole agonizing decade of material insecurity and mass unemployment, the unemployment rate was still an unconscionable 15 percent on the eve of World War II. The ghost of that decadal trauma was alive and well at war's end, and stalked the halls of Congress, impelling passage of the historic Employment Act in 1946. By that time the number of federal "civilian" employees, while still of a modest magnitude, was more than three times the 1929 number.

Since the Employment Act made the *federal* government responsible for "maximum employment and purchasing power," that responsibility could be carried out only if it was a big spender when needed. Total federal purchases, in the context of budget surpluses, in 1947 and 1948 averaged only about 6 percent of GNP. A serious economic contraction would have required an enormous percentage deviation from that base proportion. Nondefense federal purchases in those years averaged only about 2 percent of GNP, *and that proportion never became much larger.* For example, in a high-point year such as 1968, federal nondefense purchases were still only 2.4 percent of GNP.

It would take fantastically high budget deficits to pull up civilian federal purchases to the levels necessary to overcome either short-run mass unemployment or the growth of a large long-run reserve army of the unemployed. Of course, national defense purchases in 1968 were 3.8 times bigger than nondefense federal purchases. But then, military purchases are *supposed* to reflect only national security demands, not stabilize the economy and provide jobs at high employment. So the true significance of the Employment Act was its import as an historic, official, federal policy commitment on the level of intent.

The "mixture" of public and private, including all levels of government, got richer and richer for over half a century. Enrichment and persistence for so long demonstrates deep economic and cultural roots and the likelihood of fluctuating permanence rather than transience. Nontransience is still the right view of the process, even if one accepts the argument of Robert Higgs in his *Crisis and Leviathan* that government's role has grown secularly by successive leaps in response to recurrent crises of various sorts. If the socioeconomic system's evolution generates endogenous successive crises, each following its predecessor in short order, that invariably induce demands for additional government intervention, such a cumulative result still demonstrates government growth as a systemic product. If the process exhibits "ratchet effects," as Higgs believes, that only adds to its vigor and enduring power.

The advance of big government has been so powerful that it has overcome a deep-rooted, durable, vociferous sociopolitical and ideological current fervently dedicated to a small, decentralized government and low taxes. More specifically, it has been powerful enough to surmount a resurgence of that current that began with the stagflation of the 1970s and surfaced strongly in the 1990s. It has survived despite the devastating blows dealt by that resurgence to the Keynesian policy of explicit aggregate demand support by government.

To be sure, the resurgence was able to slow the outlays aspect of the government's rise after the prosperous sixties. It succeeded, for example, in reducing the annual expansion rate of total civilian federal purchases to a sluggish 2.5 percent from the early 1970s to 1994 (helping thereby to pull down the real GDP rate to only 2.6 percent a year). But on the other hand, real total *all-government expenditures* (including transfer payments) more than kept pace with real GDP at 3.2 percent annually. Real transfer payments to persons zoomed over the same years at 4.5 percent. Also, the continuing pressure for government enlargement at the grass roots frustrated the "tax revolt" by perpetrating a 3.3 percent annual increase in real total state and local government receipts from 1985 to 1994. Real purchases at the state and local level did almost as well over those years of the tax revolt, and grass-roots employees substantially outpaced the growth rate of the civilian labor force. Worse yet for the anti-governmenteers, there was a shocking 4.6 percent average annual jump in real state and local total expenditures, pulled up by the veritable explosion of transfer payments to persons.

Increase of Business's Appeal to Government

Getting down to basics, it is necessary to try to discover why the governmental juggernaut must flourish for so long. To find the answer to that question, it is essential to examine the long-run economic and social forces creating Higgs's recurrent "crises," and Schlesinger's "cycles," plus something strategic that Higgs largely neglects. That additional factor is the evolution of the larger culture as embodied in the specific human response mechanisms that, together with market system developments, ultimately determine the long-run career of government.

We first turn to the vital individual and organizational elements *within* the ever-expanding market nexus itself. Market participants, such as individual business firms and associations of firms, feel continually impelled to invoke government to intervene on their behalf, even as they rail against the costs or potential dangers of public support for other such intervention. The aggrandizing market parties proliferate and get more powerful over time with (a) the proliferation of product variety and the attendant economic sectors identified with the particular products; and (b) the parallel multiplication of blatant inequalities and internecine conflicts among them.

As the various departments and levels of government respond to these piecemeal, micro-level pressures by costly balancing acts, concessions, supports, regulations, and fiscal measures, intervention of all kinds accumulates. Thus over time unfolds the vast structure of business-oriented grants, mining and grazing subsidies, price supports, tariffs, export aids, tax expenditures, "industrial policies," research and development and educational subsidies, loans, and bailouts.

Two Expansion Requirements in the Market System's Larger Setting

Big parallel changes also develop in the market's integument. Specifically, the growth of the technologically advanced market economy brings with it two long-run developments that have little if anything to do with intermediate "crises," but have a lot to do with long-run augmentation of government's role. The first is the increase in socioeconomic infrastructure requirements of an ever larger and more diversified market economy. The second development is the increasing amount of damage to both the physical environment and the well-being of the human population that accompanies modern economic development.

Most of the infrastructure development has to be public, either because it is providing a public good or because business is unwilling to make the necessary large-scale, long-run commitments at prices and quantities acceptable to the community. This infrastructure growth requirement can be illustrated by a glance at a sample of activities at the state and local level covering the approximately four decades beginning in 1950. We can total the state and local expenditures for education, highways, sanitation and sewerage, parks and recreation, water supply, electric power supply, gas supply, and transit systems. The total for this selected infrastructure group in current dollars amounted to about 64 percent of all-government civilian G in 1960, following the first decade and a half of explosive infrastructure rebuilding necessitated by the lean years of the Great Depression and World War II. By 1990, total expenditures for the group still amounted to 64 percent of all-government civilian G. But in ratio to GDP, the infrastructure group had gained from 6.8 percent to 8.5 percent. In real terms, the sample grew almost 4 percent a year, 1960–90, in the context of a real GDP growth rate of a bit over 3 percent. Even omitting the big educational component, the infrastructure group grew at a substantially faster rate than real GDP.

This is not to assert that the public infrastructure growth in the postwar era was necessarily adequate to the expanding requirements of the socioeconomic system. Indeed, as is well known, there were widespread, rising complaints, particularly during the infrastructure slowdown after 1970, that in this sphere there was an emerging crisis. However, the point here is simply that economic growth requires parallel public infrastructure growth at a rate probably approximating at least the real GNP rate. The record after World War II is quite consistent with this proposition. Infrastructure will unquestionably remain a significant contributor to government's and the economy's long-run rise.

A second long-run development in the integument encompassing the growing market system, including its household partner, is the spread of environmental impairment. The injuries to the environment are again generated by the evolving physical implements and operations of firms and households themselves. They are "endogenously" produced.

The social and governmental policy response, which burgeoned after World War II, must grow in the future even more rapidly than the public civilian infrastructure increase because population growth, technological advance, and rising per capita investment and consumption continuously generate *accelerated* damage to the environment. Meanwhile, the environmental movement, now global in scope and enjoying business participation, has established such deep roots in the community consensus that public policy and material resources will inevitably continue to be addressed to the problem.

The vigor of this likely process is borne out by recent trends in the government's response. For example, real all-government pollution abatement and control expenditures rose over 4 percent a year between 1972 and 1990, and real solid waste management outlays increased at a shocking annual rate of almost 7 percent between 1980 and 1991. Even the much lower business outlays for pollution abatement rose 2.74 percent a year, 1972–90. The upcoming enormous and inestimable public works effort for cleaning up nuclear wastes and dismantling nuclear weaponry has already been noted earlier.

Society's political response to accelerated environmental damage is but one outstanding example of a large and diverse set of demands on government: broad social groups that perceive themselves as adversely affected by the market system's changing impact on them pressure the government to intervene to correct those perceived adversities. They become public interest groups, invoking either direct government support or a reshaping of the specific ways in which market participants (including, perhaps, themselves) operate. Intervention accumulates piecemeal but adds up to an ever larger total.

Growth's Public Budget Demands

As long as the community is committed to continued economic growth at some rate, certain types of government-expanding policies will be required. These policies are the kinds that are often connected with government budgets.

A basic impelling consideration in this matter is the fact that traditional reliance on business fixed nonresidential investment (I_f) to carry the primary burden of GNP growth has been a chimera since about 1910 in the United States. It was in the years surrounding that census year that the business structures component of investment began a drastic long-run slowdown that pulled down the I_f/GNP ratio by several percentage points (or about 20 percent less than in the 1869–1911 period). That lowered average ratio persisted for the rest of the twentieth century.

The gross investment demand drop after 1910 so cut into the long-run GNP rate that it fell from over 4 percent a year on the average to somewhat over 3 percent. The post-1910, twentieth-century record has made it clear that fixed nonresidential investment (I_f) follows expected sales (GNP) so as to yield an I_f/GNP ratio of about 10 percent. As a contributor to the growth of production capacity and to the spending stream, it can support at least a long-run 3 percent plus growth rate. But it has been doing so since the Great Depression only because government purchases G has interceded to sustain the growth of aggregate demand necessary to support the 3 percent GNP growth rate (less after 1970). Meanwhile, G has risen in size and performs its growth underwriting role by remaining absolutely bigger than investment. Thus, the essential aggregate demand condition for sustained growth is that G must rise at a rate at least as vigorous as the targeted GNP rate.

As a corollary to this relationship, it is most probable that the size of the federal debt, and of the publicly held portion of it, will continue its long-run absolute increase. This hypothesis fits the community's hostility toward federal tax increases, together with the necessity for federal expenditures to contribute to the growth in all-government expenditures. Moreover, the community, including business, state and local governments, foreigners, and households, has acquired an enormous stake in its holdings of that debt and the income payments it provides. Significantly, there has developed no interest-group constituency demanding that the debt be retired—despite all the talk about the horrors of the current budget deficits.

Administrative Management

As discussed in detail earlier, government growth has been shifting away from a relative rise in public spending and public employment to a large expansion in administrative management of the economy and society. Public managerial and even entrepreneurial functions can be expanded with but little addition to government outlays or employment. The important aspect is the enlargement of direction, control, regulation, resource allocation, and supervised privatization. These activities are almost impossible to measure. All that can be said is that the proliferation of interest-group pressures accompanying socioeconomic development ensures the continued proliferation of public managerial activity.

If Wagner's Law is measured by public spending and employment, a limit long before total governmentalization can be expected. While some limit on the long-run growth of administrative management can also reasonably be expected, that limit cannot be pinpointed with the degree of confidence that can be extended to the spending-employment maximum. It must be open-ended and left with the loose forecast that public management of economic and social life will continue to increase and contribute to government growth in the broadest sense of the term. It promises to be the chief vehicle of expansion of the public sector in the future.

One important source of fuel for that expanding public managerial vehicle is the growing influence of international relationships. As discussed in Chapter 6, both the economy and government policy are caught up in an ever-larger network of connections with the rest of the world. While this change has potent implications for the size of the federal budget, it also means that federal worldwide administrative responsibilities will continue to multiply.

Of perhaps preponderant significance in this trend is the apparent determination of the government, backed by powerful constituencies, to pursue a superpower role in world affairs. Americans seem willing to accept, for example, a military budget and the resources necessary to provide for two simultaneous "small" wars of intervention. "National security," the euphemism for superpower global interventionism, permeates foreign aid allocations, Third World debt negotiations, international weaponry sales, enforcement of the Nuclear Non-Proliferation Treaty, all relations with the United Nations and North Atlantic Treaty Organization, trade policy, and the increasing concern for industrial policy and technology exchange bolstering U.S. international "competitiveness."

But there are other budding administrative strategies that have less connection with the superpower role, that nonetheless express the continuing expansion of upcoming global undertakings. Interrelated examples of the areas or institutions on which such assumed responsibilities are focused include: foreign exchange policy, General Agreement on Tariffs and Trade and the World Trade Organization, coordination of domestic monetary policy with the foreign balance of payments, pursuance of trade protections in the context of a trade balance relatively and absolutely much larger than ever before in history, antitrust controls over international cartels, support for foreign affiliates of U.S. multinationals, regulation of international airlines, international aspects of basic labor standards and food safety laws, global pollution controls and natural resource conservation and preservation (e.g., the rain forests, the International Nuclear Liability Treaty), the world oil situation, suppression of international drug trafficking, concern with the domestic policy issues in other countries (e.g., Japan, Germany, the European internal market), Organization for Economic Cooperation and Development relations, and the impact on the United States of future changes in Eastern Europe.

So much for a partial summary of the international administrative and budgetary issues treated in Chapter 6. There are clearly few larger domestic sources of federal management expansion than the sources making for this package of expanding international involvement.

Bureaucracy

The major thrust of this work is that the influence of the government establishment itself on public-sector growth should be relegated to a subordinate status. Aside from some minor exceptions to be examined in the immediately following discussion, it is hard to find significant, autonomously waxing public agencies on either the state and local or the federal level.

The references to the public bureaucracy issue herein are not, as with Max Weber, the internal interpersonal relationships of the public agency. And certainly a large public instrumentality is not viewed as a bureaucracy per se. Rather, the focus in determining the possible existence of bureaucracy is the agency's relationships over time with outside entities, such as its political and economic constituency or the group(s) it is set up to service. Unfortunately, general empirical measures of autonomous, bureaucratic, administrative management increases are almost impossible to find. One is therefore forced to revert to either budgetary or employment criteria if an objective, nonanecdotal indicator of a bureaucratic juggernaut is to be located in the historical record.

A bureaucracy, as defined here, is an agency that is likely to coercively substantially increase its staff, especially after about 1970. However, a government agency is not viewed here as bureaucratic if its enlarging staff is concurrently providing an increasing amount of public services or responding to augmented constituency pressures. A post-1970 slowdown following a long-run expansion is the pattern shown by both the GNP and many public and private economic institutions. Even if a public instrumentality has a constant staff after about 1970, it is not considered bureaucratic. As a criterion, the changes in constituency or sector served are always to be compared with agency staff changes in order to test for bureaucracy.

Partiality toward a constituency—for example, Pentagon purchasing rules that permit $435 hammers—runs up government purchases because of excessive cooperation with the interest group. It may approach fraud, if anything, but nevertheless the government is essentially a "cooperating dependent variable" and the enlargement is an expression of private interest group initiative, not government bureaucratic coercion. Of course, the public at large suffers the cost.

It is antibureaucratic if an agency tightens its purchasing rules to cut its costs. It is not bureaucratic, although it may show partiality, for an agency to encourage technological innovation in its private constituency. The agency is *serving* its interest group. Initiation of a new government agency, such as the National Aeronautic and Space Administration, is not evidence of bureaucracy since it serves not only the affected enterprises and their workers but also a national purpose emanating basically from a public consensus—a general interest, not a special interest alone.

In general, if a public agency's real expenditures (managerial activity) expand more slowly than agency employees or constituency, there are two likely interpretations. One is that employees have been unable to build a bureaucratic empire. Another is that employees are getting less efficient, which of course is not necessarily inconsistent with the first interpretation. Unfortunately, neither interpretation tells us whether or not the public agency is serving its interest group well by conserving on outlays.

To try to resolve such a dilemma, comparison can be made between the rate of employment or agency appropriations growth and some other changing phenomenon, such as labor force, GDP, a relevant sector of society or the economy, perhaps the nation's general interests, or the behavior of other nations with the same problems. On the state and local level, expenditures have been surveyed previously. State and local government accounts for the overwhelming bulk of both rising civilian public purchases, and also the growth of civilian public employment. Within state and local real purchases, it has been noted that infrastructure outlays rose over the very long run at a vigorous pace, but that the pace slowed as time passed, when education is included. That very important expenditure component of the total direct state and local outlays drifted down over the long run. The state and local departments responsible were apparently not able to continue to expand their empire as powerful bureaucracies would be expected to do. However, they were able to perpetrate real outlay expansions in tandem with, and in some instances at a slightly higher rate than, the economy's sluggish growth after 1970. All of this seems consistent with the interpretation that the infrastructure agencies were simply sensing the economy's requirements.

As for state and local full-time employment equivalent (FTE), there were a number of strongly growing activity categories in the postwar era. Cases in point are education, health and hospitals, public welfare, and police. Moderate growers with modest staffs included highway departments, sanitation and sewerage, parks and recreation, natural resources, and financial administration. The discussion of infrastructure in Chapter 3 treated several of these.

Education was big in employee numbers and a strong grower at the state and local level, but only until about 1970. In the seventies the annual employee growth rate was much less than half that for the sixties, and after 1980, education FTE employment grew at a rate somewhat less than that for the civilian labor force.

It must be acknowledged at once that the widely dispersed and administratively separated character of public education makes it an unlikely candidate for the bureaucracy label. It may well be that at some state, county, or municipal levels educational public bureaucracies have developed. But uncovering such is not possible or relevant here; they must be left to the grass roots to appraise either their contribution to overall state and local government growth or their possible excessive size.

In any case, a survey of the totality of public education is not likely to uncover much in the way of bureaucratic influence on the public sector's long-run rise. Such a survey would have to focus on public elementary and secondary education, the heart of the public education department. If it did, it would find only modest intimations of inordinate rise. The acid tests would have to address themselves to developments in the last quarter-century, after the baby-boom hump in elementary and secondary school enrollments. Examination would discover that, for example, the pupil/teacher ratio in 1994 at 5.8 was higher than the 4.5 ratio for 1970, when it probably should have been lower on efficiency and nonbureaucratic grounds. Similarly, the total elementary and secondary school employment relative to enrollment rose by about 11 percent between 1970 and 1990. The interpretive problem here is that the possible quality improvement of educational service is ignored by the figures. Also, the 1970 base for comparison may reflect some employment lag relative to the baby-boom enrollment explosion.

Another possible test might be made using teacher salaries trends. This would show that the CPI-deflated average salaries, which jumped over 30 percent in the decade of the baby-boom, low-inflation sixties, plateaued in the next quarter-century with an annual growth rate of only one-third of a percentage point. This looks very much like concordance with the stagnation of real labor compensation in general in that period, and hardly suggests bureaucratic power at work. The same flatness characterizes the ratio of state and local government FTE employment in education to total state and local government employment. Little coercive power is evident in that case, either. And real expenditures for elementary and secondary school operations rose annually at only a moderate 2.3 percent from 1970 to 1992.

One should probably conclude that even by looking at the heart of public education in general, there is little cogent evidence of bureaucracy in the historic years of general economic growth slowdown. Additionally it should be noted that fiscal neglect in the last quarter-century was accumulating an enormous, multibillion dollar backlog of unmet physical plant requirements in the public education sector. Any bureaucracy worth its name would not have permitted that to happen.

Emphasis on the slowdown is not designed to deny the possible significance for other relevant changes of the rise in absolute numbers of state and local employees from 10 million in 1970 to 16 million in 1995. But certainly the state and local bureaucratic world after 1970, if it existed, was grim compared with the heyday of postwar expansion beforehand.

It is informative to glance at two of the specialized human services: health and hospitals, and public welfare. Together they had 768,000 FTE employees in 1960. They grew fast in the next thirty years, reaching 1,895,000 by 1992. This was a high annual rate of 3 percent, about the same as staff in education and much faster than the civilian labor force. (Incidentally, if FTE employment in these two departments and in education are deducted from total state and local employment, the remainder grew at only 2.5 percent a year—merely one-half of a percentage point faster than the civilian labor force.

These two agencies had a functional connection with the growth of the state and local transfer payments, since they were major dispensers of such payments. Transfers helped greatly to raise total real state and local expenditures to a growth rate approximating that for real GDP. As for employment, the total for the two agencies amounted to a noteworthy 14 percent of all state and local government workers in 1992.

We know from the earlier discussion of the welfare state that certain human services agencies and their health and welfare transfers grew rapidly because of the upsurge in prices and the community's social welfare demands. Whatever legitimate criticisms may be leveled at these programs, that of being autonomous, self-aggrandizing bureaucracies exercising coercion would be difficult to support.

The particular state and local instrumentalities just discussed accounted for about 59 percent of all state and local government employees in 1960 and 64 percent in 1990. Significant self-augmenting capacity of these departments does not seem to be indicated. The noneducational state and local agencies, accounting for 36 percent of FTE employment in 1990, will not be examined for Leviathan tendencies here. Rather, a brief review of four big instrumentalities in the federal government is more appropriate.

Federal Agency Expansions

The four federal agencies to be examined are the "civilian" Department of Defense, the Department of Veterans Affairs, the Agriculture Department, and the

Postal Service. Employment in the four in 1991 accounted for 71 percent of all federal civilian employment (78 percent in 1960). The largest of the agencies thus omitted are the Treasury, Justice, and Health and Human Services departments. However, these have been treated earlier in other perspectives and sufficiently to indicate that they would be unlikely candidates for coercive bureaucracy presumptions. They are, on the other hand, instrumentalities with considerable promise of significant future growth contributions to the overall size of the federal establishment.

Employees in the four selected agencies as a group increased at an average yearly rate of only one-half of 1 percent between 1960 and 1991. Bureaucratically speaking, this is a pitiful performance. And they did not grow at all from 1970 to 1991. If one were looking for Leviathan, one would no doubt find this discouraging. However, a brief, more specific look at the four provides a more complete interpretation.

The Department of Defense (DOD), together with its armed forces, is notable for close ties with its economic-political constituency. That military-industrial complex has been briefly treated earlier. What is needed at this point is some additional treatment to test the perspective of the self-generating, coercive, autonomous government Goliath argument. This should also provide a basis for estimating the likely contribution of the DOD to government's future growth.

In the case of the DOD, the support sources include not only the specific, vested military contract interests but also society's general interest in national security and jobs. This powerful combination produced a unique coalition between constituency and agency in the Cold War era and the hot wars contained in it. One might well expect enormous agency expansion.

Who had the initiative in the coalition? The answer is neither component of the complex. It was a cooperative, mutually reinforcing institution. No major element in the eager private constituency had to be coerced by the DOD to participate in the expansion of military purchases.

The expansion power of the coalition fluctuated in the intermediate period largely with phases of general interest in national security. However, neither the private special economic vested interests nor the DOD could prevent the slowdown in national defense purchases (NDG) after two hot wars and their absolute decline after the 1987 peak year of the Reagan military buildup. Also, real NDG had been arrested in the seventies by a competing general interest dedicated to containing government growth. That competing "general interest" acquired additional constraining force in the late eighties through an antideficit upsurge following the Reagan budget deficit explosion.

The two hot wars in the quarter-century after the end of World War II carried real NDG and DOD employment to intermediate peaks in 1952 (Korean War) and 1968–69 (Vietnam War). Real DOD payrolls and payroll per employee peaked in 1972. This peaking phenomenon around 1970 is noteworthy. To be sure, the DOD's link with national security endows it with special characteristics. Still, its resemblance to the grand periodization for government's general growth pattern in the whole postwar era is remarkable: rapid rise to the early seventies, slowdown thereafter. For the DOD, its post-1972 slowdown fits the general pattern better functionally because the hot war influences were past. In any case, the slowdown is always inimical to the long-run Leviathan hypothesis.

But the DOD–industrial complex career is particularly hard on such an hypothesis. During the Cold War and after the hot wars, the DOD could barely hold on to its established position. Real NDG languished after its second hot-war peak of 1968 until exactly twenty years later, when the Reagan buildup brought it back to the same level for that one year but below the level of 1955–65.

The Reagan expansion program brought DOD initiative into the limelight to prod its willing constituency to sell more military goods and services to the federal government. The DOD was transformed into a reactivated bureaucracy for a brief spell of eight years. The resulting jump in military prime contract awards to business firms in the country lasted only until 1985, however. The DOD's next initiative period, prodded by Congress, was destined to be contractive because of the Cold War's end.

The DOD was able to raise the number of its employees only by 11 percent as of 1989 from its post-1950 nadir of 948,000 in 1980. The total staff was the same in 1991 as it had been in post-Vietnam 1972. Indeed, it was slightly less than in post-Korea 1958! The 1991 level pulled down by the end of the Cold War: the department employed 1,085,000 in 1985 and 880,000 in 1994.

But there is more to add to skepticism about a DOD Leviathan. Observe the record for the department's real total payroll, for example. It was $22.5 billion in 1965, *the same* in 1980 and 1982, and again *the same* in 1989—*before* the Cold War's end! And the record is astonishingly similar for real payroll per DOD employee: $21,799 in 1965; twenty years later, $21,482; and $21,162 at the Reagan peak in 1989! Such a record of constancy for real average employee compensation rivals the grim history of real average weekly earnings in all private nonagricultural industries, which were $262 in 1960 and $264 in 1989 (constant 1982 dollars).

An agency enjoying a public-contract–hungry civilian constituency and the enormous influence of national security that does not grow vigorously is not a self-aggrandizing, bureaucratic juggernaut. In the long run the DOD was practically through adding to government growth by 1955. From that year to the Reagan peak of 1988–89, real NDG grew at less than 1 percent a year, and DOD employment failed to grow at all. This is the record for the federal government's very biggest agency.

The DOD was in the position of serving the armed forces. The question is, did it exploit its situation in order to build a growing administrative and servicing organization relative to the body of military personnel in its care? After the Vietnam War, the number of military personnel on active duty plateaued. The Reagan expansion added about 4 percent to the armed forces. Accompanying this comparative constancy, the ratio of DOD employees to active military personnel hovered narrowly between 47 and 50 percent. It had been 51.6 percent as far back as 1950. Hence, DOD workers were definitely not gaining on their military associates. If the department was overstaffed with a ratio of 54.5 in 1991, then it was already overstaffed in 1950.

Stability also marked the department's efficiency measure—that is, the ratio of real NDG (1987 dollars) to employment. In the quarter-century preceding the Reagan eighties, that output proxy per DOD employee averaged about $195,000. The Reagan expansion of real NDG in the eighties outran the modest staff increase of 1.2 percent annually, so that this productivity indicator rose markedly to an average of about $248,000. That figure was far above any past hot-war level. But the gainers from the productivity increase were not the aggregate of department payrollers, as would be expected from a bureaucracy as defined herein. They were the military contractors and related beneficiaries—the department's civilian political and economic constituency. Hence, there was no government agency feathering its own nest at the expense of its relevant public on the basis of this critical criterion.

Barring some new, major national security alarm or unbridled global interventionist binge, the foreseeable future promises further reductions in the DOD staff and NDG. The federal government's largest agency will therefore be something of a drag on federal, and to a much lesser degree all-government, growth. But it would be a rash forecast indeed to expect anything like a return to the levels that immediately followed the end of World War II.

The second largest federal agency in employee numbers is the Postal Service (PS). Regular PS employees in 1950 numbered 364,000, or about one-half the DOD number, and in 1990 they were equal to almost three-fourths. They were about a quarter of all federal civilian employees in 1992.

The number of workers in an infrastructure sector of the economy and society such as the PS would be expected to grow with the real GDP over the long run. They did increase, but not at a rate that suggests a bloated, bureaucratic expansion. Specifically, PS regular employees increased in number at a yearly average rate of 1.77 percent from 1950 to 1991. For comparison, recall that the total civilian labor force grew at 1.72 percent and real GDP at 3.15 percent. Therefore, as a public infrastructure agency in the communications sector of the economy, the PS was basically an unassuming service organization.

Such a judgment is further borne out by the fact that the modestly increasing number of postal workers were handling ever more mail per person. The total amount of mail handled rose at a rate slightly faster than real GDP. Hence the average number of pieces of mail handled per regular PS worker increased from 90,000 to 208,000 over the 1950–94 period. This is a first-class productivity record—over 2 percent a year. For comparison, output per hour in the nonfarm business sector increased at 1.63 percent annually during 1950–91.

Also, the PS became increasingly reliant on its own revenue sources rather than on government financial support. Federal government appropriations for the agency, as a share of its total revenues, fell from 17.6 percent in 1970 to 1.3 percent in 1991. This kind of quasi-privatization development undermines the notion of public bureaucracy status.

The PS clearly fits the criteria of a nonbureaucracy as conceived in the present analysis: the staff grew modestly, it exhibited a good productivity record, its costs to the government were minimal, and its employees' real pay trend was hardly excessive. On the matter of pay trends, including fringe benefits, the following comparisons for yearly percentage growth rates are revealing:

	Real compensation per hour, private business sector	Real average salary per PS employee
1960–75	6.37	3.25
1975–91	0.42	0.85
1960–91	3.30	2.00

PS employees' wages did worse than workers in the private economy over the long run. What is more significant for present purposes is the collapse for 1975–91 in the PS real salary growth rate, more or less paralleling the drop in the private sector. Such a drastic fall does not fit the self-reinforcing bureaucracy hypothesis. Rather, the total PS record suggests a basic public infrastructure establishment that expands pari passu with the economy and society. It can be expected in all probability to continue to participate similarly in government's future growth.

The Department of Veterans Affairs (VA) is today the third largest federal instrumentality as measured by employees. The department had 175,000 employees in 1952 and 262,000 in 1994. At the outset, let us note that this represented an average annual increase of slightly less than 1 percent over the approximately four decades. On the surface, this is an extremely slow growth rate.

But it is too facile to brush off that record as suggesting little likelihood of a bureaucratic tendency. First of all, other cases have served warning that a growth rate break in both the economy (indeed, in the world economy) and in government expansion occurred in the early or middle seventies, with strong increases beforehand and a distinct slowing down thereafter. But the VA is full of surprises. VA employment showed no growth up to 1970, which is contrary to the usual pattern, as just mentioned. Hence, if we calculate the annual employment growth rate taking 1970 as the initial year, then with 1994 as terminal year, we get almost 2 percent. That rate slightly exceeds the yearly percentage for the civilian labor force, and it is contrary to the usual post-seventies slowdown pattern.

percent rise—needs to be shown as warranted in some respect if the criticism of self-aggrandizement is to be rejected. One reasonable check on this matter is to ask the question: Was the department's workload, or output, increasing proportionately to its staff after about 1970? A legitimate indicator of workload in this case is the number of veteran beneficiaries (persons directly served, clientele, immediate constituency) on the department's rolls. That indicator shows a rise in rolls up to the early seventies, when VA employees over time described a rough plateau, and a fall after the mid-seventies, when VA employment was rising. On that simple criterion, the record looks good in the early phase but suspiciously like bureaucratic overstaffing in the later phase. And it should be borne in mind that over the whole period 1952–91 the number of beneficiaries on the rolls increased annually at a minuscule 0.30 percent. If the rolls are a proxy for the department's output, then its labor productivity is good before 1970 but very poor thereafter. Specifically, the ratio of veterans on rolls to VA employees (output/labor input) was 18 in 1952, up to 28 in 1970, and 13 in 1993!

It seems reasonable to conclude that the bureaucracy picture for the VA is blurred. The staff element in the picture clearly reveals overbuilding. However, it would be persuasive to expect that a continued fall in veterans on the rolls must sooner or later pull down the bloated staff. In such case, it would begin to act as a drag on all-government employment. And from the pecuniary standpoint, the real total VA budget—a congressional policy matter, falling absolutely since 1975—must also have a restraining impact on all-government expenditures. Such has already been the case for some time. The lack of growth in the real VA budget has made no contribution to the 2 percent annual increase in the real federal nonmilitary purchases between 1972 and 1994.

The last agency that will be examined for bureaucracy here is the federal Department of Agriculture. That sizable department and its articulate political constituency reach far back into the laissez-faire era. They will reach far forward into the future.

Employing the usual periodization for the World War II era, we get the familiar staff growth pattern exhibited by other government instrumentalities and the economy. Departmental employment rises quite strongly by over 2 percent annually from 1952 to 1970, and that is followed by extremely slow growth between 1970 and 1994. The real total budget of the department, a congressional policy matter like the VA budget, misbehaved by hardly rising over the standard expansion period, 1960–78. By 1994 it was slightly below what it had been in 1980. Such patterns do not come through as representing a bureaucratic juggernaut at work.

It seems rather pointless to compare that record with such agricultural phenomena as the fall in total farm employment from 5.6 million to 3.2 million and the rise in farm output by 1.3 percent annually over the same period. After all, farm employment is not analogous to veterans' beneficiaries, and farm output hardly reflects appropriately the vast variety of conditions directly or indirectly connected to agriculture. A community consensus, focused on the diverse activities surrounding agriculture, demands that numerous government agencies give their attention to these conditions. The agencies include not only the federal Agriculture Department but also a far-flung network of state and local instrumentalities with which the department cooperates. The multiplicity of conditions and related programs include, for partial example, farm commodity production, storage, and prices; land and water use and conservation; credit availability; youth; homemaking; forests; electricity; education; pesticides; foreign aid; insurance; food and nutrition; research; and experimentation. Many of these matters have required, with public initiative and acceptance, increasing Agriculture Department attention over the years. The VA had no comparable array of programmatic responsibilities to warrant its staff increases after 1970.

It should also be borne in mind, before making any judgment about possible future bureaucracy tendencies, that consideration must be given to the powerful influences exerted by the farm lobby and the farm bloc in the Congress. The political power of farm firms has much exceeded their production share of GNP. Additionally, there is operating always the deep-rooted, pro-agricultural ideology of the great mass of the American people. Agency and congressional response to such ideological authority and to organized constituency pressure is not, in this case, autonomous agency empire building.

Community ideologies can be nonbureaucratic in their impact on an agency's growth, provided that the agency's response passes its other bureaucracy tests. On the other hand, those tests may indicate bureaucracy behavior, in which case it can be concluded that the agency *exploited* the supportive ideology in order to build its own overweening size and authority. The state and local education superstructure appears to illustrate exploitation of the widespread ideological esteem for education. The Agriculture Department illustrates a constructive and constrained response to the community's romantic but obsolete belief in the beneficence of the family farm.

The role of the Agriculture Department as contributor to future government growth would appear to be slightly positive. But it seems unlikely that the contribution will be in the sphere of federal government employee growth. More likely is a sluggish rise in the agency's budget and its administrative management of both farms and the many socioeconomic activities, processes, and conditions related to agriculture.

The four federal agencies selected for examination here account for the bulk of all federal civilian workers. For example, in 1994 (preliminary estimate) the sum of the four staffs was 2,084,000. This was 70 percent of all civilian federal employees. On the criterion of staff, the federal bureaucracy thesis would seem to have little support, with a noteworthy exception in the case of the VA. On the state and local level, the thesis has some support in the career of the educational establishment.

The larger question initially broached in this chapter is whether all-government growth, measured in several ways, is reversible or can even be brought to a halt in the foreseeable future. The general answer given by the record is that absolute growth will necessarily continue. But that answer could not be based to any significant extent on the hypothesis of bureaucratic agency Leviathans. It would be foolish to deny the existence of aggrandizing *coalitions* between constituencies and government instrumentalities. But the record as interpreted herein exhibits only weak support for primary determination of the government growth process by agency rather than constituency or beneficiaries.

The aggregate of constituencies and beneficiaries, the main target of the anti-bureaucracy school, was unable to prevent a relative fall in federal civilian (including the DOD) employment from 3.3 percent of the civilian labor force in 1960 to 2.3 percent in 1994. Total federal civilian employment in 1994 was a mere seven-tenths of 1 percent above its 1967 level! It is only when we turn to the category of transfer payments that important increases in expenditure power can be found. Those increases and their societal sources have been treated in the previous discussion of the welfare state.

The employment records of the selected state and local and federal agencies suggest continued absolute growth at a modest rate for the group as a whole. The rate will no doubt be much dependent on the economy's pace, as observed in the two postwar periods ending and beginning around the early 1970s. But as noted in Chapter 3, it is probable that the era of *relative* government employment and real budgetary growth has ended, and Wagner's Law will take the form of ever greater administrative management for an indefinite period. Thus, the government growth slowdown on nonmanagerial criteria after the early seventies was prophetic, although somewhat accentuated by the economy's poor performance in those two decades.

Privatization

It may be presumed by some that future government expansion will be significantly restrained by privatization of some important public instrumentalities or activities. But it is difficult to find the emergence in recent times of much empirical evidence upon which to base such an expectation.

In the first place, the U.S. political economy differs sharply from certain European countries where privatization has had some important effects by virtue of major industry denationalizations—for example, steel, railroads, banks. Indeed in those nations privatization has largely meant denationalization. But in the United States, in peacetime, the power of anti-government sentiment has effectively prevented public ownership, operation, and financing of big economic activities, except in special cases of major bailouts. Notable exceptions, such as certain local public utilities, the Tennessee Valley Authority, the Canal Zone Government, and the Panama Canal Company, do not add up to much in the way of government budgets or employees. There comes to mind, of course, two big institutions that are publicly owned and also operated by personnel who receive government paychecks: the Postal Service (PS) and the public educational establishment. Of these two, only education might be a possible serious candidate for some form of limited privatization.

The privatization of the Postal Service—an ambiguous concept at best—would have little effect on the pecuniary size of the federal government. That institution, known as the federal Post Office Department before its reorganization in 1970, creating the Postal Service, always relied for the great bulk of its revenues on postage receipts. The federal treasury paid out to it only enough to cover the excess of its expenditures (including, of course, employee compensation and all employee benefits) above its receipts. The postal workers' paychecks and pensions, while emanating from the federal treasury, had their chief source outside the tax revenues or borrowings of the federal government.

As examples of the small public budgetary commitment and its trend, in 1975 government appropriations for the PS amounted to $1.5 billion, which was only 13 percent of the institution's total revenues. These magnitudes over the long run declined, so that by 1991 the government appropriations were only $562 million—a mere 1.3 percent of PS total revenues in that year. Privatization of this big institution, with its 820,000 nominally labeled government employees and operated much like a regulated private business, would have practically no effect on the size of government. This proposition adds a lot to the conclusion in the above bureaucracy discussion to the effect that the PS has nothing significant to contribute to accusations of self-aggrandizement by federal agencies. Indeed, it is obvious that there are good reasons for omitting the PS entirely from the government instrumentality rubric and viewing it as a publicly regulated, semi-private institution.

The public educational establishment is definitely a different matter. This is clearly a very large public institution. Of the $391 billion school expenditures in 1992, over 80 percent were public monies and those outlays absorbed 14 percent of all-government direct expenditures. In the case of education, private institutions have always existed alongside the public ones, however. This makes it quite different from the mail delivery service, even though in recent times private parcel service, FAXs, and E-mail have become increasingly noteworthy in competition with the PS. But private educational institutions have enjoyed a substantial and longstanding rivalry with the public, and that fact contributes some plausibility to the chances for privatization. However, those chances at this point in history are highly speculative. On the one hand, some public schools have been replaced by private (but regulated) ones. Some public schools have been turned over to private administration but remain publicly financed. Many Catholic schools in particular have been losing enrollments because of the growing shortage of Church-connected staff. We cannot reasonably predict the direction and magnitudes of the future public and private trends. The U.S. National Center for Education Statistics projects the public institution share of total enrollments at all levels of education to be about the same in 2003 as it was in 1980 and higher than in 1955.[1]

It should be added, as a general judgment on privatization behavior, that the meager steps in that direction that have been taken in the United States have almost invariably entailed continued public financial support and/or supervision of some sort. For example, in the cases of certain privatized local public services, "government intervention is required . . . in order to ensure that sufficient services are provided to residents."[2] Privatization in the widespread form of contracting out with private vendors—as, for example, Pentagon military contracts or hazardous waste disposal—leaves major production methods in the hands of private firms, but the government determines the output or service volume and pays according to contract specifications (allowing, perhaps, for overruns!). In the also widely used franchise form of traditional privatization, such as trash collection or operation of a "private" public utility, the government still regulates the level of service and the price charged.[3]

Other types of "private" service provision employ vouchers, but again the government still performs the strategic funding role of supporting some targeted level of services. The Hartford, Connecticut, Board of Education was proceeding in July 1994 to privatize the city's thirty-two public schools, but the for-profit firm that would take over the schools would only manage the buildings, supplies, transportation, and security. Educational matters, including teacher qualifications, curriculum, and labor-management relations, would remain under the control of the board, with the private firm performing only a consultative role.[4] What is this quasi-privatization?

These types of privatization have existed for a long time, particularly on the local government level. However, on the public employee test, the long-run rise of local government employees from 1950 to 1985 much exceeded the annual percentage rate for the civilian labor force. It is hard to believe that the marked slowdown in local employee growth rate to 1.25 percent annually in the years 1980–93, was due to any significant degree to privatization. Hence, it seems reasonable to reiterate the conclusion that the record so far indicates but little privatization effect in the dominant local government sphere.

Notes

1. Calculated from *Statistical Abstract,* 1993, p. 147, No. 221.
2. Yolanda K. Kodnzycki, "Privatization of Local Public Services: Lessons for New England," Federal Reserve Bank of Boston, *New England Economic Review* (May/June 1994), p. 32. The immediately following references to privatization types are loosely gleaned from the same excellent essay.
3. Ibid.
4. George Judson, *New York Times,* July 23, 1994, p. 10.

INDEX

ABOUT THE AUTHORS

John F. Walker is the author with Harold G. Vatter of *The Inevitability of Economic Growth* and the *History of the U.S. Economy since World War II* (M.E. Sharpe, 1996). His articles have appeared in many economic journals, including *Challenge, Journal of Post Keynesian Economics, Public Finance/Finance Publique,* and *National Tax Journal.* He is on the editorial board of the *Western Tax Review.*

Harold G. Vatter, Professor of Economics Emeritus at Portland State University, is a specialist in the history of the American economy since the Civil War. He has written books covering most of the post–Civil War era from the *Drive to Industrial Maturity, 1860–1914* to the *History of the U.S. Economy since World War II* (M.E. Sharpe, 1996), as well as many other books and articles on economic topics.

DATE DUE

GAYLORD			PRINTED IN U.S.A.